IN AFRICA
WITH
SCHWEITZER

IN AFRICA
WITH
SCHWEITZER

Dr. Edgar Berman

NEW HORIZON PRESS

Far Hills, New Jersey

Distributed by

Macmillan Publishing Company, New York

Photos courtesy of The Albert Schweitzer Friendship
House, Inc.

Library of Congress Cataloging-in-Publication Data

Berman, Edgar.
  In Africa with Schweitzer.

  1. Berman, Edgar.   2. Surgeons—United States—
Biography.   3. Surgeons—Gabon—Lambaréné (Moyen-
Ogooué)—Biography.   4. Schweitzer, Albert, 1875–1965—
Friends and associates.   I. Title.   [DNLM: 1. Schweitzer,
Albert, 1875–1965.   2. Surgery—personal narratives.
WZ 100 B516]
RD27.35.B46A3   1986   610.69'5'0924   86-23694
ISBN 0-88282-025-7

Book design by Joan Ann Jacobus

Dedicated to the many who may yet become aware of Albert Schweitzer's "Reverence for Life," leading them to an inner peace individually and a better world collectively.

Schweitzer's "Reverence for Life" is epitomized in his paraphrased sentence:

"A farmer working to earn his daily bread may cut down a million stalks of grain, but on his way home he should consciously crush *Not a Single Flower*."

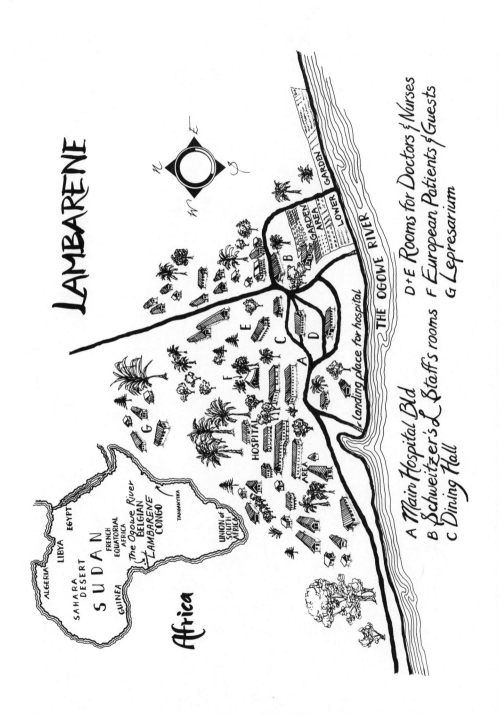

LAMBARENE

A Main Hospital Bld
B Schweitzer's & Staff's rooms
C Dining Hall

D+E Rooms for Doctors & Nurses
F European Patients & Guests
G Lepresarium

THE OGOWE RIVER

landing place for hospital

GARDEN AREA

LOWER GARDEN

HOSPITAL AREA

Africa

SAHARA DESERT
ALGERIA
LIBYA
EGYPT
SUDAN
GUINEA
FRENCH EQUATORIAL AFRICA
The Ogowe River
LAMBARENE
BELGIAN CONGO
TANGANYIKA
UNION OF SOUTH AFRICA

Contents

Preface

As a practicing surgeon in Baltimore, I was president of Tom Dooley's Medico, an international organization that sent American physicians to work to developing countries for short periods. In the fall of 1960, Dr. Schweitzer requested a surgeon from Medico to come to Lambarene as a temporary replacement for his chief surgeon. I volunteered (along with my wife, Phoebe). However, my personal motives for going were less medical than was my interest in one of the few great men of our century.

My medical experiences in Lambarene were of a kind that I could never have anticipated. Much of the conversational parts of this book are verbatim—extracted directly from my diary. Other parts are distilled from my memory of those talks at the instigation of jottings in the diary. Most was corroborated by my wife's better memory. However, I'm not quite sure whether some of the large amount of my Schweitzer reading, both before and after my visit to Lambarene, may not have seeped into parts of my written dialogue. This cannot be helped because of the twenty-five year hiatus since my stay in Lambarene.

In September of 1983 I went back to Lambarene to refresh memories and possibly assess his impact on that society.

There are many misconceptions and myths about this gentle heretic which I have tried to resolve. But more importantly, my objective in writing this book was not only to relate my adventures but to give more insight into a man who was a spiritual and intellectual phenomenon unsurpassed in this century. Even more, I hope this book will keep alive some of Schweitzer's philosophic and spiritual thoughts which are so relevant in our troubled times.

1

THE ODYSSEY—
THE CONTRACT

At about dawn we met our pilot with his single engine airplane that looked like it had been assembled out of spare parts.

As we became airborne, flying very low, we could see Brazzaville, capital of French Equatorial Africa and the capital of the Belgian Congo—Leopoldville's two concrete highrise urban areas split by the wide swiftly-flowing Congo River. Just a few minutes out, the land was totally encompassed by a vast emerald jungle. The only signs of habitation were tiny groups of thatch-roofed huts, miles apart, buried in the thick multi-hued green carpet below. We could see thin lines of well-worn foot pathways intersecting a wide orange-colored, dirt road which the pilot followed.

In less than a half hour the polyglot plane's engine began to sputter, and we had to set down at Pointe-Noire for repairs. Two hours later, a little more shaky regarding the safety of our transportation, we were again airborne and heading for a brief stop to refuel in Libreville, the capital of

Gabon. From there the pilot followed the Ogowe River to Lambarene.

Skimming along in the small plane at treetop level, Phoebe and I saw the glinting corrugated iron roofs of the Schweitzer Hospital shimmering in the soggy October equatorial heat. Fading now, they had been painted red with white crosses, to discourage German bombings which had taken place in the vicinity during World War II. I could see many one-story wooden buildings of various sizes, separate and in clusters, close to the smooth, swiftly-moving Ogowe River— one of the much-used waterways in that part of Africa. Once the river had been a main thoroughfare for hauling lumber to the coast; it was now used mostly for the mail boat and merchants hawking their wares to the villages. On an uneven grassy airstrip near Lambarene, across the river from the hospital, we made a rough landing.

A *pirogue* (a long dugout native canoe) manned by Schweitzer personnel waited for us on the river bank. The rainy season was about to begin, and the river was high but would soon be twenty feet higher. Rolf Adler, a young, very pleasant German doctor from Schweitzer's hospital, greeted us and immediately provided Phoebe and me with pith helmets—*de rigeur* for any white person (male or female) working with Schweitzer.

The hand-hewn *pirogue* had to be balanced precisely and we were carefully placed fore and aft along with our baggage. The oarsmen who stood ready were all arrested lepers, easily recognizable by their missing fingers and toes, and their leonine facies caused by the disease's characteristic lumpy thickening of the facial skin. When we were settled to their satisfaction, we pushed off.

The hospital was directly opposite us; but from the swift flow of the river it seemed certain that we'd be swept downstream if we attempted to go straight across. The expert oarsmen, however, immediately set off upstream against the flow. Chanting in unison and sweating profusely in the dank heat, they paddled hard for about a half mile upstream. Then, they put even more muscle into their job and angled us across the swift current. As we neared the opposite shore they let out a high-pitched shout, almost a scream, interspersed with their rhythmic chant, to alert those waiting for us on the dock. The rowers were expert at gauging the flow of the river and the distance, and we arrived downstream exactly at the hospital landing.

As we touched land and tied up, all the bells of the hospital began to ring—a ritual announcement for new arrivals of staff or distinguished guests. A good proportion of the staff—doctors, nurses, aides, even the cook—came down to the dock to give us a profuse welcome; introductions were made. Of the two other doctors at the hospital, the first to greet us was Rolf Mueller, a tall, handsome, very efficient Swiss. The other was Richard Friedman, recently from Israel and a former internee of a concentration camp. He was rotund, heavily moustached, in a way a young version of Schweitzer, with, as we would discover, a whimsical sense of humor.

It was then that I caught my first glimpse of Albert Schweitzer. He was coming down the hill toward us, somewhat bent but agile and walking at a good clip. He was eighty-five years old. On his head was the pith helmet, encased in a stained white cover, and what we would discover was his usual dress: gray baggy chino pants, a short-sleeved, open-neck white shirt, and well-worn heavy shoes.

He was lean, larger than I imagined, and as ruggedly handsome as portrayed in his pictures. His large head and strong features were topped by a shaggy white mane flowing down both sides of his head and matched by a bushy moustache. His nose was strong, widely splayed; his eyes were deep blue and, as I later saw, could change almost instantly from a kindly twinkle to sharp anger. Though his skin was pocked, this did not intrude on his good looks. As a result of his outdoor work—building and repairing—his arms were very muscular and deeply tanned.

He appeared vigorous and joked with some of the younger nurses as he passed them, while clapping his hands to shoo a pet chimpanzee from the path. He came to the landing, shook hands with me, kissed Phoebe's hand in a courtly way, and made a little speech in French.

"Thank you so much for coming so far to our poor hospital to help us out." Then with a twinkle in his eye he continued, "Our hospital isn't exactly Johns Hopkins and our accommodations aren't like your Hilton Hotels." Then pointing to Dr. Friedman, he went on, "But as you can see, we are all fat and happy." Then, seeing our pith helmets on, he nodded, pointed to them and said "You've passed the first test."

Without further ado, and with the word *"allons,"* he placed his arm around my shoulder and led us up the hill toward our quarters.

"Do you speak German or French?" he asked in rather hesitant English.

"French," I replied. I understood French better than I could speak it, and he understood English. He was most comfortable speaking French or German, so with intermittent help from different staff people who could interpret questionable phrases, we conversed very well.

"No matter. Languages only clutter the mind," he said. "I'll show you the way to your room and we'll have lunch." This businesslike, if not unpleasant, attitude made me a little apprehensive about our future relationship—the ultimate reason I was there.

We walked up the hill in silence toward the place

where Phoebe and I would live, going along a short well-worn path bordered by heavy green jungle shrubs toward the main unpaved hospital square, actually more of an avenue between hospital buildings. In the square was the natives' living and social center at the hospital. It was a gathering place for ambulatory patients, families, native visitors, a conglomeration of various animals, and a temporary palaver (negotiating) place. Here, it was business as usual with daughters and wives, the most expensive cash crop if not the principal one, routinely traded and marriages arranged by the male establishment during a relative's hospital stay. Besides the financial deals, it was a place where aggrieved parties might settle their differences or family squabbles.

Under the protective shadow of the large overhanging iron eaves, small groups of the families of the sick squatted side-by-side, minding their children, nursing infants, or doing various outdoor "household" chores. Some prepared meals in large black pots over small wood fires; some sat in circles on their haunches, talking, arguing, or just watching the busy Schweitzerian world go by. One young woman braided another's hair and some had just come from the river with their wet laundry.

There were many children, mostly naked. Some played and kicked a ball around near the open smelly concrete sewer running through the length of the compound; all were shoeless, many with large ulcerous leg sores which didn't seem to impede their game.

We picked our way through this morass of people interspersed with dogs, wandering goats nibbling at just about everything, and an assortment of fowl, including geese and one turkey. There were also a few chimps wrestling, then chasing each other, overturning any obstacle in their way.

As we went along, natives stopped Schweitzer and asked in a French patois about a family matter or a patient.

He patiently answered each of them. At one point, Joseph, one of his most-trusted *infirmiers*, (hospital aides) waved him over to a building to show him a sick infant in its mother's arms. Schweitzer gently took the child, asking Joseph a few questions as he cursorily examined it. Then he called to Dr. Mueller, who walked behind us, telling him to examine the baby more thoroughly later.

The buildings in the square were constructed of rough-hewn mahogany and other hardwood frames, with screened sides, with the omnipresent corrugated iron peaked roofs coming down in eaves low to the sides. The eaves kept the sun and the driving rains out and provided protective outside living and cooking space for the patients' families.

There were many different types of buildings. Some were long with separate rooms for different purposes such as a simple laboratory. Others, like the operating room and the storage room, stood alone and were not screened but completely encased in wood. There was a special compound for the professional staff and white patients (see map, page ____). This latter may sound like apartheid, but the real reason for it was basically sound, as I later learned. The dining hall and open wards were also long, low individual buildings.

The Leper Village buildings (constructed with Schweitzer's 1952 Nobel Peace Prize money), which I saw only later, were much newer but built along similar lines with bamboo siding. The Leper Village was removed from the main compound, probably because of the ancient stigma of the disease. But the tuberculosis ward was almost in the middle of the compound and just below the room where we were to stay.

Many of the professional staff of about twenty-eight whites (mostly European) and some nonprofessional black aides and white volunteers followed us. The doctors wore tan chinos and short sleeved shirts as did the black *infirmiers*. The white nurses, mostly older, were always dressed in white as were the female volunteers. Most of them spoke English rather well.

Breaking the silence, I told Schweitzer that Phoebe and I had stopped off in Kamakura, Japan; and I had a personal letter for him from Daisetz Suzuki, the renowned Zen scholar. He was pleased. "I remember Suzuki fondly," he said, "Mrs. Schweitzer had always been particularly interested in him and, of course, I came across his work when I was learning the oriental religions."

We continued our walk, lapsing into silence again. Then, giving me a sidelong glance, he asked, "Dr. Berman, we're all very happy that you've come to help us, but why should a busy surgeon, researcher, and professor back in the United States, where you have everything, come to this poor hospital in the depths of a jungle to do such simple work?"

It was not an unexpected question, but it occurred unexpectedly soon. After all, he knew me only second-hand through the flattering letter regarding my abilities from Tom Dooley of Medico (of which I was then President), and through Erica Anderson, the world renowned photographer, who knew me well and whom he trusted. He was canny enough not to accept at face value my affiliation with the Johns Hopkins Medical School, knowing just as I did that many reputable surgeons with large practices, publishing erudite treatises, are frequently poor in judgment and poorer in skill.

"To be perfectly frank," I answered, looking searchingly at him, "I didn't come out here to just practice surgery, which I hope you'll be pleased with; I do enough of that at home." I paused, then said, "Nor am I that much of a do-gooder or religious enough to have been prompted to come many thousands of miles to alleviate human misery. We have plenty of that, too, back home."

Schweitzer stopped. He turned to Ali Silver, who was

walking just behind us, for an interpretation, as if he wanted to make sure he had heard right. In some of our subsequent talks, Miss Silver, a middle-aged nurse, was frequently an interpreter. He nodded his head as she translated what I had said to German. Later she told me that the phrase that stumped him the most was "do-gooder."

Turning back to me, his large blue eyes crinkling with interest, he said, "So?"

Still not knowing how he would react, I continued, "Both my wife and I really came to try to get to know you." His large, somewhat stooped frame straightened a bit, as if waiting for more.

He then started off again up the path; his hands clasped behind his back, as they often were; his head bent down. He remained silent. A few steps further on, he stopped again. As I looked at the place where he stood, I saw that he was staring at two concrete crosses in a small cleared space. He said nothing for a moment or so, then lapsed into German, Ali Silver interpreting as he spoke.

"That's where my wife is buried and also Emma Hausnecht" (a long-time friend and devoted nurse). A sadness seemed to come into his eyes, and he put his hand gently on one cross. Then abruptly he turned and we continued our walk. He again put his arm around my shoulder and said, in effect, "It's a deal. If you're a good surgeon and a hard worker and do the job, we'll get to know each other."

His words were a great relief to me, but I didn't know then how closely I was to be observed and the trial I was to go through before he passed judgment.

Halfway up the hill, just past the tubercular wards, Schweitzer left us for his own screened-in room in one of the long rows of wooden sheds. We were shown to ours by Dr. Mueller.

Our room was about ten feet by eighteen. (As I later

observed, it was not much smaller than Schweitzer's.) The walls were mostly screening; first, because of the rampant malaria there, and secondly, because it let a breath of air, though rather damp, into the rooms. Dense vegetation surrounded the building. There was no electricity or running water. The furnishings consisted of two iron cots with straw mattresses and pillows, a potty under each cot, two kerosene lamps, a handmade table fashioned from crates, a similar wooden chair, and a separate smaller table with a huge old-fashioned ceramic bowl and pitcher for washing. There was also a bottle of boiled water for drinking and teeth brushing. A two-holer outdoor latrine was about a hundred yards one way, and an outdoor rainwater shower barrel about a hundred yards the other.

I was well acquainted with simple quarters and living conditions, having been with the Marine Corps on Guadalcanal, Guam, and Okinawa, but I knew it would be a lot tougher for Phoebe. Our only consolation was that the great Albert Schweitzer lived in a room, not unlike ours, under the same conditions.

We would learn later that the primitive living arrangements were strictly by design. Schweitzer was not only thrifty to a fault, knowing the cost of electricity and running water, but he had strong ideas about the staff not living differently from the natives and the patients. Simplicity was an abiding creed with him.

On that first day, I had been up since before dawn and was really bushed, but I had hardly gotten settled before I was called on to prove myself.

2

THE TRIAL—
THE CONTROVERSY

Schweitzer didn't waste time taking my measure as a surgeon. An hour or so after our landing, he found the perfect opportunity to get a fix on my abilities. This "test" was not just of my expertise: it was also the proof he needed as to whether his poor black tribal patients would be getting the best treatment.

I had just changed into chinos and a short-sleeved shirt, and washed up for lunch after the long trip, when one of the nurses appeared on our porch. "There is a case Schweitzer wants you to see right away." Dutifully, if somewhat self-consciously, feeling a little ridiculous (and looking even more so), I put on my white cloth-covered helmet for the second time. I followed the nurse down the hill past the tuberculosis ward and onto the bustling main square.

She led me into one of the wards. Here tatter-clothed families grouped themselves on both sides of the aisle and at the bedsides, constantly feeding and caring for their sick. The babble of the bush people was held to a low drone, as busy hands gently attended the patients' needs. Schweitzer had been severely criticized for operating a hospital this way. Even I had been skeptical; but after a few weeks' experience, I was convinced. It not only made sense, it worked.

As we entered the ward, I saw Schweitzer standing beside an occupied hand-hewn wooden bunk bed surrounded by other staff members. Without a word, but with a kindly smile, he pointed to the patient, then nodded to Dr. Friedman.

In a nasal twang and singsong cadence, Dr. Friedman gave me a short history of the patient. Friedman was a general practitioner at the hospital, as most of the doctors were, but assisted and did some minor surgery. He also fancied himself a psychiatrist of sorts.

I examined a groaning, writhing black man of about fifty. His thin face was contorted in pain. It was soon obvious that he had a strangulated hernia (a loop of bowel caught in an enlarged hernial ring of the groin), not an uncommon male problem in Africa. The man's history showed that the strangulation was of three days' duration—too long a time, I reflected. "With his high blood count and rise in temperature, the bowel is more than likely gangrenous," I told Schweitzer. He readily agreed.

Since there were two younger physicians, Adler and Mueller, at the bedside who could easily have taken care of this particular patient, there was little doubt in my mind that this case had purposefully been singled out to test me. Knowing this, I was sure Schweitzer was going to be at the operating table, if only as long as it took to gauge my judgment and technique. It gave me my first insight into the shrewdness and also the integrity of this man.

It was a most convenient coincidence for him that this type of case was available so soon after I arrived. A strangulated hernia provided the means of assessing my surgical skill as well as my judgment. In cases of strangulation, after surgically relieving the constriction of the bowel, a fine judgment frequently must be made at the operating table as to whether the bowel is viable (capable of remaining alive). If it is pink and shiny, it is viable. The bowel is then simply dropped back into the abdominal cavity and the hernia repaired. If the blood supply has been constricted for too long and the bowel appears dull and blackish blue, the judgment would be that it can't be saved. The dead portion must then be removed with the added risk of infection from the open ends which are then pieced together. And there are many borderline cases.

The decision must be made at the operating table. If the surgeon has misjudged the viability of the bowel and drops it back, he could be leaving a lethal piece of gangrenous gut in the patient's abdomen. On the other hand, unnecessarily cutting out a piece of viable bowel exposes the patient to peritonitis from the always-contaminated cut bowel ends. The decision depends on the acumen of the surgeon. As it turned out, this case was borderline. With his vast clinical experience with hernias, Schweitzer was well aware that a decision would have to be made as soon as the abdomen was entered.

The patient was sent to the O.R. for prepping, Schweitzer left the ward, and I went to scrub. There was a generator, used only for the operating room suite (it also provided power for an antiquated and rarely used—about 100 times a year—x-ray machine) which was started up. Over the months I spent at the hospital, I always knew of an imminent operation when I heard the start-up whine of the generator and the steady thrum of it giving power for the lights. So electricity was easy to provide, at least for the O.R.; running water was not. As I scrubbed, a native aide poured soapy liquid over my hands, then rinsed them with sterile water—the excess running into a galvanized tub.

The scrub-up room was a simple roughboard cubicle about six by ten feet, off the operating room, which was larger but just as rough. Except for the modern shadowless operative light, there was no resemblance to any up-to-date operating rooms. From here on, the resemblance to any modern operating units ceased. There were no tiled walls or floor, no glass shelving, no spic and span instrument cabinets, and no explosion-proof flooring. There was no blood bank or pathology lab to immediately examine specimens for malignancy. There was one anesthetic machine of ancient vintage for nitrous oxide, but no oxygen.

My assistants for this operation were three elderly Gabonese: Nyama, a tall robust man (who was still alive, retired, living in the same single room hut when I returned there in 1983) and Joseph and Pierre, men whom Schweitzer had trained for the past forty years. They were all very businesslike and taciturn, yet pleasant and intelligent. They had been with Schweitzer almost since the first clinic in the miserable chicken coop that the Paris Missionary Society had afforded him when he first came to Africa. He had complete confidence in each of those men. And it seemed to me that they, especially, were told to assist me instead of a doctor— just another part of Dr. Schweitzer's testing pattern.

Later, Schweitzer informed me that Pierre was rarely wrong in the operating room and Joseph rarely wrong in the wards. Nyama ran the whole O.R. suite. After I'd been in Lambarene for a while, I watched Pierre, under supervision, operate to correct a simple hernia and do it as well as any of the younger surgeons there. And Joseph had almost a sixth sense in diagnosing certain tropical diseases. He would take a history and examine a patient thoroughly, as he was taught, and, though he was always checked by a physician, he also was rarely wrong. His powers of observation were amazing. As surgical assistants, they were both superb—not only in their dexterity with instruments but in anticipating my every move. The correct instrument was in my hand before I could ask for it.

After I finished scrubbing, I gave the patient a spinal anesthetic; something I had not personally done in perhaps fifteen years. In a matter of minutes he was anesthetized from his waist down. As I turned away from the patient to change my gloves for the operation, there was Dr. Schweitzer puttering around across the room as if he were looking for something.

I had expected Schweitzer to attend the surgery for perhaps five or ten minutes. However, he remained throughout the entire two-hour procedure, standing on a stool, looking over my shoulder.

Though I was too preoccupied to think of it then, I later realized that he was in that room for only one reason and that was to make sure this one lone black man, whom he had never seen before and who lived some hundreds of miles away, was treated properly.

Later, I continually observed the gentle empathy and compassion with which he treated his patients, black or white. Which is not to say that he was not frequently exasperated with and stormed at them about some taboo or their laziness when they were in their more healthy states.

We operated in T-shirts and regular chino trousers under heavy rubberized aprons with good modern O.R. gloves. Our bare arms were continuously wiped by a native aide to keep the sweat from the incision.

By the time the anesthesia was effective, I had rescrubbed, the patient was draped, and we were ready to begin. I immediately made the incision through the various layers, clamping bleeders, opening into the hernial sac, then pulling out the thick purplish loop of bowel caught in the hernial ring. There was, of course, normal pink bowel leading to and from the strangulated loop. Having released the strangulation, I hurriedly wrapped the affected piece of bowel in warm sterile saline compresses to try to bring the blood supply back as much as possible before passing final judgment on its viability.

While waiting to see if any changes would take place, I asked over my shoulder, "Dr. Schweitzer, what do you think?"

"It's beyond saving," he answered without hesitation. I was relieved that we were both of the same opinion. "Just do your colostomy," he said matter-of-factly.

The last word caught me by surprise. "A colostomy?"

"Of course, a colostomy."

I sensed trouble. This was not the judgmental test I was expecting.

"Dr. Schweitzer," I said, trying to be diplomatic, "Colostomies are not done for these problems anymore; we resect (cut out) and do an end-to-end anastamosis" (sew the ends together).

"No," he said, "Not here; it's dangerous that way; we've had poor results with resection." Little did I know how much he ran his little fiefdom with an iron hand. No one ever even argued with him; they knew how utterly stubborn he could be. I had not as yet seen the extent to which his anger could mount. So I unknowingly challenged him.

Stalling for time, I tried to adjust my thinking from the ambience of a super sterile operating room in Baltimore to the radically different circumstances under which I was now working. I came to the conclusion that conditions within that abdomen on the operating table weren't that different and that these people were probably much more immune to infection than the average city dweller in the United States.

"May I ask how many resections have been done here?"

He didn't answer directly but snapped back tersely, "It's too much of a risk." It was obvious that he was annoyed.

"The chances of a wound infection and disability, with the help of antibiotic therapy, should be no greater here than anywhere else," I told him, trying to support my judgment. "Also, to have to open the abdomen again in five or six days in order to close the colostomy is another major procedure and, in the long run, probably much more hazardous."

He said nothing.

The sweat pouring down my back was not completely due to the heat in the O.R. I continued, trying to convince him, "I think it will work well if I resect. The patient will be better off and out of the hospital in seven or eight weeks."

He still said nothing. The tension was razor-sharp.

I looked at the others in the room, hoping to get some sign of encouragement. My plea for support not only went unheeded but I couldn't get anyone to even look me in the eye. I began to get shaky. Maybe I was taking a life-threatening chance with the patient (if what Schweitzer said turned out to be correct). I was certainly taking a chance of not gaining any rapport with him by denying his experience and judgment. Keeping my eyes trained on the incision, I said apologetically, and I hoped without the arrogance of righteousness, "I must do what my own experience tells me is best for the patient."

I went ahead with *my* method. But, as I proceeded, I tried to placate him. "You've had only young untrained surgeons here with little experience. I feel sure that what I'm doing is right."

He still said nothing.

I cut out about fourteen inches of blackish, gangrenous bowel, sewed the two healthy ends together with as little contamination of the peritoneum as possible, and dropped the reconstituted gut back into the abdominal cavity. I then quickly repaired the hernia. When I was finished, I turned, peeled off my gloves, took the heavy apron off, and shed my sweat-soaked T-shirt. He was still there, impassive, with no show of emotion, but looking very tired. Then, without looking at me, he said simply *"Danke"* and left.

I realized then that he was not used to being contradicted. Even though the technical part of the surgery went well, I could only imagine the worst of what he thought of my disagreement with him, especially in front of his aides.

I dried off with a towel, put on a clean O.R. shirt, and walked back to my room. I was depressed, bone-tired, and hungry—I had eaten no lunch (but, then, neither had Schweitzer). I had been on the go since that morning. As I thought over how much had transpired since 5:00 a.m., the contretemps at the operating table kept coming back again and again. How did he feel about my medical heresy in *his* operating room? Did he resent my opposing him in front of the others? Was his colostomy operation really safer and a better idea here in Lambarene? Then I wondered how he would react when we next met, and did my actions alienate him to the point of destroying my hope of private talks with him?

I was exhausted and still perspiring as I entered our little cubicle. I knew both my and his doubts would be present for at least a week, until that patient was on the mend. It was the longest week of my life.

Phoebe was napping, the hair on her forehead matted with perspiration. I didn't want to disturb her so, in my sweaty state, I flopped onto the straw mattress and was instantly asleep. It seemed that I had just put my head down on the crackly straw pillow when I was awakened by the ringing of the dinner bell. I awoke as if I were in another world, my bed damp, my clothes clinging to my skin. It was 6:00 p.m.; more than two hours had passed.

Foggy-headed, I arose, swinging my feet over the side of the bed. As I did, I noticed old French and German newspapers scattered on the floor at our bedside. Trying to get my bearings and yawning sleepily, I asked Phoebe, now awake, what the papers were doing on the floor. "You remember Marie-Louise Cullum, the beautiful American volunteer we met at the landing. She said that all sorts of diseases are caught by walking barefoot anywhere on the compound—even in this well-scrubbed room."

I knew about hookworm which was very prevalent in the southern United States. It penetrated through the soles of the feet and caused severe anemia. (It was once thought to be the cause of laziness in the Southerner.) Later I was reminded that one of the most common African diseases is schistosomiasis (also called Snail Sickness). The water-borne parasite (the schistosome), carried by the snail, invades through any part of the skin; in its adult form, a worm, it invades the bloodstream, intestine, urinary tract, and liver. From then on, we spread the newspapers six thick every day, especially during and after our "showers."

Removing my sweat-dampened clothes, I said, "I would give anything for a shower." The outdoor rain barrel shower arrangement was some distance from our room. Phoebe and I discussed alternatives. Necessity mothered a very simple solution. I stood naked, feet together, in the narrow washbowl that had been on the bureau. Then Phoebe poured a stone pitcher of tropically warmed water over me. I lathered with a bar of hotel soap (fortuitously snitched from our last semi-civilized bathroom), then she poured a second pitcher over me as a rinse. I felt a renewal that no shower at the Plaza Athenée in Paris could have ever achieved. I then gave Phoebe the same luxurious pleasure.

We dried, dressed, bundled the wet papers from the floor into a rattan wastebasket, put dry ones back, lit our lanterns, and walked up to the dining hall. We took the places set out for us, just opposite Dr. Schweitzer. The meal began with his saying grace. He was pleasant as we ate, saying nothing of the operation room controversy. Dinner was followed by a hymn sung by all, with Schweitzer accompanying the voices on a piano, and then a reading and interpretation by him of one chapter in the Bible.

He left immediately for his room, with no request for me to follow. Phoebe and I were again introduced around to the other staff people and some visitors and temporary volunteers who had not been down at the welcoming ceremony. There was a Swiss carpenter, Siegfried; a Japanese doctor, Takahashi, who was in charge of the leprosarium; and others, nurses and guests among them. We talked for awhile, then each of us left for our rooms.

I was tired but even more depressed. I again mentally kicked myself; maybe I should have gone along with his decision in the O.R. Would he ignore me now? I had dragged Phoebe three-fourths way around the world on our first time off in three years when we could have been in Paris or the Caribbean. Yet here I was in a jungle with a self-made problem. I spent a restless night.

It was not until about four days later that I was to know where I stood.

3

THE INSIGHTFUL BELLS

As his temporary surgeon-in-chief I had daily contact with Schweitzer, but there was still not a word from him about our agreement to talk. I still did not know whether the bargain we had struck during our walk up the hill on that first day would be consummated. It was now four days after that first operation; my patient had done well and was soon to be discharged. During those days of waiting in that post-operative period, I began to get an insight into the personality of Albert Schweitzer.

First, I found he was watching and assessing me. At mealtimes he probed with little subtlety, delving into my thoughts on various medical, political, and social subjects, and also on my relationship with his staff. When I was operating he would just happen to visit the O.R., or he would suddenly appear on the wards when I was making rounds. I was also told he would *just happen* to check every patient upon whom I had operated. He obviously was not going to make a snap judgment. His faith in someone had to be built with time and on his own shrewd, studied observations.

But while he was checking up on me, I, through less direct means, was learning what he was really like. At the same time, I was being well indoctrinated into the everyday routines of life at Lambarene and obtaining a deeper understanding of the man. Naturally, I talked to most of the staff and got insight from them, including his right arm, Ali Silver, the tactiturn Dutch nurse with the severe short grey hairdo, who daily gave out many of the assignments to the black staff from her porch steps in the morning. There was also the tall, erect Alsatian nurse, Mathilda Kottman, another overseer of the menial work to be done. Then there was the lovely, soft, compassionate, middle-aged (also Dutch) nurse, Marie Langendyk, very religious and very bright. Though very loyal, all three gave me objective insights into the complexities of Albert Schweitzer. There were many diverse opinions of him. Initially, all attested to the depth and versatility of his genius; but this had little credibility for I found that most of them had never really had enough intellectual relations with him, other than the hospital business at hand. Though generally congenial, his preoccupations and unavailability made him aloof, but this was obviously necessary to accomplish the immense amount he did.

Some things could be learned about the man in simple ways. For instance, the bells that awakened us every morning and sent us on our way to work, to meals, or to prayer. Only a mind born of and influenced by German genes and culture could have been so disciplined. As untidy and undisciplined as the native part of the hospital seemed to be, those bells and their regularity implied the rigidity by which the compound was run.

There were three kinds of bells, each rung with equal vigor and on-the-minute accuracy, by various staff people.

The special bell in the Leper Village, donated and inscribed by an East German religious group (itself paradoxical in that supposedly atheistic state), was used mainly for special occasions such as birthdays, holidays, or the arrival of prominent visitors, of which there were many. Then an ordinary bell of indeterminate origin was situated near the dining room and pealed out the daily schedule: especially, awakening at 6:30 a.m.; the end of the day at 8:30 p.m.; and, on Saturday noon, the end of the work week. The third bell was a huge, flat piece of iron that was sounded by striking it with a piece of heavy metal. This last signal, of unusually sonorous timbre, served as a reminder for daily hospital call or Sunday prayers for staff and workers alike. This "bell" hung at the bottom of the hill in the open square (formed by the hospital wards, operating room, and pharmacy) and was also the bell rung a half-hour before mealtime.

Breakfast was at 7:30 a.m., lunch at 12:30 p.m., and dinner at 6:30 p.m., except on Sunday when breakfast was at 8:00 a.m. Services followed at 9:00.

The dinner bell was continuous and was followed in a minute or two by ten or twelve single strokes, which by some strange quirk emitted sound waves evoking a terrible din of howling (in exact pitch) by every one of the numerous dogs on the place. The noisiest bell was near the dining room and also rang out the back-to-work signal at 8:00 a.m. and 2:00 p.m.

But the ringing of the bells was only one of several rituals that ruled the compound. There was always a special ceremony for a birthday, which Schweitzer hugely enjoyed. One of the nurses would get a woven coconut mat about two by three feet long and have someone paint something (either serious or comical) on it, appropriate for the birthday person. The night before, everyone, including Schweitzer, would sign it in indelible ink and each would leave a gift. A cake was baked; and, at the first breakfast bell, a large tray with the cake, flowers, and the gifts was brought outside of the celebrant's room. Then, all the doctors, nurses, and Schweitzer would crowd outside of the room singing hymns. The birthday person stayed in his or her room; then, after the hymns were over, the tray was brought in with the cake, simple gifts were presented to him or her, and everyone filed in to give congratulations.

At lunch on that special day, the mood was very festive; some of the staff even loosened up under the influence of the wine that was served. When the meal was over, Schweitzer would get up and make a very humorous speech. Then at dinner, just as the meal was finished, instead of hymns and a sermon, there was a choir of children on the porch singing various French and Fang (a native tribe, formerly cannibal) songs, ending up with a beautiful birthday song. These children were all from the Leper Village.

Another routine occurred for celebrations on religious holidays—not just Christmas and Easter, but for some of the lesser saints. For instance, on December 6 (St. Michael's Day), there were gay decorations in the dining room on the table, on the porch, and in the clinic. A gingerbread man had been cooked showing the saint's switch with which to paddle bad children. These holidays, I felt, were not taken very seriously but certainly helped break the monotony of daily routines. It also reminded the natives (who loved any reason for celebration) that Christianity had its joyful side too.

Certain other fixed routines reflected the man. Mealtimes, especially, followed specific sequences that were every bit as rigidly adhered to as the chimes and the holiday festivities. They were somewhat alleviated by bits of quiet conversation and the nightly guessing game.

The latter was always intriguing; it was to fathom the exotic, if unappetizing, animal or vegetable matter that had been set before us (among which were elephant, crocodile, and buffalo). Guessing the answer frequently lay more in deciphering the odor than the taste. The native root, manioc, in sticks, or cooked into a tapioca-like gruel, was easy to spot unless the cook was bored or had a creative urge and decided to camouflage it differently or mix it with a fruit. Fried plantain, a non-sweet, large banana-like vegetable with a potato-like taste was sometimes ingeniously disguised in ways a three-star chef would have envied. There was frequently hash, powdered potato, papaya, and mango. On Sunday night, there were usually cold cuts and cheese (the meat was mostly canned). Sunday afternoon was the big meal, sometimes with wine or beer and occasionally the more tasteful parts from the buffalo.

Part of the dining routine was the pleasant preprandial loitering—standing around talking shop or gossiping about recent radio news of the outside world—while waiting for "le Grand Docteur" (a title lovingly bestowed by his patients). Then the relaxed atmosphere was over. We sat only after he had entered, taking our set places at a long table. Schweitzer presided at the middle of the table's length, flanked by his two trusted female aide de camps—Ali Silver and Mathilda Kottman. Phoebe and I had been placed facing this triumvirate.

The first of the many parts of the mealtime ceremony was the swallowing of the bitter, yellow anti-malarial quinine pills that were placed beside each setting. Next, Schweitzer, his bowed head resting on his large but sensitive young-looking hands and muscular forearms, would say grace in German. The meal would then begin. Breakfast and lunch were preceded by grace only with no other religious service. Dinner was different, with a semi-fixed protocol after the meal.

Breakfast was usually a gruel of oatmeal or wheatena, with bread, butter, jam, and tea or coffee. Dinner menus included soups and gruels, which Schweitzer seemed to particularly enjoy, dunking the coarse homemade bread in both. He saved every scrap of leftover food and either fed it to his aging and somewhat moth-eaten-appearing dog—always under the table at mealtime—or took some back to his quarters for his pet pig, antelope, turkey, or owl.

During meals he frequently seemed preoccupied and far away, sometimes fingering the edge of the table as if it were the keyboard of his organ. At other times he would remember something he wanted to discuss with a staff member or, with his incisive wit, joke about some happening of the day. When telling one of his own funny stories, he would be so voluble, gesturing and laughing so heartily and infectiously, that he himself frequently drowned out the punch line. But the somber atmosphere of mealtime was lightened only momentarily by the somewhat hesitant response of the staff's half-hearted smiles. Had they been less in awe of him (which he tried to disabuse them of with little success), meals would have been much more relaxed. To my mind it was the staff, not le Grand Docteur, who influenced the almost churchlike mealtime ambience.

The twenty-eight regulars at the table, by their own rules not his, spoke to him only when spoken to—a protocol usually used by the Vatican in audiences with the Pope. Whenever I think back on the general atmosphere of the meal—the long table and the deference to Schweitzer sitting in the Jesus position—it evokes an image of Da Vinci's *Last Supper*.

When dinner was over, well-worn Bibles and ancient hymn books were passed around. Most of the hymn books were in German; a few were in English. Miss Kottman had Schweitzer's Bible ready, which he had marked for his reading. He would then take his old-fashioned metal-rimmed glasses from his shirt pocket and begin.

Pulling the old kerosene lamp closer to him, and in his strong and well-modulated voice, he would name the hymn and page. (The first few nights he took Phoebe's English hymn book and turned to the page for her.) Then, pushing his chair back, he unwound his large, slightly stooped frame, and with a sort of shuffle he would go to an old upright piano, where a kerosene lantern was perched on a movable arm, the wick turned high. He would swing the light over the keyboard and play that evening's hymn. He didn't sing, but the entire group at the table accompanied the piano.

He would then shuffle back to his place to read from the Bible. Occasionally, he would explain beforehand what he was going to read and why. Then, depending on his mood or what was brought out by the text, he would elucidate as he went along; either with twinkling blue eyes and great humor, as in the story about St. Augustine's conversion, or in deadly seriousness about biblical characters such as Isaiah or Daniel. He emphasized certain passages of the text with his large-muscled forearms and his long-fingered, expressive hands. Sometimes these lectures would last for a half hour or more.

One evening he read from Amos and went on to explain at great length that this was the first time that God was mentioned as being for all people and not just the people of Israel. The next evening he went on to tell how this came about. At another time, Schweitzer read three passages from Hosea; it was a time just before Amos, and it was the first preachment of humanitarianism and thinking of and helping your fellow man. Hosea, like Amos, mentions a God for all people.

Frequently he talked of Isaiah and the siege of Jerusalem, when the prophet told the Jews not to surrender—that God would save them. Schweitzer had historical evidence that Isaiah had infiltrated among the Syrians (the ones laying siege) and had noted some cases of plague; and sure enough plague spread among the Syrians, and the Jews were saved. He then went into a long description on disease and how it changed biblical as well as modern history.

Every dinner reading was a fascinating one. Sometimes he subtly brought in his own theories that a certain passage in the New Testament, though condoned by the Church, was not necessarily accurate.

He frequently read from other books—usually a philosophical text—then elaborated with his own interpretation of the subject. On Saturday or Sunday, an extra hymn might end the dinner hour.

Dinner the second night was unforgettable in that his interpretation of the Bible was so lucid. I had never heard each phrase of it dissected so minutely. He read three paragraphs (he usually read three) from the Prophets Elijah and Elias, then interpreted the text in great detail. He noted in those few paragraphs the first mention of others in the Old Testament. In this instance he interrupted himself to explain, from his own studies, that when John the Baptist asked Jesus if "He were the one" there was no implication that Jesus was the Messiah, though Jesus Himself thought He was. According to Schweitzer, John instead thought that Jesus may have been the Prophet Elijah, who was supposed to return from heaven to announce the Messiah. Schweitzer then read a small biblical sequence explaining each word of Jesus' reply. Actually, he was really explaining how his own book, the *Quest for the Historical Jesus,* came about.

There was never an evening when something unusual wasn't explained. His interpretation of just one phrase placed in the context of its time put an entirely different emphasis on its meaning. And as I later learned from him, this was the pivotal fault that he himself had discovered that put a new light which so upset the Church hierarchy on the historical Jesus.

After closing the Bible that second night, and for the next four, he talked extemporaneously about St. Augustine. He explained how Augustine grew up as a Christian but that when he went to Carthage as a student he was attracted to the fleshpots of that ancient culture and gave up Christianity. Later, this then non-sainted man was influenced by St. Ambrose, a great public speaker; so Augustine began to read the Bible aloud for the sole purpose of polishing his oratorical technique. Since he had to make a living he studied rhetoric, going to Rome and Milan to teach it. But, as Schweitzer explained, this was the beginning of Augustine's re-conversion to Christianity.

With a smile playing at the corners of his lips and with obvious pleasure, Schweitzer, nodding his bent head and wagging his finger for emphasis, went into great detail. He described how, through his Bible-reading exercise, Augustine gradually became so entranced with the ideas of Christianity again that his original oratorical interest waned as his Christian feeling waxed. So it was, by this circuitous route, that Augustine again took up the faith, became a believer, and in time gave up his lustful ways for more saintly ones.

Sunday was always a special day, as we awoke and ate later than usual. On that day, for some reason, only Dr. Friedman or Dr. Takahashi rang the bells for prayer. And only Dr. Friedman and Dr. Mueller and Dr. Adler preached in the clinic square, mainly to Blacks. This was what Schweitzer himself did for some forty years and which, as he said, he had always looked forward to.

The doctors usually set up an outdoor pulpit, had a reading from the New Testament down in the hospital square, then gave a sermon for twenty minutes to a half hour, with Frederick, a gaunt, greying, serious-minded man, another of Schweitzer's trusted *infirmiers*, translating into the Fang dialect.

To me there was little interest and even less understanding shown by the natives in those sermons. Some of them stood with exposed breasts, nursing; most of them squatted, scratching or chewing tobacco leaf; some even cooked; but they knew they should be there. At first, Schweitzer said he would know who didn't attend; and when the time came for their treatment he'd bring it up with them.

I asked Joseph to interpret for me as I asked a few natives some questions about their understanding of the sermon. They saw in the Bible only what they usually saw in their own spirit world: mainly good and evil, taboos, hexes and curses—but little ethics.

When meals were over, everyone rose; Schweitzer either left or lingered to draw someone aside to give instructions or just chat with a visitor. He then went back to his room. At 8:00 p.m. the bells rang signalling the end of the official day, but certainly not his. Many a night, returning to my room at one or two in the morning after a late emergency, I saw him, his profile silhouetted by his lamp's rays, writing.

During those first few days, while Schweitzer continued to maintain silence as to my status, I was in and out of his office, which was in the pharmacy shed overlooking the square, with administrative and medical problems, especially those of a tropical nature, with which I was inexperienced. I also learned much about him. In those meetings, I observed him in his day-to-day routines and his reactions to various incidences. Little things—an argument with a tribal leader; incidents with those around him—staff, patients' families, and native workers—both pleasant and unpleasant; his concern for animals; his overly-diplomatic manner with the local gendarmes; even the way he was overseeing his construction work—made indelible impressions on me that would have been unobtainable by the most direct of questions.

I could never forget his anger the time he found two of

the vegetable gardeners sleeping off a hangover on a Monday morning. I'm sure it cured them for at least a few weeks. Or the time he caught a young family visitor stealing a fish from the pantry. He personally took the complaining boy, practically by the ear, down to the river bank, put a fishing line in his hand, and made sure he stayed there all day.

What I noticed even more, especially at the dinner table, were his varying moods, which ranged from absolute silence to exuberant joking.

I soon realized Schweitzer was rarely impulsive or open with strangers. It took more than a few days of intermittent contact for him to show even a glimmer of his private side. One volunteer said she spoke no more than a few words with him for almost a year. Certainly no politician, celebrity-seeker, or journalist could accurately assess him on their hurried fly-in-fly-out visits. As he himself once said, "one rarely gets totally inside of another's head no matter how close."

Just before my arrival, there had been some visitors of note at Lambarene, including former presidential nominee Adlai Stevenson. Once back in civilization, these visitors, while acknowledging Schweitzer's talents, offered the media off-the-cuff opinions of his personality and medical contributions, usually wrongly based on their few almost-instant observations. This was coupled with loose gossip by unhappy members of his staff. Few if any of those short-term critics were capable of offering valid conclusions on the man's humanity or character, much less knowledge of the hospital's accomplishments, which they were certainly not equipped to judge. Yet their statements were immediately latched onto by the worldwide press, giving an unfair picture of the doctor and the hospital.

Shortly after the evening meal on my fourth or fifth day at the hospital, I heard Schweitzer say to Ali Silver, "In about ten minutes." That was the usual signal meaning he would see someone in his quarters. During those first few interminable days I had strongly questioned whether I had come this great distance, and lived so uncomfortably, for naught. But that evening the "in about ten minutes" was for me. I was summoned down from my tenterhooks. Ali came over and said Schweitzer would like to see me in his room. By a not too strange coincidence, the patient upon whom I had operated that first day had been told that morning he would be able to leave in a few days. I guessed that I had passed the test, and this was to be the first of our conversations.

THE HERETICAL
QUEST

I hurried back to my room to freshen up, excited about seeing Schweitzer. As I was going out the door, I saw on the homemade scrap-wood dresser the letter from Daisetz Suzuki I was to deliver to Schweitzer. Picking it up on the fly, I hurried out across the pitch-dark compound, my kerosene lantern throwing magnified ghost-like shadows on the thick foliage along the path. As I drew closer to his room, I could see the famous profile bent over his desk, dipping and writing, dipping and writing with his old-fashioned pen and ink.

Two topics were on my mind. The first was to gain some personal background from him as to how and why he was attracted to certain disciplines, such as music and religion; and secondly to ask how he came to write the *Quest for the Historical Jesus*, which had evoked so much controversy and so much Church opposition in 1910. Of course, I didn't know how far I'd get with either goal.

His pet pig lay sleeping on its bed of straw on the porch upon which I creakily stepped. Schweitzer immediately came to the door and quickly drew me in. He joked, "I won't let the anopheles (the mosquito, carrier of malaria) incapacitate a good worker."

It was my second reassurance that I had been accepted and the bargain Schweitzer and I made would be honored— we were to talk. As was to be frequently the case when we met, Ali Silver (or one of the other English-speaking nurses or doctors) was there to help if needed as an interpreter. This first time, her frigid stare and pursed lips made it obvious that, unlike the good doctor, she had not yet passed on me. I remembered her wincing at my candid conversations with him, just as she did on that first day on the hill. I was sure she had heard via the hospital grapevine of my confrontation with Schweitzer at the operating table. As Friedman told me, everyone else had. Later, I could feel she especially resented my casual and frequent joking with him during meals. It was almost a jealousy, as if I were encroaching on her relationship with Schweitzer. And I could understand that: even after her years of dedication to him I rarely saw him laugh with her.

Schweitzer's room was no larger than ours, except that it had an alcove for his organ and a corner that was sectioned off with chicken wire for his orphan antelope fawn. The organ was special; it was zinc-encased to prevent rust and termites from getting at the wood—an absolute necessity in the tropics: even hard wood could not cope with the equatorial climate and the various insects it spawned. The instrument, which was actually a piano fitted with organ pedals, had been given to him by the Bach Society of Paris not only for leading the organization some years as a founder but also for his many contributions, mainly his Bach interpretations and writings.

The room, lighted by two green-bowled kerosene lanterns, appeared to be in complete shambles. Papers and books were heaped everywhere, including on and beneath the iron cot where Schweitzer slept. The floor was a minefield of bundled papers through which I had to carefully pick my way. Sheaves of papers tied with string hung from nails on the wall and on the exposed ceiling beams. It must have been more systematic than it looked, for during our succeeding conversations he was always able to put his hands on anything he wanted immediately.

One of the many books by or about Schweitzer that I read in the weeks before we embarked cited his "filing system." He always worked on two or three projects at one time. During the time I was in Lambarene, he was writing the third volume of the *Philosophy of Civilization* and another volume on Bach. His research material for the various chapters was neatly stacked in ten or fifteen piles around the floor, reflecting the orderliness and simplicity of his mind.

"My only concern, besides my friends dodging their way through the maze," he said, "is that the cleaning woman will knock some over and put them back in the wrong order. It would take me a day to reorganize them."

Each chapter of each book was bound by string, waiting to be put on the weekly boat that would send it on its way to his publisher in Europe. His desk was piled high with opened and unopened mail as well as half-answered letters written in his small, precise handwriting not yet ready to be taken to Lambarene village to be mailed. Most of the hundreds of letters that came with the supplies on the weekly riverboat was answered by nurse Silver, but some he personally answered in longhand. I had yet to see a typewriter on the premises.

Schweitzer looked drawn and gray that night, not the healthy pink he usually exhibited in the morning. He was now in his ninth decade and still working fifteen to eighteen hours a day. As I came in with him, he drew a backless stool over to his desk and gently pushed me onto it. The fawn, a beautiful golden tan spotted with white, which he continuously petted while we talked, was sitting, her delicate front legs tucked under, at the side of the desk. His greyish-brown owl, eyes tightly shut, was perched on one of the rafters. Schweitzer sat in his chair and rubbed his eyes with the back of his hand like a small boy who had just awakened. Then he leaned back and came right to the point.

"I'm now living up to my end of our contract, so we'll talk; I know you've lived up to yours." He put his large but delicate hand on mine. "I guess you know I've been watching you as you've involved yourself in our lives. I'm pleased—you not only get along well and have been good for my staff and the patients, but you've shown us new things (obviously a reference to the bowel resection), and you've worked hard."

He smiled and winked. "Please tell your beautiful wife I appreciate how much she is doing." (Phoebe was working in the *pouponniere*, the baby clinic.) Schweitzer continued, "When you came I didn't know I was getting two for one."

The mention of work set him off on another track. "Work is good for the body and spirit." He gazed off for a moment. "If the natives here could only learn how good it is to work, especially with their hands. . . ." For a while he was quiet, fingering the edge of his desk as if it were a keyboard as he did so often.

Then he focussed on me again. It seemed he did not know where or how to begin our talks. This was understandable; after all, he knew little of me or why I was so interested in him. He finally said, "Do you see this old softwood desk? I made it myself out of lumber that the U.S. military gave me from a torn-down barracks after World War Two." He surveyed his handiwork, covered as it was with books and papers. "The United States has been good to me and my patients. My lectures there earned me a great deal of money for the hospital." As an afterthought, he added, "The tuberculosis ward was built partly with American money."

The mentioning of his lectures in the United States seemed to remind him of other things.

He went on, not at all vindictively but somewhat defensively, "A foreign press that has mere glimpses of one or that asks, at most, a bare handful of questions or has a ten-minute chat may create a picture, most of which is not very accurate. It's not that it's always bad; sometimes it's very good. It's just that it's more imagined than correct." Then he laughed. "When I first read one of their accounts of me, I wasn't sure whether they had confused me with an angel or a devil. As you know by now, I'm just another human," then, with his usual wit, "with equal attribution from both above and below."

At this early stage of our relationship, especially so soon after the operating room incident, I was not about to discuss the criticisms I'd read about him relative to the interviews he had given. So I mentioned that it wasn't only the glimpses that journalists got of him; that his whole background reflected so much more than that of even an extraordinary human being. How many people in this world have four doctorates; a dozen honorary degrees from great universities; separate careers in music, theology, philosophy; and have published public sermons and criticisms of our society?

And how many individuals from the sophisticated environment of an intellectual European home, with all the amenities, would give up everything to work in a chicken coop (his first hospital—the only one the Paris Missionary Society allowed him) in the loneliest, most foreign and disease-ridden part of the globe?

And then, the Nobel Prize did not exactly detract from his credits.

I had decided on my way to his room that I would be as direct with him as I hoped he would be with me, but would also take care not to offend him in any way.

I couldn't help but smile. Instinctively deflating my flattering appraisal, he said with a straight face, "You didn't mention my medical achievements."

Joking back at him, I said, "Not to be disrespectful, but I don't think you'll ever get to heaven for your 'kitchen table' hernia operations."

Ali Silver gasped as Schweitzer turned to her for help in getting the full gist of the remark. Roaring with laughter he came right back with, "No, but I'm sure most potential saints get there much quicker being a doctor than a philosopher or musician."

Taking up on the word heaven, he said, "I don't believe in it, at least as it's usually meant or described,"—not surprising in view of his unorthodox views of other Church doctrine—"But," Schweitzer continued, still in a jocular mood, "if there *is* one, I doubt that I'll be admitted, and not because of my poor surgical skills. Do you know of even one saint who got there by writing things the Church thought were heresy?"

He was, of course, referring to the *Quest for the Historical Jesus*. I had had a vague recollection of the book from my comparative religion class in college. Then when a friend of mine knew I was coming to Lambarene he gave me a copy. I reread it hurriedly, and although I didn't quite understand all of it, I could see why the Church was so disturbed by it.

"Do you know because of the *Quest for the Historical Jesus* the Paris Missionary Society turned down my first application for my mission to Africa? One of the provisos on which I was allowed to go was my promise not to preach. I agreed because if I could not preach what I believed, I certainly would not preach what *they* did. Even then, they wanted me to go before a Christian tribunal and answer their questions. I politely refused, saying the age of inquisition was past.

"Do you know what finally convinced them to let me go? I guaranteed I'd pay my own way, bring my own medication, and maintain the hospital myself." He squinted his eyes and murmured to himself, "Not very Christian."

I decided to ask him the question that had been in the minds of many people for over fifty years: why a man with all his talents would put up with all of this and have to beg for that lowly Mission.

He explained it slowly and, at times, painfully. "I was only twenty when I decided if I were to repay the grace of talents that had been visited upon me, the best way was by relieving at least some of the physical misery of our world. Also, spiritually, I felt a deep responsibility to all men." Just saying this seemed to sadden him.

"This decision was not made overnight; it was a gradual affair, and Africa was not my first choice. My first choice was right in Strasbourg, trying to socially rehabilitate discharged prisoners. It didn't fulfill my needs. Neither was it doing the most for the tragedy of the worst.

"But I also realized my *Quest* had created a problem for Christianity. With so many theologians not willing to accept my thesis on Jesus, I decided that I'd make my life my argument—going to Africa was living it.

"I had always thought of Africa as a continent mired in misery, illiteracy, and pain, having no way to help itself. I also knew that it was only because of ignorance and lack of opportunity and that, by simple logic, the more fortunate had to help. It was by sheer chance that I finally made up my mind. One day I came across a missionary report with the description of the many problems and illnesses that black Africa was heir to. I felt that that was where I could help the most. So, after three doctorates, I began medical school."

Then he made a small confession—"selfishness": "I also thought I would be less distracted in Africa so I could think and write at the same time. I thought then that Europe pulled at me in too many ways."

He stopped and gazed off as if thinking of those first years. "I mentioned my chicken coop hospital before and I'm sure you've read about it. Someday I'll show it to you; it's not far from here."

I guess he'd never forgotten that the Church didn't even want to give him the tiny Mission he finally got. It took all of his minister father's persuasiveness to get that job for him, even with all he had to offer. Much later, realizing his preaching talent, the Church allowed him to begin formal preaching. But he had already been preaching in a round-about way for years.

For the first time I realized that he still had lingering anatagonistic feelings against the Church hierarchy—and not only because of its criticism of his book and the Church's later dogmatism as to the truth about Jesus, so different from his own. He also resented what he felt to be the Church's cupidity and, most of all, its callous disregard of the medical needs in Africa. He strongly felt that that particular group of Christians had too little empathy for people and no heart for misfortune.

As he went on, he became more relaxed with me and began to reveal some of his inner feelings.

"Though all religions and especially the life of Jesus had fascinated me since before gymnasium (high school) days, my first and greatest love had always been music and the organ," he confided. "It has given me the greatest pleasure and still does. I learned long ago that, even though love of something like music may be overriding, other unexplainable internal drives and curiosities must be satisfied. Sooner or later one must choose an order of priorities. As I grew to know them myself, I came to know more unconscious compulsions that I could not really avoid. And the top priority which obsessed me was the life and ethics of Jesus Christ.

"Even as a child in Sunday school I'd wondered about Christ. Why was Jesus' family so poor? His father was a carpenter; and then the three Wise Men had brought Him so many gifts at birth. Also, I questioned what happened to those three Wise Men; and, if they were that wise, why didn't we hear from them again? Was Jesus really God or the son of God? If He was God or the son of God why should He suffer? Later, as a student of theology, what I questioned and what I found out about Jesus didn't make less of Jesus either as a man or as a special son of man—not God, as the Church described Him and which He proves wrong from the Scriptures alone.

"I couldn't understand why they wouldn't accept Jesus as a philosopher and a mystic *and* a Jew in a Jewish milieu. My research showed without question, and with hard evidence, that Christ's preaching of the coming of the Messiah was in the Jewish tradition of His times."

It was strange that the Church should have taken such public affront at Schweitzer's writings; after all, he was just a student. Actually, his thesis in the *Quest* hinged as much on Jesus' new humane psychology and His new ethics as on His supernatural beliefs.

He went on, "Theology was not just mystical but philosophical; and certainly philosophy was partly theological.

"I maintained they both depended on truth and evidence, and that's what the *Quest* was about. But since the death of Christ the great simplicities He preached became bogged down in interpretations which eventually became dogma. I approached the historical Jesus scientifically and, as many scholars still think, I showed sound evidence for my interpretation.

"However, I also know my explanation of Jesus has been attacked many times. Christian theology just would not accept my ideas. But to my knowledge they have not been refuted—as yet. All I did was use the scientific method in interpreting Jesus' history from the words taken from Mark and Matthew, which I think were the earliest and truest writings about Him. These show that Christianity has now created a dogma and gotten away from the truths of Christ— that man must understand the worldly kingdom of God. Moreover, the less blind faith our society has, the greater its faith will be. In our era of investigation and enlightenment, the Spirit of Christ will live yet another three thousand years or more. Without it, it cannot survive."

I interjected that blind faith is what the average religious person lives by—not evidence.

"That may be the main trouble—faith without thought," he answered. "Faith will only endure when it is thought through. But this is no different than what Christ really preached. Rote belief is dead in this enlightened age."

He explained further, "The Church is still answering crucial questions, even as to Jesus being God, regardless of new interpretations. What's more, since they've been comfortable living by their dogmatic doctrine for thousands of years there is no reason to change. They seem to be more interested in sin and the Virgin birth than showing man how to understand God and His Kingdom."

I suddenly realized Schweitzer implied that Jesus' Spirit had already lived three thousand years not the nineteen hundred and sixty years that had passed. I asked him what he meant.

"No one knew exactly when Christ was born. Some of the Gospels, especially John's, show flaws of authenticity anyway. All anyone really knew of Jesus' life was for maybe six to twelve months at most, when He was preaching. The Dead Sea Scrolls suggest that Christ may have been an Essene anywhere from one hundred and fifty to fifteen hundred years before. Moreover, our second-hand histories by Mark and Matthew were written maybe a hundred years after the death of Christ; yet they were the most reliable evidence I could use in my interpretations. Even then, they were so different from the dogmatic interpretations of the Church."

"If your work was so logical and you had so much basic evidence, why was the Church so upset by your interpretations?"

He took his time answering. "After teaching what they had for so many years, it's understandable that they considered my work heretical." He zeroed in passionately on that one word. "Was it heretical to bring out facts rather than vague feelings based on shaky interpretations? Was it heretical that I claimed that the Church should not have asked its constituency to worship Christ as a god, when He Himself never thought He was a god? Was it heretical that I interpreted Jesus' words through those of Mark and Matthew, whom the Church so wholeheartedly believed in? Could that be a slur on Jesus as a man, if obviously a man of divine spirit?"

He'd always believed, he said, that man is not just flesh and blood but also spirit. It varies in degree in various men. "Without the brains of man to think and to think at times of why we are here, he is then without spirit—not really a man." He added, "An animal is a creature of God—a living thing—but it may not have a spirit. I don't know. I think to have a spirit one must know that it has one, and I'm not sure that animals do, but it is ethical to think that they do." He was alluding here to his Reverence for Life philosophy.

"Frequently the Church is its own worst enemy," he mused. "It discourages the spirit in those who are enlightened and presents it like a fairy tale to the unenlightened. It seems to separate the people from Jesus." Shifting again, he said, "We'll talk about it more some other time. We're getting much too serious for our first talk."

"Will you bear with me for just one more moment?" I asked hesitantly.

He nodded.

"Why did you choose to go into medicine so late in life?" He was thirty-five.

"It was a simple expediency if I were to do some good in Africa." Then he smiled, and his eyes twinkled. "It may have never got me a prize in science (referring back to my joke on his hernia surgery) but it has been a handmaiden to enhance my own spirit in helping those miserable and diseased here."

As I suspected, it was an expiation, or better, a giving back, a repayment for all that he was endowed with at birth.

"Were you endowed from birth with all those talents or do you think your training was more responsible," I inquired.

"Well, if I wasn't so fortunately endowed," he said thoughtfully, "I don't know why I was taken with music so early (at the age of four) when other children weren't, or why I was so curious about Jesus and God and life when my own small friends were only interested in soccer. I don't know.

"Certainly my parents didn't push me into music or philosophy. But the study of organ music and theology went back a hundred years in my family."

He paused. "I guess I was guided to a certain extent,

but the necessity of thinking things out came to me, on my own, very early. Later, my great urge to write my thoughts down was purely instinctual—with no guidance at all." As he put it, "I could not but do what I have done.

"I never understood why," he said, shaking his head, "Why I always had such empathy for my poorer classmates in school in Gunsbach."

Whatever their origin, his natural urges overcame his grandfather's wish that he be a comfortable cleric in a European parish or his father's hope that he become a doctor—even if not a contented Strasbourg doctor. "So here I am in Africa, neither all one or the other, but a little of both.

"As to my medical career, science had never been my greatest drive but, once in it, I became intrigued by its discipline. It is so different from philosophy or theology—so exact. Evidence in science is so concrete, so sure, as distinguished from the humanities. However, even before I came into science I figured that the only way to prove something was by putting it through my own version of the scientific method, which was so important in my research."

Schweitzer rose suddenly. "It's getting late; we'd both better get to bed."

Though I didn't get all that I came for—mainly, a more detailed explanation of the historical Jesus—I had learned more than I had ever hoped to in our first meeting. Hearing about some of the parallel aspects of his youth and his drives opened up a whole new part of Schweitzer's life to me.

As I got up to go I remembered Suzuki's letter. I handed it to him at the door, apologizing for almost forgetting it. Schweitzer opened the letter and smiled once or twice while reading it. It was not a long letter, and I didn't even know the language in which it was written, but I imagine it was in English. He folded it and put it into his back pocket, where he seemed to stuff so many other papers. I was dying to know what the letter said, but he never mentioned it again.

As we stood there he said, "I wish I had more time to study the oriental religions." Actually, I had read he had studied them intensively. "Whatever the religions of man, they are no different in the early stages of their development and in the thought of an Almighty. From there on the differences are superficial. All of them start the same, either in fear or hope. But then they gradually get refined and polished differently by time and the particular culture they find themselves in. Yet, whether Eastern or Western (he did not include African), they all wind up not differing that much, except in ritual."

At that point, I was still too unsure of my footing with him to carry the discussion further. Instead, I mentioned that Suzuki had twice warmly brought up Mrs. Schweitzer and how much he enjoyed her letters.

"He thought she had a very original mind," I told him.

Schweitzer nodded. "Yes, she did have and was a great help in clarifying many of my thoughts." (It has been implied more than once that she helped coin the term "Reverence for Life.") "She was a special favorite of Suzuki's and I think they corresponded for over seventeen years."

We talked about Mrs. Schweitzer for a while. Of Jewish stock, Helene Bresslau had been educated in history, and edited most of the work of her father, a well known historian. "She was always rather sickly, but when she knew she was coming to Africa to work with me she took up nursing. She died of tuberculosis—probably contracted here at the hospital where it is so prevalent among the natives."

As he talked of her I formed a picture in my mind of a bright and probably very powerfully-willed woman. It had struck me, that everything belonging to the hospital was stamped H.S.B. (Helene Schweitzer Bresslau) as if she were the real spirit of the place. I later found out this was a common European tradition.

"There's an interesting sidelight behind that Suzuki letter," I said.

"So?"

"When I visited Suzuki in Japan I told him I was on my way to work with you. I had read some of his books, but I had wanted to meet him just as I had wanted to meet you." I paused, reflecting on my own motivations for coming to Lambarene.

"Also, in America, the youth are now getting into Zen and other of the more exotic religions." I thought this might trigger Schweitzer's revealing his ideas of why our young people were being attracted to the oriental religions.

"Zen is not so exotic," he responded. "Only very different in that it negates the worldly life, whereas our Western religions affirm it—or at least should. There is not a great difference in religions, if they begin at an equal cultural level. You can't compare the primitive tribal beliefs here with a religion of the Chinese or Japanese—people that have much older, more sophisticated cultures."

I wanted to ask why some areas of the world had such advanced cultures so long ago, while the Africans didn't advance, but I refrained: I didn't want to appear to denigrate Africans. Yet he partly answered the unasked question.

"Here in Africa, there may be separate differences in beliefs for each separate tribe—and separated by only a hundred miles—but, with the lack of communication or at least a network of dedicated evangelists, how do they coalesce and grow?" He repeated, "Basically all people are the same in their fears, their attachments, and their joys. Beginning in childhood, they fear death; they hold onto life at its lowest, almost subhuman ebb; and they are closer to family and friends than to strangers."

Suddenly Schweitzer broke off that train of thought. "So, what about the story you started to tell of the letter?"

I explained, "One night in Tokyo, I was talking to an art critic friend of mine about this celebrated Zen scholar and he said his family knew Suzuki and could arrange for me to meet him. It was done by phone.

"The next day Phoebe and I drove about fifty miles south to his home in Kamakura. He lives with a young Japanese-American woman in an abandoned temple on top of a hill. I think he is ninety; yet he walks up and down those hundreds of steps each day to get his mail.

"We had a long talk at lunch that lasted well into the afternoon, continuing for an hour or more over a specially brewed dark-green bitter ceremonial tea. It's sipped over a sweet mint held on the tongue. It reminded me that my grandmother, born and raised in Russia thousands of miles away, drank her boiling hot samovar tea over a lump of sugar. I wondered how this cultural similarity came about, so far apart."

Schweitzer disregarded the tea-sipping technique and immediately picked up on the "they" and "them." "Is he married?"

"No, I don't think so; he was with—I suppose you'd call her his paramour."

"His paramour," Schweitzer repeated, giving me a glance of mock disapproval by furrowing his forehead and pursing his lips.

"I don't know what the exact relationship is," I said, "but she is at least sixty years his junior. Anyway, she's very attractive, about twenty-five years old. Let's say she's his secretary and lives in the same house with him." I went on quickly. "She told us how they came to live together. She was a student when he was teaching at Columbia University in New York and he was about to go back to Japan for good. She took the last course he ever taught, and, the first day after the first session, she said, 'I knew he was *my* man.' Those were her exact words. So she brashly went up to him and said, 'I'd like to study with you wherever you go, whenever you leave.' And she did.

"Anyway, when Suzuki heard I was going to see you, he said, 'I must send Schweitzer a note,' and, as if not to forget, he immediately took the first piece of paper he could lay his hands on, off a nearby table, and wrote in ink a rather lengthy letter on one side. As he finished, his young friend, sensing something awry, went over to him and peered over his shoulder. She saw that the letter was written on the back of something important, and there was an argument. She finally took the paper from him, and scolded him gently. Then she gave him a clean sheet to write on.

"Shaking his head, he wrote another, shorter note on the paper she had given him. He seemed to be a little disturbed, but took it in good humor. As he handed her the second note to put in an envelope, he murmured to me, 'She's a typical American—no respect for her elders. Besides, whatever was written on that other paper couldn't have been that confidential.' "

Schweitzer laughed heartily.

It was then about 11:00 p.m., and le Grand Docteur looked very tired. As I grew to know him better and observed him more, I realized how his appearance changed not only with fatigue but with his mood.

Saying I had stayed too long, I broke off the conversation. He didn't protest.

5

ADAPTING
TO LIFE
IN THE RAW

One stifling morning about two weeks after we arrived at Lambarene, Phoebe and I were given another look into the Schweitzerian character. As we approached his quarters on our way to breakfast, we saw him standing on the porch shaving his rugged face with a straight razor before a small mirror hanging from a nail on a post. As we passed, we nodded good morning to each other as if it were perfectly natural for him to be performing his ablutions in the open; it made sense, considering the darkness of those cubicles in which we all lived. It didn't dawn on me right away, but then I realized he was wearing his shirt. Few men put their shirts on before shaving; they don't want to get the collar wet and smeared with shaving cream.

As we continued on our way, it suddenly occurred to me that he also was not intermittently dipping his razor into a bowl of water, as most of us do. Only when I turned around for another look did I see that the unshaved part of his face hadn't any cream on it. He was shaving dry. I winced at the thought of it. I wondered if it was some type of self-imposed asceticism or if it was his usual abiding dislike to waste? By small signs I soon found out it was the latter.

Not that dry-shaving is necessaily a sure sign of frugality; it just brought to mind other examples of his saving habits. Each hospital day brought forth an example of his efficiency and abhorrence of waste.

I had read how difficult it had been for him just to keep alive those first few years after his arrival in 1913. He told me, though not really complaining, "Imagine yourself after a long sea trip greeted with an infested house unlived in for four years, an old chicken coop for surgery, no one to interpret or help, a hundred cases to unpack, and patients already waiting with strange diseases you had only read about."

From what I heard, when he first arrived the living conditions generally were not too much superior to the jungle around him. The food was barely edible and the climate unbearable for a European. He had only the medications he brought himself, and these were soon in short supply, with a six-week wait for more.

Later in one of our talks, Schweitzer told me that during the hardships of the First World War, when no outside supplies came in, even the Christmas candles were hoarded—lit only for a short period so they could be used the next year and the next, if necessary. This intense aversion to wastefulness, however trivial, from conserving table scraps for his animals and straightening bent nails to writing rough drafts on the reverse sides of old letters, continued to that day.

However, I had more trouble adapting to the somewhat more modernized semi-comforts of the hospital in 1960 than he had in the raw jungle in 1913. Just to physically keep up with a man forty years my senior in everyday chores was difficult and embarrassing. But to see his shadowy profile night after night writing till very late made me, at the age of forty-three, feel hopelessly inadequate in just simple endurance if nothing else. Those evenings in which I didn't have a session with him I collapsed in bed at 9:00, totally spent. And, getting up for breakfast in the relative cool of the early morning dawn—about eighty degrees—I was still fatigued.

Coming from a comfortable urban existence, with every convenience from supermarkets to air conditioning, we thought that the heat alone was enough excuse not to raise a finger all day. It was much worse for Phoebe, who was more susceptible to extremes of temperature, especially to heat, and much more sensitive to her surroundings than I and more devastated by other, personal facets of life in the jungle hospital.

Despite her refined classical features, blue eyes, natural burnished-copper hair and lovely figure, Phoebe was not a hot-house flower. She could still ride a horse in the morning, work in her garden for six hours, manage a large home and then go to a symphony that night as fresh as when she had awakened.

The first indication of the cumulative effect of this primitive life-style reached a breaking point that very morning we had noticed Schweitzer's manner of "shaving." We both had had a fitful night's sleep. The humidity, even for this rain-forest climate, had been terribly oppressive. Then, in the middle of the usual breakfast of cereal, coarse homemade bread, jam, and coffee, there wafted into the dining room an odor that could only be associated with the mordant decay of flesh.

Phoebe and I glanced at each other. We looked across the table, but there was no evidence that Schweitzer took notice of the odor. Nor were the staff regulars reacting. So we tried not to notice until I saw Phoebe pale, beads of sweat appearing on her upper lip. She lay down her fork and hurried to the door. Schweitzer, without alluding to the stench, asked me if she were unwell. I simply told him that she had awakened with a headache. He still did not acknowledge the obvious. Soon, Dr. Friss, the visiting Danish philosopher and one of the translators of some of Schweitzer's work, headed out the door, his color turning an unhealthy green.

I excused myself as unobtrusively as possible and went looking for Phoebe. She was halfway down the hill toward our room, retching unproductively at pathside. There was no sign of Dr. Friss.

We learned that the morning's horrendous stench and the specific stimulus ot our emetic centers came from the bimonthly arrival of the local butcher. This time he brought elephant meat (frequently he also brought crocodile tails or buffalo steaks and chops) in his open-air *pirogue*. Refrigeration was unknown in those parts of the African bush, except in the more sophisticated environ of the Relais, the small hotel in Lambarene. There an ancient generator did its best, at least during the waking hours. This was the hotel where we would go late Saturday afternoon or Sunday for the luxury of a luke-warm shower and a passable meal.

Not only was the meat of that butcher open to the elements in the *piroque*; but in over-110-degree temperature, odor or not, it was covered by a clambering host of brightly-colored insects of every conceivable species with new insectivores waiting to climb aboard at every stop in every village along the river. So, by dint of the prevailing winds, the rancid odor of the butcher's side of elephant had preceded itself. This was called fresh meat, which in the Gabon is a relative term ranging in meaning from just killed to maggot infested.

In between the butcher's visits, there were even more

A passport to the Gabon

Arriving in Lambarene

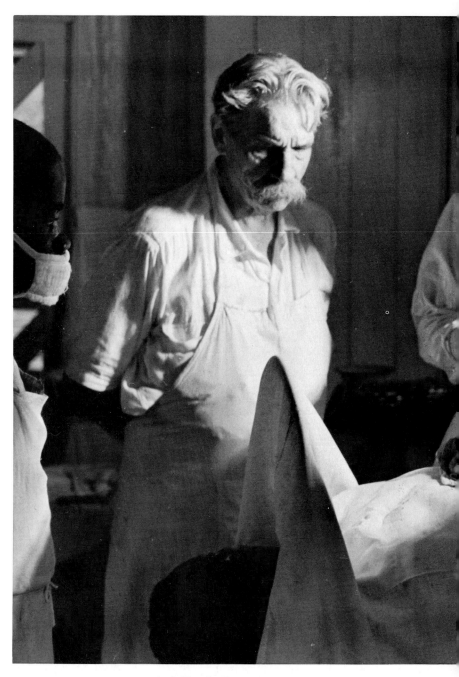

A difficult decision

The Main Street and Wall Street of the hospital

One of the early Last Suppers

disturbing daily and nightly irritations. One involved the necessity for privacy in very personal functions. Having had a three-year Marine Corps stint in the South Pacific where I used silt trenches out in the field side-by-side with my fellows-in-arms, "civilized" accoutrements of certain natural functions were not as necessary to me so I wasn't as affected as Phoebe by the one and only staff privy. But Phoebe opted for the semiprivacy of the potty under her bed—a situation I couldn't fault her for. No event could be as ignominiously embarrassing as when five or ten of your male and female colleagues face each other each morning waiting patiently for the use of a lone privy.

The place of encounter, an outdoor "two-holer," was midway between the two long, low, tin-roofed wooden buildings in which we all lived. It was set over the edge of a small precipice. There were no distinctions as to sex in this facility; it was divided side-by-side, French style, by a plywood wall that extended only from knee to neck. After breakfast, as was natural, there was a lineup of the sexes, face to face, waiting their turns. This scene would have tested the *equanimity* of the world-renowned Dr. William Osler of Johns Hopkins, popularizer of the word *equanimity*.

Everyone put on a show of nonchalance. No female or male eye ever met the other as all of the usual sounds and other airborne emanations exuded from within. Everyone had his or her own little ruse to avoid the embarrassment of the wait. Mine was a precious, month-old *New York Times* classified ad section held in front of my face during the entire wait. (After a month or so, I could recite from memory every help wanted ad, with job description, on that particular paper.)

When one came out, he or she, still not meeting the eye, quickly passed the key along to the next in line and disappeared as fast as possible. The next then went in even more quickly and locked the door from within. It was a relay. Inside, six-inch squares of French and German newspapers hung neatly on a nail.

If only I could have avoided looking down into the privy on our first day I would have saved myself a vision that affected my diet for the rest of my stay. The privy opened below onto a twenty-foot drop on the side of the hill that was easily accessible to the compound's flock of hens. These poultry, the sole producer of the compound's eggs and the occasional source of a tough chicken stew, were down there in force nurturing themselves among the excreta, the maggots, and other repulsive crawling fauna. From that day on, I could never face the scrambled or fried produce of that flock.

This impingement on Phoebe's most intimate privacy, along with the daily abrasions of her other senses, culminated that day in an explosion of emotion that could easily have ended our stay there.

I left her that morning when she began feeling better. She was getting ready to go to the children's ward where ulcerous legs, snotty noses, and wormy diapers awaited her. I went down to the surgical ward to make preliminary rounds on a few of the sicker patients and then to the operating room for a scheduled procedure. Just before I began to scrub up, Joseph called to me, saying my wife was outside and wanted to see me immediately. Having only seen her half an hour before, I was puzzled.

As soon as I saw her I knew something was radically wrong; her recent pallor had been replaced by flushed cheeks and an agitated eye. She took me hurriedly aside and made sure we were alone.

"I've got to get out of here," she said almost hysterically. "I can't take it any longer."

"What's happened now?" I asked placatingly.

Her lips tightened. "I can't take it any longer. Not

only did that same man with some fingers and part of his nose missing (an arrested leper) bring our water pitchers in today; but, when I went to brush my teeth with it, it was full of bugs!"

"Bugs? It can't be. The water's boiled; it's always been clean."

Her blue eyes flashed and her face reddened. "Bugs, millions of them," she repeated. "You can stay. I'm getting the next plane out." She flounced off toward our quarters.

I told Joseph to hold off a few minutes and dashed up the hill after her. It happened that Dr. Friedman was just coming out of his quarters and he stopped to say hello. I told him the problem. Strangely enough he smiled and went into the room with us. I looked into the water; and, sure enough, there were "millions of them." I gagged, but he only grinned more broadly, and, as he went toward the door, said, "Just malarial larvae; you can drink a bucketfull of them and they won't hurt you."

I breathed a sigh of relief; but Phoebe collapsed on the edge of my bed; her head in her hands. "It's just too much. Everything I touch seems to be darting or wriggling; every diaper I changed in the children's ward yesterday was crawling with a tangle of worms. Now this."

Her eyes misty, she flopped on her own bed, her head in her straw pillow, and didn't move for about ten minutes. I wanted to comfort her but didn't know what to say. Neither of us expected Lambarene to be as primitive as it was. But even though she'd been born and raised on a farm, walked five miles a day in all kinds of weather from a one-room schoolhouse where she later taught, nothing had ever been as earthy, as uncomfortable, or as repulsive for Phoebe as what she had been through the past couple of days.

Unexpectedly, her spirits revived. She got up. Without a word, she went to the washbowl, poured some of the "live water" in and washed up. "Well, let's go down," she said with an abashed smile. "Wiggle or not, stench or no, if you can take it so can I. At least I'll give it another try."

So there was no premature disgruntled departure. But it was mainly because we both began getting so fond of Schweitzer.

And as difficult as life was then, I couldn't imagine how Schweitzer had weathered his early years of struggle, saving and building. From what the older nurses told me, the conditions then would have made the most profligate of men into the most miserly of hoarders. Spending most of his time and effort raising and collecting edible food, waiting for months to get a supply of simple quinine to treat and prevent malaria, or being so short of paper and pencils just to keep his medical records, unquestionably had a lasting effect on him. Even after he had built his new hospital in 1913, life was made harder yet by the intervention of World War I, when he finally had to close the hospital.

At that time Schweitzer was working in a French-occupied nation and was declared a prisoner of war and placed under house arrest for two years. (Schweitzer was from Alsace, then a province of Germany.) He laughed when he told me about his being under house arrest in Lambarene with two French soldiers as his guards—as if he could escape anywhere in this jungle. But, as he said, "All of my time was not wasted. During the long interlude as a prisoner of war in Lambarene, then in France in a prisoner exchange, I not only memorized dozens of scores of Bach and Brahms but finished four books, one of which was on Bach."

During that time in Europe, Schweitzer underwent two operations for a tropical disease, the exact diagnosis of which he never disclosed to me. Because of the hints he dropped, I always thought the first operation may have been a possible bowel resection and ileostomy (like a colostomy) for a persistent tropical bowel infection and the second operation a closure of the ileostomy.

When he returned to Lambarene post-war, Schweitzer said, he was shaken by the looks of the old hospital he had spent so much time fixing up. "It was termite-ridden and a shambles that the jungle had retaken. I then decided to make the break I had contemplated for some time." But it was not only to move up the river to a better location, it was also a subtle break with the Church. The government had given him some two hundred acres on the old location of Trader Horn (now moved to the village of Lambarene) for his own hospital.

As he said, "I was starting all over again. Planning everything from getting the best price from the lumber merchants, ordering nails and iron roofing from Europe, putting together bunk beds out of raw wood, and even determining the best angles for the roofs and the best locations for protection against the sun and driving rains. Getting labor to scratch out space in the jungle was always difficult. The natives would show up as they pleased. Then, putting it all together was just overwhelming. At the end of the day I was not only fatigued but my hands were blistered from the hammer or shovel, and my calf muscles cramped while sleeping."

He let slip more than once that this new hospital had little formal Church connections. It seemed to me that while he couldn't forget the early treatment he received from the conventional Church, the final break was amicable and subtle. His excuse for moving was the state of the old hospital, the necessity for a larger one in a higher, healthier location, and the need for a more enduring type of architecture. "I again had the struggle of building a larger hospital while still carrying on my burgeoning practice," he said, shrugging as if he still didn't know how he'd accomplished it.

Now, in 1960, in addition to feeding and treating tens

of thousands of sick natives on resources that would ordinarily wind up in the trash cans of most hospitals, every one of the hundreds of staff and patients depended on him. He supplied the wherewithal for their nutrition, housing, water supply, and even counselled personal problems. As I also learned during my stay, no more than one or two people in the entire compound knew how a pump or generator worked; but Schweitzer did. I could only imagine what his problems must have been like some twenty-five years before.

Little by little, by 1927 the material shortage was solved; but there was still the twenty-four-hour-a-day tropical heat, the strange diseases, and the most exotic (if at times repulsive) diet for a sophisticated European to be exposed to. Thirty-three years later, in the era of refrigerated and packaged food and the technology explosion of the mid-twentieth century, most of the same conditions still prevailed.

This included Sisyphean refurbishing. As everlasting as mahogany is supposed to be, the wood that Schweitzer took from the primeval forest to build his simple wards, operating room, and living quarters began to rot in that formidable climate even before the last nail was driven in. The most durable of those natural materials held up for only short periods. Once sodden with rain and parched with heat, the wood became very conducive to the well-being of the all-consuming termites.

Ordinary metals rusted out in short order. This made necessary the special galvanized iron roofs seen glinting in the sun from across the river. That most precious commodity was of overwhelming importance to the maintenance of the all-wooden structures that it protected beneath long overhanging eaves, and was even harder to come by and more expensive to ship because of its bulk and weight.

Schweitzer's daily ongoing battle of propping up and replacing structures against the unceasing onslaught of nature was no less trying and frustrating than treating his human patients against the same aggressions of nature in this backwater of the world.

It was as if nature was trying to prove his efforts of no avail, to break his will.

"I only survived by conserving soap or paper, pinching pennies, and day-by-day patching and mending both people and shelters," he told me. Once, when in Lambarene and a poor old man asked him for alms, Schweitzer told Ali Silver to give him five francs (about ten cents). She said she had only fifty francs; and he asked her did she want to break the hospital.

He had to have had a will of iron, perseverence, and an indomitable spiritual drive just to maintain his sanity at the beginning, much less minister to the needs of others, in that environment.

Yet even under these debilitating circumstances, the measure of this man was not his survival but his superhuman creativeness during those doggedly-trying times. While attending the poor and disease-riddled villagers day and night Schweitzer still managed to write seven or eight books, update others, and produce over fifty shorter treatises in theology, philosophy, and medicine, in addition to keeping up with his organ practice, correspondence, his lecture tours, and his anti-nuclear peace initiatives.

6

A PERSONALITY
OF PARADOXES

Because of his reputed humanitarianism, the kindly facade, and the disarming personality he presented, no one would think of Albert Schweitzer as a revolutionary. Yet, as a youth he discovered new truths in theology; he created fresh interpretations of Bach's organ music and formulated the unique "Reverence for Life" theories of man's responsibility to his brother animal. Later, in Lambarene, he founded a pioneering hospital in the midst of a primitive environment. He was an uncompromising intellectual rebel, a destroyer of dogma and icons—even those of the fabled Jesus. To him, dogma was always guilty until proven innocent. His conclusions, once reached, brooked no interference. He was indifferent to the resulting ostracism no matter from what rank or level of sanctity. Though challenging conventional truth for truth's sake, he also sought that same truth by which to live.

I expected Schweitzer's nature to be complex and even enigmatic, but found it more so. As I began to know him, I

found he was compassionate, yet tough; simple yet complicated; adamant yet compromising; fearless yet careful; stingy
yet generous; officious but lenient; loving but indifferent;
tempestuous but calm; sensitive but hardened; and, above
all, a perfectionist with many imperfections.

To many, the most misunderstood of his contradic-
tions was that this highly gifted man would bury himself in
the primitive milieu of an African jungle: here was the author
of the Church-shaking *Quest for the Historical Jesus*, and his
humane, if misunderstood, "Reverence for Life" choosing to
sacrifice his talents to the cerebral and social sterility of a
Stone-Age culture, gearing down to the level of Gabonese
tribal life, opting for an almost cloistered intellectual existence. Even to his colleagues and his family (mainly his
mother), his self-imposed exile was incomprehensible at first.

At the time, I, like most others, thought it was surely a
lifelong sacrifice of himself, his talents, and his own ego—a
waste of all the worlds he encompassed. However, in time, his
reasons became clearer to me.

He was unlike other extraordinary men who lived the
good life and rationalized that only thus could they nurture
their talents in the interests of society. They usually enjoyed
their status in a rich, comfortable, cultural, urban environment.

What people couldn't possibly have known without
being with him was that Schweitzer's self-exile wasn't willful
or volitional. He actually had no emotional alternative, as he
later explained. Because of his all-abiding spiritual responsibility to the "brotherhood of those who bore the mark of
pain," it was a compulsion that he was powerless to deny; and
he knew it.

Though he said he was going to give up most of his
intellectual pursuits in order to treat the sick and preach the
word, his talents grew and could not be thwarted, even in

that jungle life. We'll never know whether he could have accomplished even more in Paris or Berlin.

One of the great sources of his productivity in Africa was his almost superhuman power of concentration. It seems that he could work as well in the maelstrom of his pharmacy office as he could in his study. At times, he seemed to enjoy interruptions by the most trivial of distractions; but was always able to get back to his writings without missing a comma.

As I watched, I wondered at this talented colossus spending half an hour or more discussing with a native chief the most propitious spot to build an outhouse or just passing the time of day with an itinerant vendor of elephant meat. I witnessed him intent on measuring off and sawing a two-by-four in the construction of a new tool shed or raging at or joking with a crew of laborers as he directed them in the fine art of pouring cement.

I would get a flash of his character, often by a simple phrase or a casual action, at the oddest of times. At first, he revealed his character to me grudgingly and piecemeal; later he was very candid. Once, when we were genially talking about some of the reasons he took up medicine to come to Africa, he shocked me by impulsively blurting out, "Do you think I enjoy living here?" Of course, I thought he did, but I didn't pursue it at the time.

As disciplined as he was in conserving his time, he spent some of it with the strangest things and people. One of the most curious was the relationship he established with a diseased and possibly demented pygmy lady who frequented the hospital compound. She spoke no known language or dialect; they communicated by sign language alone. I was most fascinated, if puzzled, by his interest and rapport with her.

Mama San Nom (no name) was tiny, about fifty years

of age, totally unkempt, filthy, usually entire naked, and misshapen and diseased. Her facial appearance suggested leprosy, but Schweitzer told me it was never proven. She had the usual myriad other diseases including tuberculosis, syphilis, and gonorrhea. (Almost all of the women in Lambarene had gonorrhea, supposedly brought in by the white lumbermen in the nineteenth century.) Gonorrhea was, of course, a sort of blessing in disguise. It at least produced an infertility that helped to keep the birth rate down and by the same token prevented a number of vesico-vaginal fistulas (a tear between the bladder and vagina) brought on by numerous births.

Mama was of unknown lineage, place of origin, and of questionable sanity.

One of her less endearing traits was her penchant for one of her particular gourmet delicacies—a spiny, yellow-furred caterpillar, which usually came out of the ground after a downpour. Just after a hard rain she would disappear, maybe for days at a time, and return with a cache of those formidable-looking creatures. Then she would spend part of each day in animal husbandry, tending them in a cardboard box and foddering them like a farmer his cattle. When they grew fat and tempted her palate, she would cook a passel of the most appetizing of them in a pan of palm oil over an open fire. She always generously offered to share these enticing delicacies with anyone around. The refusals didn't seem to bother her one bit.

She would drift in and out of the hospital compound, staying sometimes a week or a month, then disappearing for varying lengths of time. No one knew where she came from or where she went when she left. Schweitzer always seemed delighted when she reappeared. But it was more than just a curiosity or a compassion for her.

Schweitzer had long been interested in abnormal mentalities and human behavior. He wrote one of his earliest treatises, *The Psychiatric Study of Jesus*, while he was a medical student—before the era of Freud and the quasi-legitimization of psychiatry. From what his record of accomplishment showed in every field in which he had concentrated, his creativity undoubtedly would have also contributed profoundly to psychiatry had he followed that interest.

The pygmy lady was obviously a unique case study: here was a dementia not, as is generally conceded, resulting from the modern family and the fast sophisticated living we endure, but derived from the most primitive milieu. Schweitzer considered it a window into that rather inscrutable art—psychiatry.

She was of an unusually pleasant nature and seemed to sense any patient's, or patient's family's, plight or problem. She was always immediately helpful in any way she could be: baby-sitting, cooking a meal for a fatigued busy mother's family, or tending a sick patient all night long. Not even Joseph, with his vast knowledge of Gabonese dialects, could understand a word of Mama's gibberish.

Schweitzer told me that he had a standing order to everyone on the compound that she should have the run of the place and that he would have her treated with no less than the utmost of respect and compassion. He saw to it that she was well taken care of with a place to sleep and enough to eat. Sometimes he went out of his way to bring her little presents: once a tiny doll that delighted her; another time, near Christmas, a slight variation from her rather exotic dietary penchants—some hard candy.

I remember once seeing him rooted to a spot for maybe twenty minutes quietly watching her as she ministered to a dying old man. Because of Schweitzer's interest, I also watched her as she went about whatever she had to do at the time. I was never sure just how crazy she was. For, as she sang her own tunes and cavorted to her own choreography in a sort of shuffling rhythmic dance, she seemed to have an eye out for her audience, as if to placate or amuse them. Whether by design or happenstance, the other natives always caught her happy spirit, forgetting their many woes as they clapped and chanted to her rhythmic beat.

While the doctors and nurses talked of her as a loon or daft, the look in her eyes was far from demented. They were extremely expressive, even sensitive, especially when she was around children or someone very ill. She seemed to have a maternal, or maybe it was a childlike, instinct. She would hold infants lovingly or play as an equal with the older ones (who always enjoyed her) for hours on end. The fact that the kids had enough of their own diseases without needing to acquire any of hers didn't faze the families, even after Schweitzer's almost-five decades of teaching basic public health.

In return for her helpfulness, many favors and treats were bestowed on this kindly, if unwholesome, creature by the patients. There was little doubt that, though xenophobia was a survival necessity by which all natives lived, Mama was an exception: the tradition of shunning any stranger unless associated with family, tribe, or village of origin was set aside in her case.

Once, as we both watched her out on the hospital plaza, I asked Schweitzer how he felt about her, especially about her mental state. "She's obviously not sane; yet she fits into no usual pattern of abnormal behavior. Perhaps it was the influence of her primitive upbringing and the society she had always lived in that has ameliorated her actions and made her such a unique mental patient. She may have stranger habits than most of us, but maybe we have worse ones that we tightly control. (At this, I thought of the rumors I had heard of his own periods of depression).

"Though she's unconventional she is certainly self-sufficient; and not only doesn't bother anyone, but seems to live more by the golden rule than the rest of us." Then, squinting his eyes in the process of thought, he said, "I'm not quite sure what, but I think we could all learn something from her." In a sense, these words bespoke his own kindred heretical individualism as he, similarly, went his own way. After seeing him with her at various times, I was convinced that his interest was part of another compulsion to study human nature in all of its variability. He once said, "the clue to the nature of man is at its purest in rural Africa because there was no need to peel off layers that cover more sophisticated societies."

In his everyday life in Lambarene (except in his writings or music) Schweitzer led a rather routine jungle existence. He took in stride the absence of the ordinary comforts and stimulation that he left behind in tiny bucolic Gunsbach or the more cerebral Strasbourg. It was a paradox that he did not miss just the peacefulness of it. Why should he still remain in Africa after his more than forty years? He had fulfilled more than his share of responsibility to his *brothers*. And, if he had still "so much more to accomplish," why would it be more conducive to productivity to be bothered with lack of water because the pump was broken or to think and write in that enervating heat and humidity? It all came back to his feeling of penance for the "sin" of being born with so much more than anyone else.

Ruminating over this, in a less spiritual and more psychological vein, I saw that there might be two reasons: one, that he was so immersed in his responsibility to the natives that he couldn't go home again; or two, that his atonement was as lasting as his productivity. Perhaps, I decided, it was somewhat of both.

For example, in 1939 he had sailed home to Europe just as World War II broke out. Knowing it would be a long war and that if he were caught in it he would be kept from alleviating the misery of the people he loved, he decided, on the spur of the moment, to turn around and take the next boat back. Yet he also took a large risk in going back, because if Germany won he would again be an internee and an enemy alien.

One of the more blatant paradoxes of Schweitzer's life was that, though he had such love and empathy for that huge mass of village people and patients unrelated to him, he seemed to have so little for those in his immediate family.

One could say that though Schweitzer was an intensely loving man, the long hours of hospital work and building plus his many mental preoccupations may have precluded a loving personal relationship to a woman or child. He was no doubt less a husband and a father than a thinker and doer. Then again, his available time for family in his later years was further denied by involvement in worldwide philosophic, political, and artistic concerns.

In this respect he was not unlike other great men of his or of any time. Both Albert Einstein and Winston Churchill had the poorest of family relationships which surfaced publicly in their problem children. (Einstein had one child residing in a mental institution; Churchill had an alcoholic daughter). Their connubial stresses were less publicized. Churchill's "Clemmy" was supposedly an unhappy, lonely woman. Einstein divorced one wife, then had marital troubles with the second because of his incessant philandering. It seems inevitable that some great men in their efforts to develop and exploit their rare talents to the fullest are loners;

and some, in a sense, so egocentric that they are unable to enjoy a family life. In these, it is certainly apparent that nothing—mother, wife, nor child—has priority over the thoughts roiling in their brains.

Schweitzer, unlike many celebrated men, had never been known to sacrifice his talents to romance. In Schweitzer's case, there were other, stranger, aspects of this distant family life relationship. Part of it occurred long before his talents surfaced.

One of the people who had been with him for over twenty-five years said that Schweitzer, in his youth, had not a thought of marriage until the subject was broached to him by the woman he eventually married. If he had come to Lambarene with a woman in the world of the sexual permissiveness of 1983 rather than under the Victorian mores of 1913, she assured me, he would never have married.

It's been said that he never had a romantic attachment prior to his marriage in 1912 at the age of thirty-seven. The marriage ceremony, before their departure to Africa, was the first occasion in which he had ever kissed a woman "romantically." Even then, the idea of marriage, broached by the then-Helene Bresslau, his closest female friend and admirer, had been presented as a means of keeping his reputation beyond reproach in Africa. She had had her heart set on going with him, and marriage was the only way.

Helene was a brilliant woman, speaking seven languages. She was also a superb editor for him years before their nuptials. There is no question that before this "marriage of convenience" she was helpful to him. Afterward, in Africa, she was indispensable.

Only a vague history remains of their earliest association. She was obviously in love with him for years during his Strasbourg University days, but he seemed not to know it. He was a constant visitor with her father, an eminent historian at the university (a known atheist, formerly Jewish, later converted to the Moravian brothers).

When she first heard of his resolve to go to Africa, she even took up nursing in order to go with him. There, she was not only his sole companion but his administrator, practical nurse, editor, assistant, and a homemaker in the bush. But the hospital talk also had it that after her intermittent illness her working and wifely mission with him declined.

When Schweitzer returned to the hospital in 1927, after World War I, and his fame had spread even more, many more volunteers began coming to help. At that time, every housekeeping and administrative chore at the hospital, down to the most minor detail, was done for him first by younger women like Emma Hausnecht, then by Ali Silver and Mathilde Kottman. Simultaneously, Helene became more sickly and had to spend most of her time in Europe. Though she was dying of tuberculosis, she still tried to help Schweitzer; but, for her own good and possibly of his own need for freedom, he did not want her back in Africa. It seemed to many that family ties were only an intrusion into his busy world.

Even Schweitzer's relationship with his daughter, Rhena (born on his birthday, January 14), though seemingly a loving one, was sparse and then only occured on his occasional visits home when she was a child. She stayed mostly with her mother in Europe and didn't visit Lambarene until the age of twenty. At that time she wanted to become a doctor and possibly follow on her father's footsteps in Africa. This he wouldn't allow. I once asked him why, and he replied, "It is not the life for anyone who doesn't have an overwhelming religious and philosophical mission to work here in the bush."

According to more than one observer at Lambarene, Rhena went back to Europe in a rage, got married against his wishes, had four children, was unhappy, then divorced, and became a lab technician (also against his wishes). She would then come to Lambarene for a month or two at a time and work in the lab, but it seemed that she spent no more time with him than did any other staff member.

Beside his family life, one other aspect of his life must have been even more difficult for him to sacrifice. After almost five decades in Africa and his deep involvement in worldwide human affairs (especially the anti-nuclear peace movement), how could he relinquish the opportunity to meet and communicate with an Albert Einstein, a Daisetz Suzuki, or an Adlai Stevenson (other than by mail) in order to treat the same scabrous ulcers on the bodies of black jungle natives or observe a demented pygmy? How unusual, in our self-centered times, for anyone so steeped in knowledge about the multifarious problems of war and peace, the reasons for our life in the universe, and the evolvement of the human mind, to give up his precious time and stay up all night with a diarrheal infant, giving it teaspoons of sugar water in an effort to keep it from dying of dehydration!

Nevertheless, as I began to know him I could see how he would have been driven to distraction in a more modern Western society with his extreme sensitivity, his natural tendency to dominate, his stubbornness, and his impatience to solve problems his way. At least in Lambarene, even under the worst of conditions, he could deal directly with problems on his own terms at close quarters; and there was no one who dared stop him or tell him how to do it. What's more, he could see immediate relief and get immediate satisfaction.

The whys and wherefores of what else drove Schweitzer intrigued me. But, as much as I explained it to myself, I still couldn't help but wonder if the many inconveniences, such as sleeping on a rough, hand-woven sheet in a bed of straw at his age, had not blunted both his intellectual and his spiritual drive. Yet he would still sit night after night at his packing-box desk, by a flickering kerosene light, correcting a score of a Bach organ work, writing to the leaders of the "Ban the Bomb" movement, or putting down new ideas in the third volume of his *Philosophy of Civilization.*

To my mind, his unique quality of creativity came about by a combination of means. Primarily, there were, of course, his innate natural talents. Then there was a tough, objective, introspective mind, his extraordinary power of concentration, and his absolute belief in himself. All—even his hereticism—were integral parts of his vast intellectual productivity.

The overwhelming strength of his curiosity and the compulsion to satisfy it were instigated by a razor-sharp perception—which distinguished truth from fiction and dogma—of what he read or what he saw around him. Then, once pursuing an idea, he demanded evidence to answer every question in his mind on that particular issue, down to the finest point. I saw a good example of this as he explained to me, point by point from beginning to end, how he nailed down every truth and discarded every fiction in his *Quest for the Historical Jesus.* Once convinced, he rarely backed down or compromised. Which of course was one of his problems with the Church.

As we talked, I found he'd had a multitude of doubts in earlier years about many issues now taken for granted— even about his own religious affiliation, if not his belief in the spirit and ethics of Christ. For instance, in discussing *The Origin of the Species* he described how he changed from once thinking man a finished product to a strict Darwinian explanation that the human brain was still evolving. He constantly probed the reasons of many of his earliest thoughts.

Schweitzer also had an intense absorption in and the need to know as much as he could about the psychological aspects of human life at every level. He was a prober—though not an aggressive one—for answers to so many questions. As he once said, "A person's inner life confessed to a friend usually comes out only in a spirit of love and trust; and that takes time—frequently a lifetime."

Taking stock in the pharmacy, shoring up a rotten timber, or adjudicating a quarrel among his native help or staff, he seemed to learn from every facial nuance or phrase in every incident he'd been involved in. He once said to me after questioning a gendarme, "That man was lying and I knew it just from watching his movements during his explanation." This sensitivity to people's true motivations may have been one of his most important talents, resulting from his many years of studying the human behavior of probably everyone he'd ever known.

Schweitzer endured more boredom with friends or family than when by himself within four walls. As he once put it, "By myself I've never been lonely a moment in my life." Was he lonely in company? "There is always too much to think about and not enough time to think it through." He was obviously driven by the busyness of his multi-faceted brain, which in the ordinary mind would have contributed to frustration, frenzy, and, possibly, mental illness. Yet he rarely showed it.

He employed his multitude of talents more honestly than most and with no excuses. He received great public acclaim because of the paradox of his situation in a primitive milieu with no societal rewards contemplated: this great brain, this compassionate soul developing and creating in a chosen jungle existence.

I believe he knew that he had responses and sensitivities and an understanding of people that most of us don't have. Nevertheless, in the simple handling of people who worked with him, he frequently failed; and, though he was contrite after the fact, daily life was very unpleasant at times.

Schweitzer's *modi vivendi* and *operandi* were eminently unique. His life was more intriguing than those of other great men. Many of our geniuses may have lived less than conventionally as they created their masterpieces but few followed their spiritual bent as completely as Schweitzer did; few risked both death and the death of their talents. Schweitzer, alongside of them, was the rarest of creative intellectuals—true to both himself and his extraordinary inheritance. I tried to imagine others approaching his monumental intellectual level—a Tolstoy, a Goethe, or a Beethoven or a more modern-day scientific genius such as Einstein or Oppenheimer—living their own truths as they used their talents under primitive circumstances. I couldn't.

7

A PRACTICE PRIMEVAL

One evening dinner concluded with a talk by Schweitzer on Jeremiah concerned with people becoming impatient with the "Coming." During their entire lives, they had heard so much about the Messiah they grew tired of waiting for the one who never came.

As he talked, I wondered whether the natives there in the jungle realized that their Messiah had come. For before he came, if any people anywhere had reason to pray for the coming of a kingdom of heaven, these benighted suffering people certainly did.

Schweitzer was as close to a Messiah as any man could be. He relieved their pain, cured many of their horrible diseases, and saved many lives. If they believed in prayer they had to believe that at least a physical savior had finally appeared in the person of Albert Schweitzer. Before he came many had died for want of a single pill.

Some of the diseases I saw in Lambarene I had only

read about in medical texts. I had never seen such advanced stages of other, more common, diseases which would have been cured early in more advanced cultures.

One such case was that of an old man with elephantiasis of a testicle (as large and as heavy as a watermelon) which he trundled it in front of him in a makeshift wheelbarrow. He had never known he could be helped until a friend in a neighboring village, about five miles away, told him of the white doctor. A young woman lived with a brain tumor which had gone on so long that one eye was protruding at least a half-inch out of its socket. (Later we could only remove the eye, not the tumor.)

The rancid odor of infected yaws ulcers (carried by a spirochete-like syphilis) and those very common tropical phagedenic ulcers of the legs permeated the ward, often nauseating those who treated them. Some suppurated down to the very bone. The fetid pungency would make me hope for some emergency operation that would allow me to skip the clinic whenever such cases appeared.

With the relief medical missionaries offered I could see why they, more than most other missionary types, had as much success with conversions as they did. But those who had been helped must also have wondered why the God-like man, who could help them so much, would preach to them of another Messiah—Jesus Christ, Whom they had never seen and Who had never done anything for them.

Many of the diseases that showed up at every clinic period were either too far gone or incurable, but the most common ones could be relieved by very little medication (one penicillin shot cured the festering sores of yaws even in tots). The wonder of it all was how much Schweitzer did with so little for even the most terrible diseases. He had so few supplies and such primitive equipment. What was done there was remarkable and, generally, done well. This was, of course, further limited by money and the difficulty of attracting trained physicians for any length of time to the conditions at Lambarene. How much more could have been accomplished with some very simple, if expensive, additions, such as a larger generator for electricity, better medical diagnostic and therapeutic equipment (even a better x-ray machine), and better trained doctors and nurses.

At the very least, in this age of the airplane there should be a speedy means of sending both diagnostic and possibly major curative problems to a large city hospital. But the one in Libreville, the capital of Gabon, was hardly as modern or equipped as even an average small county hospital in the midwestern or southern United States. And even though the facilities in Libreville were somewhat better than Schweitzer's, the personnel were not as well trained to do some of the more major operations, especially on brain or chest diseases.

Well-trained foreign specialists would not come to Lambarene for the relatively meager pay and trained Gabonese were few and far between. The French Provincial Hospital just down the river was a waste. Though a bit more up-to-date and better equipped than Schweitzer's, it did very little other than clinic work under Schweitzer's friend, Dr. Weisberg. On weekends there was a sign outside that hospital, "Closed until Monday, go to the Schweitzer Hospital."

An ordinary day of medicine at Schweitzer's hospital can only be described as a hurly-burly of atypism. No two days were alike. Plans and schedules seemed made to be broken. And though operations were scheduled it seemed urgent medical interruptions were always occurring, taking us away from more routine work. This is not to mention other interruptions such as the day a most elusive goat got into the operating room and knocked over everything in sight before being captured. Or the pandemonium in the O.R. when a giant hairy tarantula climbed out from between some sterile sheets.

After breakfast I would usually make rounds, check the progress of patients, look for complications, and, if necessary, do dressings, remove stitches, and change medications. Then directly to the O.R. for scrub-up and operating, using mostly local and spinal anesthesia. After lunch and an hour's siesta (demanded in temperatures over a hundred degrees), I'd work in the clinic, first with new patients. Those who had been to the hospital before wore cards, frequently on strings around their necks, with their past illnesses and medications listed on them. Some of these cards were as much as twenty years old and almost illegible from wear and tear. If the patients were to be admitted (with the whole family) one of the aides under Kottman or Silver would show them where to go and indoctrinate them into the routines of obtaining food and cooking oil and show them where to cook.

Much of our afternoon was taken up with dressing wounds and follow-ups of discharged patients. Just before going up to our rooms to clean up for dinner, ward rounds on very ill patients would be made again, because in the afternoon patient temperatures are usually the highest and this gave us a head start on some wound infections or pneumonia therapy.

But that routine was only as scheduled. On one day I vividly remember, my schedule included an ordinary hernia, which, for some unknown reason, was probably the most common operation in Lambarene (especially in the males) and on practically every operating schedule. After which a hysterectomy on an old woman who had a tumor the size of a grapefruit was scheduled. The third procedure that morning was for another case of elephantiasis: a woman who had a leg as big around as an elephant's and probably just as heavy. There were also two minor operations; one of which was a biopsy of leperous lesions, which was done routinely to evaluate the effect of the medical therapy.

After I had finished the hernia and was to start the hysterectomy, a three-year-old deathly-pale child was brought in with teeth clenched in a typical *risus sardonicus* (sardonic smile). All of her other muscles were in spasm, her neck muscles especially standing out, and her body in typical *oposthotonous* (rigid back muscles with the spine stiffly arched). She had a full-blown case of tetanus. She had not eaten in two days, because her mouth could not be opened. Her saucer-like eyes showed how terrified she was. I had never seen a case before. Luckily, the other doctors had.

Three of us feverishly worked over her, administering serum and penicillin for the infection, fluids intravenously for her dehydrated condition, and tranquilizers and muscle relaxants to try to alleviate the musclular rigidity. The other major operation had to be cancelled temporarily, since we weren't finished with the child until noon. Thank goodness we were successful and eventually she got well.

During lunch that day, an emergency call came from the Leper Village. I rushed over. The village was about a five-minute walk from the hospital through a path in the jungle. Dr. Takahashi, the taciturn, dedicated Japanese physician who was spending his life with lepers, met me, and told me the history as he took me to the bedside. The patient was a young man about seventeen, with typical signs of leprosy, who had suddenly collapsed while lifting a heavy table. With the exertion, he was breathless, with lips as blue as dye, but in no pain. His problem obviously had nothing to do with his leprosy, which had no such complication. The lack of pain, his youth, and the sudden shortness of breath, just about excluded cardiac disease. All of this gave me a sudden insight as to his diagnosis.

I put my stethoscope to the young man's chest. His

heart was pushed to one side and in normal rhythm. There were breath sounds (sound of the lung expanding with each breath) in his right chest only. He had had a spontaneous pneumothorax. A bleb (blister) on the lung (most likely from tuberculosis, so common there) had obviously blown out, had let air into the pleural cavity (which contains the lungs) on that side, collapsed the lung, and pushed the heart to the opposite side. He was breathing with only one lung.

I ran back to the hospital O.R., got a large needle with a two-way stopcock, a large 50 cc syringe and sterile rubber tubing, and sped back as fast as I could. Sweat ran down my face by the time I got back to the Leper Village. We cleaned and sterilized the area high on the affected side of the chest (where air rose to the top) with alcohol and iodine and inserted the sterile needle after giving a shot of local anesthesia. A large amount of air was instantly aspirated through the needle, and one could see the patient's color change with every syringe-full of air removed. His breathing became less labored as the lung expanded. The needle was then connected to one end of the rubber tubing; the other end put into a bottle of water on the floor. With each breath now, he would be forcing air out of his pleural cavity into the bottle of water without sucking more air back in. The whole episode took only about forty-five minutes, but they were precious minutes when life and death was decided. In a few days we removed the small plastic tube and the needle, and he was fine.

Catching my breath, I went back to the dining room and had a bland bowl of cereal with powdered milk. I had had enough excitement for one day. Everyone had already left. As I went out the dining room door, the back-to-work bell sounded. I went straight to the clinic and examined some patients for possible surgical admission.

I was occupied dressing some post-surgical cases when an urgent call came from the O.R. One of our native female helpers had fainted, and I was the closest doctor around. She was small, emaciated, covered with sweat, and lying on the floor, very quiet. I looked closely at her conjunctiva (the mucous membrane of the eyelids): they were almost white, as were her fingernail beds. The woman was terribly anemic. After a hurried abdominal and rectal examination, the diagnosis was simple. She was pregnant and full of large ascaroid worms, as thick around as a pencil. I admitted her as a patient for deworming and a decent diet. (We had no blood transfusion, which she needed badly.) Anemia from worms was a condition common in practically all natives; it was a rare admission to the hospital that wasn't anemic. The "natural" native lethargy alleged by white settlers in Africa in many cases was due to the enervating lack of red blood cells caused by worms.

Since I was already in the O.R., I decided to send for the two minor surgical cases—a shy, nervous leper for routine biopsy, and a small, sleepy-eyed man with a large glandular abcess of the neck—which would take about ten minutes each. (Lepers were biopsied about every two months and when declared negative five times they were deemed arrested. The common medical treatment was with Sulfones and chalmoogra oil, which did have an effect on many cases, though it often took many years.)

When I had finished, it was almost time to get washed up for dinner. On the way up to the room I picked up Phoebe at the *pouponniere*. She had been working with the children all day. A dysentery epidemic was raging in the vicinity, and dying children were being brought in almost every day. Phoebe leaned her head against my shoulder. She was as fatigued as I was.

As we walked slowly toward our quarters, we came upon Joseph sitting quietly in front of the Casa Riviera (the psychiatry hut) pensively looking out over the river. We sat and talked with him for a few minutes. He was a competent, proud, reflective man with a deep sense of loyalty to Schweitzer and a dedicated responsibility to the hospital and the patients. He had once been a butcher, and Schweitzer related that he would sometimes describe symptoms such as "The patient has pain in his knee gristle or the child had broken its ham hock."

As we sat with Joseph, there was a sudden outburst of shouting. Six *infirmiers*, two carrying a stretcher—one in front, one in back—with four others, came out of the bush. On the stretcher was a naked man, bearded, sort of squat, with wild staring eyes. He was bound hand and foot with heavy vines and was chanting in a high-pitched mournful voice. The *infirmiers* had picked him up in a village about a half mile away, after a hurried message for help had been received that morning from a runner. "A demented person was running amok, could the hospital send someone?" The procession of *infirmiers* was followed by the native "sheriff" of the village and a string of curious children. We followed as Friedman (the self-appointed psychiatrist in residence) met them; he arrived cursing because there were not enough psychiatric spaces. The hospital had only six, and they were all full.

The psychiatric hut was a series of pens (about five by eight feet) of heavy reinforced wood, the usual iron roof with overhanging eaves, small heavily-screened square holes for ventilation, and no sanitary facilities. They must have been beastly hot. There were no special quarters at Lambarene for mental patients who were also physically ill.

Friedman gave the man a tranquilizer and some barbiturates intramuscularly. He was left outside, still tightly bound; with one *infirmier* guarding him. The vines cut into the flesh of his wrists, biceps, and ankles. I remonstrated against this, but Friedman said that before the patient's bonds could be released he had to move one of the less violent patients in with another to make room for this one. Then the man was carried into his cell, still bound. As we were leaving, the patient in the next cell began applauding and yelling, "Bravo, bravo."

Phoebe and I had no time to "shower" and change for dinner. But when the services were over, Friedman asked me to go down to help with the demented man. As we went toward the cage, the man next door was still yelling, "That man is crazy; he threatened me with a knife. How strong is this partition? I'm glad he's in. I'm glad he's in."

Warily, Friedman opened the "cage." The man was fast asleep, on his side, on some straw in a corner. I helped cut the man loose from the vines; there were deep lacerations where he had been bound.

The next morning when the nurses went in to give him another injection, he feigned sleep, then jumped up, knocked the nurses aside, sprang out of the "cage," and dashed into the river. Luckily, he was intercepted by a passing launch and brought back. Friedman had been right in being wary of him.

Before Phoebe and I fell into bed on the night of this mental patient's admission, I was told there was a very unusual heart patient who had just come in whom Schweitzer wanted me to see in the morning. I was no cardiologist, but I guess I had more experience than the rest of the doctors.

The patient was one of the rare fat people we saw in Lambarene, but some of the weight was probably from oedema (retained fluids). On examining him, I thought that that patient's problem was most likely (without ample facilities to x-ray and cardiograph him) to be a chronic pericarditis (an inflammation and thickening of the sac around the heart that tightens like an iron band and prevents the heart from beating to its full expansion). I couldn't tell for certain, but that was my provisional diagnosis. Sad to say, there were no more expert consultants in the entire nation to refer this patient to. In fact, there was not one hospital in any of the southern African countries, much less in Gabon, that could treat that disease. No positive diagnosis was ever made. Within a few weeks the man died.

That was just one hectic day of many. During my stay at Lambarene, other than the routine scheduled and emergency procedures, I did some operations I had witnessed as an intern but had never performed myself. Among them were the enucleation of that protruding eyeball. Luckily, there were some specialty books, owned by other doctors, to refer to for procedures I was not familiar with. There was no real library, which should have been a most important part of this primitive hospital.

Among some of the more difficult cases were the obstruction and trauma of the male or female urinary tracts, caused by either venereal disease or pregnancy, which required plastic surgery. In the best of hospitals, the results were poor, just as they were here.

I treated one probable snake bite in that time, and I say probable because the definite origin of the bite could not be determined and the patient was not too sure. However, we did have serum; and the operative procedure consisted of merely opening the wound, giving antibiotics, and watching the patient.

Children's suffering was intense. One case (a six-year-old girl) was extremely gruesome, due to the mauling of her arm by an unknown animal. Schweitzer had told me that he had seen many of these, but during my stay there was only one. Trying to match the larger arteries, nerves, and muscles was a difficult, tedious task. The arm did heal back on, but, due to the nerve damage, was useless, with no function at all.

I also did Caesarian sections, which I had not done for

twenty years. In one of the first cases, the husband, a small-village chief with patterned scarified tribal marks on his face, was so distraught he had to be given sedatives. He came to see me a few days after his wife's operation and asked if she could be sterilized. My immediate thought was that he was being considerate and didn't want his wife to go through the pain again. But then Joseph told me the real reason. The man had just bought his wife that year; and, if she died in any way which could be connected with him (he was the cause of the pregnancy), it was his evil spirit that did it, and the family would try to ruin him.

In that country, with witchcraft so prevalent, every surgeon had two strikes against him before he started. In addition, he had to always keep in mind concomitant abnormalities and diseases such as tuberculosis, worms, malaria, gonorrhea, malnutrition, and early obscure cases of Filariasis (the infection that causes elephantiasis) which, in most cases, worsen the patient's principal disease. Second, the inhalation anesthesia, other than local or spinal, which could not be used except on the lower part of the body, was extremely hazardous. We did not intubate the lungs since we had no real pressure anesthetic machine, and open-drop ether was extra hazardous because of its flammability. Postoperative pneumonia was, therefore, not uncommon.

Frequently, since the natives were in poor physical condition, hungry, and disease-ridden, they would have to be kept at least two weeks before an operation, to treat and build them up. However, with all of these pitfalls, the postoperative mortality rate was phenomenally low—somewhere around 0.5 percent, which compares favorably with modern up-to-date hospitals. Of course, there were many major operations that would never even be attempted at Schweitzer's.

On admission to the hospital, every patient had a

physical examination and the most simple laboratory tests. Smears for gonorrhea and malaria were routine. Ordinary blood chemistries were seldom done because of lack of modern equipment and the time it might take a doctor. X-rays of the simplest kind were difficult to perform and were done no more than a hundred times a year, when at least a couple of thousand were really necessary for some five thousand admissions. But this would have entailed an expensive machine, an x-ray technician, an x-ray mechanic, and a radiologist to read the films. None was available.

On rare occasions, blood transfusions were given by the direct method of donor to patient after matching. Transfusions were always received with reluctance by the natives because of the possibility of transferring evil spirits. Sterilization of all supplies and instruments was by a pressure cooker over an open fire.

Schweitzer had told me that he had not seen a case of appendicitis, kidney stones, or gallstones in fifty years. These are very common in the Western world and easy to diagnose; so, in that period of time, the lack of cases couldn't have been caused merely by misdiagnosis. I had similar experiences in the tropical climate of the South Pacific when I was a Marine surgeon. I feel it had more to do with diet than with climate.

Breast cancer was rare, but the hospital treated many cancers of bone, uterus, and ovary. There were also melanomas (malignant moles—the most deadly type of skin cancer). In my experience, this type of skin cancer occurred in white patients only. Among the many cases that we saw, a good number were never specifically diagnosed since we had no pathology lab. Unusual specimens were sent to the Pasteur Institute in Brazzaville or to Basel, Switzerland, with a three-week wait for a diagnosis.

The hospital (including the Leper Village and the wards for European patients) consisted of fifteen to twenty buildings and had about eight hundred beds, almost always full; admitted about five thousand patients a year; and treated another five thousand clinic out-patients from hundreds of miles around.

Our patient load was increased because people didn't trust the French Provincial Hospital. The rumor was that the French doctor (Dr. Weisberg) would let the *infirmiers* treat most of the patients. And the *infirmiers* usually charged exorbitant fees for their medication, as did some of our own *infirmiers* before being caught. They also knew that at Schweitzer's, he himself or one of the medical doctors would at least oversee the patient, if they didn't actually treat him or her themselves. The native families also liked and trusted the white nurses.

Another reason Schweitzer's hospital was preferred was that it was run according to Schweitzer's theory. The patient should be tended and fed and be close to his or her family, just as they lived in their huts in the village. (The French Provincial Hospital had separate quarters for white families only.) While a patient was in, the family got regular rations of rice, bananas, manioc, and some palm oil for cooking. The family and patient liked the idea of being together as a family, as chaotic as it could be, even in sickness. Also, the food was better and cost the hospital nothing.

All in all, the hospital did a tremendous, if not a complete, service. There were no "quiet" signs posted either inside or outside of the large (about sixteen by eighty feet) wards. Just like the main street and the pharmacy, a maelstrom of children played and shouted, and the wives and family clustered around the patient talking or arguing among themselves or with their neighbors. Dogs, goats, and even chimpanzees, with their droppings, came and went while the nurses and *infirmiers* shooed them away and worked around them. The wards weren't spotless and it was a miracle (or the natives' built-up immunity) that there were so few wound infections, and that the children didn't come down with more communicable diseases than they did. In any event, the results were good; the patients and families were happy.

Other than the usual problems that Schweitzer had to put up with in his wards, there were social problems. There were two main tribes in that area—the Pahouins (or Fangs) and the Galoas. The Pahouins considered themselves the aristocrats, even if they were formerly known as one of the more voracious cannibal tribes (and, from what I'd heard, probably to a lesser extent still were) and also had been the keepers and sellers of slaves. They, of course, refused to be in the same ward as the Galoas, and thus had to be separated, which was not easy to accomplish in a full hospital.

The surgical mortality and morbidity was very low; and just the alleviation of much of the malaria, sleeping sickness, worms, and dysentery prevented a lot of misery. But there was a great deal of rheumatic fever in children, which may have accounted for much of the cardiac problems in adults. And even though the patients were taught preventive health measures before they were discharged, they rarely adhered to them. Many of the diseases recurred; may patients came in again and again with the same symptoms.

The dysentery I saw there was the worst I had ever encountered. Patients ran around continuously so that it was impossible to keep them or their beds and surroundings clean. At one time, when I myself developed a full-blown case of amoebic dysentery, with terrible cramps, vomiting, and a bloody diarrhea (the kind I prayed I would never get), I felt I just wanted to give up the ghost. But the hospital was so short-handed that, despite my ten pound weight loss, I continued to work.

Dysentery, whichever kind, was usually lethal for

children unless they were treated early. It was no doubt the greatest cause of infant mortality, and frequently the only fluids we had to treat the debilitating symptoms were home-made saline solutions and lyophilized plasma (dried plasma made usable by adding sterile water). The naming of the children's ward, the *pouponniere,* was apt, since poop was eighty percent of its patients' problems. At times there were so many admitted that they were lined up and bedded down on shelving as if they were being filed away.

Children especially suffered terribly from more than one illness at a time. I would say nine out of ten had large suppurating tropical sores, mainly on their legs and in their scalps. Malnutrition was rampant, as could be seen by the cases of Kwashiakor (in the late stages, manifested by kids whose bodies were just skin and bone, dead-eyed, all with large pot-bellies, and, of all things, red hair, rarely seen in Africa). Since there was little innoculation against the usual childhood communicable diseases, these were also great causes of death.

Some children were brought in and never called for. They lived at Schweitzer's sometimes for a year or two until they could be cared for. Then the village from which they came would frequently take them back and bring them up cooperatively as village children. There were also many crippled children—not crippled from birth, but because of an injury that was never treated. We were not equipped nor had we the expert personnel to do rehabilitative surgery on them. They would stay crippled for life.

It was not unusual to see thirteen- and fourteen-year-old girls, frequently married, in the last stages of pregnancy. They usually did rather well. One big-eyed eleven-year-old girl, always on the verge of tears, was pregnant with her second child, supposedly by her brother. She was as flat chested as a boy and had no other secondary sexual charac-

teristics. Incest was, of course, a strict taboo; and this may
have been why she had been abandoned.

In the Leper Village, of course, the children lived with
the family, and there were many adolescent lepers. At one
time, Schweitzer tried to separate them but to no avail. The
new Leper Village, run by Doctor Takahashi, had been
started in 1952; but Schweitzer ran out of money. It wasn't
completed until after the Nobel Peace Prize money arrived.
Schweitzer not only designed, ordered the material, and paid
for it, but he was also the foreman on the job every day.

The leper huts were made mostly of bamboo and
thatch with the ubiquitous corrugated iron roofs. The lepers
kept their huts and their village spotless. They had their own
school and were taught by one of their more literate compa-
triots, with a weekly visit by the teacher from the Mission. A
minister held services regularly. Strangely enough, the biblical bias against lepers had not disappeared. I don't know
whether it was because we still didn't—and still don't—know
how the disease is transmitted. Even Phoebe and I felt
somewhat uneasy.

What made the hectic days even harder to take were
the restless nights. We were plagued not only by fatigue and
the heat-induced insomnia, but also by the patients hacking
and spitting all night long in the TB ward below us. When a
death occurred, which was not infrequent, there would be an
all-night vigil of weeping and chanting.

All in all, as difficult as it may have been for me
personally and medically, I had no cause to complain when I
thought of what Schweitzer himself must have endured for
almost half a century, especially in those first ten years.

There were countless other drawbacks to life at the
hospital, including squabbles among the medical personnel
themselves. But weighing the pros and cons and the limitations inherent in such a situation (such as getting highly

trained personnel for long periods), I'd say it was an extremely effective institution. As Schweitzer said, "I've told you I don't want too much modernizing for many reasons. I'm well aware of the hospital's weaknesses but I'm doing what I think best right now and within the budget which I can raise."

He was, however, very concerned about the treatment of mental disease. The morning after the episode with Friedman and the mental patient, he talked to me about it. It was one project constantly on his mind.

8

MEDICINE MEN VERSUS MEDICINE

Practicing medicine at the Albert Schweitzer Hospital was difficult enough because of the language barrier, the lack of proper diagnostic equipment, and no blood bank (with about thirty percent of the patients anemic). But it was more than a drama of man against nature. It also played out the theme of man against man. First there were the fetish doctors to put up with. Every M.D. and nurse on the place had to contend with the insidious infiltration of these shadowy witch doctors who sought to effect miracle cures with their incantations and potions.

These African healers—either self-appointed, apprenticed, or brought up in the family tradition—were, if not respected, certainly feared by most natives. Virtually all backwoods Gabonese felt that if someone had the power to heal and give life that person also had the power to induce sickness and death. Those "doctors" worked their will mainly through fear, with the help of potions from homegrown leaf or bark, but also psychologically with magic chants and the laying on of hands.

Many of the patients who came to Schweitzer's did so after the fetishers had failed to heal them. This meant that they could be vengefully hexed by these native "healers" who predicted and frequently caused dire consequences to the villagers who came to the Christian hospital.

Witch doctors mainly used others to do their dirty work. Through intimidation of members of the family or hospital personnel, they somehow managed to wreak their vengeance on their "former patients" either by threats and curses or by poisons, either at home before they left or right in the hospital. The more benign of this all-male profession were more or less counselors or priests. And they didn't dress or paint up like the voodoo doctors in the movies. They couldn't be distinguished from the *infirmiers* on the wards.

Once, when Schweitzer and I were discussing his showing (never proselytizing or converting) "the Christian way" to the natives through the wonders of medicine, he said, "If they took Jesus' word seriously they would have the faith and courage to reject both the social and medical evils of the witch doctors. But many pay only lip service to our prescriptions for complete recovery, and after they have been here with some diseases which are incurable or functional, wind up back in the hands of either the village family fetisher or an itinerant one. However, the word of the proof of our form of treatment has certainly spread when patients come here from hundreds of miles away. Also, the younger natives educated in the Mission school frequently make fun of their parents and family for believing in taboos and the prophecies of the fetishers."

Still, the witch doctors surreptitiously infiltrated the

hospital wards. Almost every patient, and even the long-time *infirmiers*, were scared to death and rarely informed on them, afraid for themselves or their families' lives. The white doctors and nurses rarely knew who they were. Schweitzer had a standing order against most of them being on the hospital grounds. When they were found out, if his angry denunciation of them didn't drive them away, he'd call for the gendarmes, since no other native would chance getting in their disfavor.

Some had once been *infirmiers* at the hospital, and had learned a few therapeutic techniques and the specific pills that worked for certain diseases. They then went back to their native villages and opened their own practices with drugs or instruments that they had filched, plus the mumbo-jumbo they had seen other fetish doctors use. They actually had sort of an internship at the Schweitzer Hospital; a fact that, of course, they advertised in the area.

Like their more highly trained and diploma'd medical half-brothers in the big cities of the world, their prices were not cheap. It was well known that the more one paid, the better the chances of getting well.

Being paid for performing a service was not unknown to many of Schweitzer's *infirmiers* either. Some would even insist on a payment of five francs before they'd give morphine for pain. They'd never do this with Joseph or Pierre around. But, with no staff member present and without payment from the patient, they would skip medications and even hold back treatment (such as compresses, exercises, or dressing changes) when they could get away with it. The *infirmiers* would rarely administer to a patient taken over by a fetisher—another example of the fear these medicine men evoked in the natives. A few *infirmiers* might tell Schweitzer what was going on, but they'd rarely point an accusing finger.

I particularly recall one incident involving Dr.

Schweitzer, me, and a witch doctor. When making ward rounds, I was usually followed by two or three *infirmiers* and an interpreter as I examined patients and left orders. During one three-day period, I noticed a dignified middle-aged man whom I'd never seen before making rounds with us. I didn't bother to ask who he was; it could have been, I thought, a curious member of a patient's family, a new *infirmier*-in-training, or even a native preacher. I did notice that he would spend a few minutes with each patient, speaking with them as we went on to the next bunk, and then take up with us again. I noticed this same man in the hospital square on occasions when few doctors were around, usually during lunch and afternoon siesta time, and I'd greet him cordially.

One day, shortly after noticing this tag-along, I asked Dr. Schweitzer to see with me a post-operative pneumonia patient who was not responding to medication. The following morning Schweitzer came into the ward as we were making our usual rounds. As he approached the bed of our pneumonia patient he suddenly stopped, his facing becoming livid as he saw our "visitor."

Brandishing his muscular arms, Schweitzer went straight to the man, who, it turned out, was not only the worst of fetishers but made the mistake of using the personal French *tu*, which infuriated Schweitzer even further. Schweitzer made it clear, "I am not *tu* to a murderer. Now you apologize to the whole ward and get out of here, and you'll suffer for your evil deeds if you ever return." The terror-stricken fetisher cringed but didn't move. Schweitzer collared him, shouting as he dragged him out through the door. Schweitzer came back exhausted but still gave the devil to the rest of the *infirmiers* for not letting him or me know.

As I later learned, this fetish doctor had had four "patients" at the hospital some time before. All four had been under his care back in neighboring villages only a few miles away. When there were no results, the patients' families brought them to *Oganga* ("White Fetisher"—the name the Pahouin tribe had given to Schweitzer) and the white nurses. One patient, an elderly woman with seven children, was diagnosed as having a vesico-vaginal fistula (an opening between the bladder and vagina caused by a traumatic childbirth); and two of the others had probable malignancies, one of the uterus. I can't remember the diagnosis of the other. All four patients died. Of, it was suspected, poisoning by the fetish doctor.

This particular witch doctor also had a large out-patient practice down at the busy hospital square among the in-patients' families. It was rumored that he had some kind of financial agreement with some of Schweitzer's aides. They would tip him off as to which patients were not doing well and therefore would be the most vulnerable.

What he was doing with me was simply tagging along then telling the patient that I was his assistant and he himself was guiding the treatment. If there were tablets or capsules beside the patient's bed he'd cleverly steal them.

Joseph told me confidentially that later in the day or at night, when no one was around, the fetisher would make his own private rounds, dispense his own concoctions, and get paid. He would peddle the stolen pills in Lambarene to groups of men sitting on their haunches in their daily palaver sessions (discussing business or settling local problems) as miracle cures for practically any ache or pain.

Fetishers were known to also practice surgery of sorts. One Saturday afternoon, on my return from a semi-civilized lunch and a hot shower at the Hotel Relais in Lambarene, I was met by Dr. Mueller. He asked me to see a very sick patient that had just been brought in by *pirogue* from quite a distance downstream. I went over to the ward and there was a young man, very muscular and known as a great hunter. He had a high fever and a rigid, board-like abdomen. He had excruciating rebound tenderness (slight pain on pushing in on the abdomen, but terrible pain on suddenly releasing the pressure)—a sure sign of peritonitis.

From the pain's sudden onset, as revealed in the patient's history, the cause appeared to be a perforation of bowel; yet there were no prodromata (usual previous symptoms) of appendicitis (which was just about nonexistent in Lambarene) or any other organ that might perforate. Dr. Schweitzer had seen the case and asked Mueller to have me handle it as soon as I returned.

Dr. Mueller gave the young man a spinal anesthesia while I scrubbed. As I opened the abdomen through a low, midline incision, pus of a fetid odor (usually indicative of a perforated bowel) gushed from the peritoneal cavity. Suctioning most of it out and putting my hand into the abdomen to explore, I felt a mass about the size of a baseball. It was down in the pelvis but not attached to any organ. I went over the appendix, stomach, and gallbladder, all of which felt normal. I then "read" the bowel for perforation (taking it all out of the abdomen and examining all sides of it carefully) from the stomach to the colon, and then "read" the colon down to the rectum. There was no semblance of a perforation, healed or otherwise. I went over the other organs again with no success.

I then peeled the tumor from the peritoneum wall, and as I did what looked like a semi-rigid piece of catgut or a hard string of congealed pus clung to my scalpel. I brushed it off onto a gauze sponge and then opened the tumor-like granulomatous mass. (This is what is usually called "proud flesh" and is composed of blood vessels and soft scar tissue, which looks like a cluster of raspberries.) There were also pockets of pus within it. I was entirely stumped as to its cause and worried that I may have missed something. I didn't want to close the abdomen without knowing and yet I had to finish.

Worried, I looked searchingly up at Joseph, who was helping me. "I give up, do you know anything about this type of mass?" I asked as I was closing.

Joseph seemed frightened as he pointed to the sponge in which lay what I had thought to be a bit of hardened catgut. "Fishbone," he whispered. I picked it up and, examining it closely, found it to be a finely honed straight bone. It was frightening. This bone hadn't just been swallowed accidentally and lodged in the abdomen: it had been worked on by a human. I could see the file marks. I removed the few stitches I had already put in the abdominal wall and searched the bowel again. And again I found nothing. I drained and closed the abdomen, but I was perplexed and still worried.

As I was washing up, Dr. Friedman came in and I began telling him about the case. He put his finger to his lips, motioning me not to talk about it. This was most peculiar. I finished drying my hands and walked out with him. When we got outside, he told me he didn't want to get any of the *infirmiers* in trouble with a fetish doctor. This *infirmier* had been watching and had gone out to tell Friedman what was happening.

Friedman then related how fetishers, when treating cases of severe pain, generally inserted a well-honed, long, thin fishbone through the skin at or near the point of pain. It acted as a counter-irritant, not unlike the burning hot ointments that old country doctors rubbed into the skin to allay pain in a muscle or joint. It was also not dissimilar from acupuncture, which theoretically relieves pain and supposedly also cures by contact with nerve endings.

Obviously, what had happened here was that, over a period of time, the unsterile fishbone worked its way into the peritoneal cavity. Then the body defenses tried to contain it by building up the contaminated mass. The nonsterile infected bone then penetrated out of the mass, causing an intense purulent peritoneal reaction without perforating the bowel.

I told Dr. Schweitzer about the case just before dinner. He said that he had heard of this procedure and complication but had seen only one, and asked if the bone had been sharpened at both ends. I had it with me, wrapped in a piece of gauze, and showed it to him. He handled it and nodded his head. He also went through the same probable steps of its developing a peritonitis that I had gone through. Then he launched into a list of some of the other man-made illnesses we had to watch out for—in the main, poisonings of various degrees.

The natives in this region had rather profound faith in homegrown medications—almost certainly concocted by the fetish doctors. All of them came from roots, barks, or leaves, many of which are poisonous. (Of course, many drugs used all over the world today, such as digitalis and quinine, also come from such primitive sources.)

Besides the fetish doctor, there was occasionally a village pharmacist, usually an older woman and usually also the village midwife, who dispensed her own natural products. It was doubted how many of her concoctions, usually learned at her mother's knee, were of any value. I saw both fetisher and pharmacist were mostly fakers. Many fetishers actually considered their poisons curative, though they were often disastrous.

Schweitzer gave me some tips on the fetisher problem. "Your pneumonia patient who seemed to get worse even with penicillin therapy was typical. Whenever there are unexplainable symptoms or unattainable results with therapy, look into what the patient had eaten or was being fed. Even be suspicious if someone in the family was cooking it or feeding it to him, for whatever reason.

"Sometimes the *infirmiers* can get to the bottom of the poisoning problem by finding out if someone had a grievance against the patient."

Right after his dinner lecture he guided me over to the piano bench and continued. "The poisons they use are usually very slow to act but occasionally there are sudden deaths. If we suspect a poisoning, the first thing we do is to put the patient on a charcoal mixture (charcoal has tremendous absorptive powers) that sop up the poison; after that, we see to it that the preparation of each meal is supervised by one of our more trusted *infirmiers*.

"Frequently, the patient himself may catch on and refuse certain foods, even from a member of his family. Mental illness also occurs with some of these poisons; and when the patient is manic even morphine doesn't faze him. Especially watch out when the operative wound heals well with no evidence of infection but the patient gradually fades away." Schweitzer smiled, "As you've found out by now we have diagnostic problems you'll never have in Baltimore.

"And don't think," he continued, "that poisons are used just for vindictiveness or mistakenly used for healing. They have also been known to be used to attain *justice*." But then, using a phrase I asked Ali Silver to interpret, "There's *a hitch* to it; the judge and juror is usually the fetish doctor. If there is an argument with an accused thief, or even just a family squabble, the fetish doctor may be called and there is a trial by ordeal. It is common knowledge among the villagers that a trial will take place and everyone carefully watches the accused. If in the eyes of an honest fetisher the man is innocent, he is dismissed. If it is a minor crime, he is given a mild poison in small doses. Yet if the fetisher doesn't like the man because he is not a believer or flouts a taboo, that trial by ordeal—a strong medication he must take to vindicate himself—may end in death. They also know that the outcome may depend on who paid the biggest fee if the fetish doctor is dishonest.

"Yet," he explained, "sometimes the fetish doctor claims some amazing cures; cures sworn to by the families of the ill. Mostly, these cures are for illnesses the fetisher first gave the patient." He laughed. "He has a foolproof absolute guaranteed cure. He creates the illness with a mild poison, then cures it with an antidote and gets paid for both.

"For instance, a middle-aged native lumberman came to the hospital by boat. He had an enormously distended abdomen and was constantly retching. It was obvious he had an intestinal obstruction with no bowel movement for three days. The cause was in question, so we gave him intravenous fluids, and I'd see him five or six times a day, hoping to put off an exploratory. Early one evening, while walking toward this patient's ward, I saw Pierre.

" 'Don't see that patient now,' he told me seriously. 'He has his doctor (his fetish doctor) with him and the whole ward is watching. Don't go in now.'

"I stayed out; and, on going back later that evening, I was shocked. The patient was sitting up in bed drinking coconut juice. He had four bowel movements and felt fine. The fetish doctor had gone; and, according to Joseph, the fee was exorbitant."

But as Schweitzer once said, "Even if they become Christians, they still have their own little fetish boxes to ward off the spirits."

One night in his room, Schweitzer was telling me about an old wrinkled witch doctor who was about eighty and now an emeritus who other fetishers came to with their problems. Schweitzer related, "He was one of the few who was neither corrupt or dangerous—more a psychiatrist than a general practitioner. He came to me for help once, but secretly, so as not to blemish his standing. His second wife was sick and she had not responded to his treatment. I went along with him and put her in a private room and told no one. She had a full-blown case of Erisipelas (a fast-spreading streptococcal infection of the skin) which was cured in a few days with antibiotics. I then secretly discharged her. No records were kept, and no face was lost by my friend," he said winking.

He looked at me with a mischievious little-boy smile and asked, "Do you want to see my fee?" Without waiting for an answer, he went over to a shelf and brought out a small tin box in which there was a piece of bone that was a deep yellow color, a small ribbon, a polished stone, and a little bell. "Many people ask me for the secret of my longevity. I always tell them that I have the best of all possible worlds. If my faith in Jesus doesn't do it, my fetish will.

"You know, a fetish is supposed to ward off all evil spirits. One may have one for his health, one to spawn daughters, one to hang on a tree to be sure of a good crop, or one for any of a hundred other purposes." I asked Schweitzer if he used his for problems other than aging. He put his finger to his lips and said, "That was something never to be talked about, but mine is one of the best and most effective." I asked why, and he said because the bone I saw was a piece of human skull. (I later learned that the person whose skull was to be used as a fetish was usually 'done in' for that specific purpose.)

"It's interesting," he continued, "that the natives believe that magical powers are in the skull. Don't we think the same, even if not in the bone itself? Aren't we so proud of our brain power? Then there is the so-called science of phrenology—reading a person's fortune, as your wife told me she does by reading a hand—by feeling the skull." He continued, "I can also wish on my fetish for good or evil to someone I like or dislike; so watch out."

He closed the box and put it back on the shelf.

"If the fetishers are still so popular and feared," I said, getting a little more serious, "and the belief in fetishes so strong, wouldn't this make you feel that their faith in Jesus isn't very strong?"

"No, they can separate their beliefs. They're no different than a sophisticated, good American Christian going to a gypsy fortune teller or a good Anglican Londoner going to an astrologer. Look at a Catholic fingering his beads as he prays or works for the end of an illness or in a disaster beyond his control. We all have our fetishes, our good-luck pieces, and our superstitions; so the natives with a fetish can be as good Christians as a Berlin *burgomeister*. In the same breath, I say that is what true Christianity isn't. A superstitious belief in a fetish is merely a reflex, an instinct, or a wish. If there is true faith through our compassion and ethics, one doesn't need skull bones or beads. Many natives realize this with education; some never!"

"What if one needs neither," I questioned, slipping back into a religious vein. "Can't one be an agnostic and still be secure?"

"Yes," he said. "I guess that is possible, until a tragedy occurs—the loss of a loved one, a serious accident in which a close friend is hurt, a natural catastrophe destroying crops or a home, or just serious illness. Then only a true ethical faith can be solace. During those crises, burning candles and throwing salt over your shoulder does little good for a troubled mind."

"Dr. Schweitzer, I admit that gnostic beliefs such as yours may do wonders; but the ordinary lay person trying to make a living doesn't have the time, the talent, and the brain to really acquire an ethical spirit that would help him in time of need. Couldn't the blind faith in a fetish do as much good?

Don't you think that the honest fetishers, not the one I've met, are sort of thought of as priests and part of a religion?"

He looked at me sideways as if he didn't want to hurt my feelings. "In a conventional sense, religion doesn't necessarily mean a real belief and understanding. In any spiritual sense, one can only have true faith in thinking ethically of one's place in society and the universe. Good fetishers are like good psychiatrists—good listeners with common sense and compassion. But that's no religion unless psychiatry is a religion, and," nodding his head, "some do take it as such."

I remembered seeing Dr. Friedman with that mental patient he had brought in tied hand and foot with vines and wanted to discuss Schweitzer's thoughts on psychiatry.

But he was already rising and bidding me good night. My questions would have to wait.

9

THE QUEST
CONTINUED

On Sundays we all arose to the Sabbath bells, rung a half-hour later than on weekdays. Other than making rounds on the very ill, nothing was scheduled but the sermon in the hospital square. Afterward, Phoebe and I usually went for a walk in the jungle but never by ourselves. It was still dangerous because of wild animals further away from the hospital, so we were always accompanied by a native leading with his machete at ready. In the afternoon, we frequently took a *pirogue* ride on the river until almost sunset.

One very hazy and terribly humid morning Dr. Mueller, one of the young German doctors, very ambitious, no-nonsense, ramrod straight with barely a sense of humor, was to deliver the open-air sermon to the patients in the hospital square, interpreted by Pierre or Joseph. Just after breakfast, Schweitzer motioned to me and we went off to a corner of the dining room as the native waiters cleaned up.

By this time, Schweitzer and I had had several talks in

his room and others at his desk in the pharmacy building or just on the grounds as we ran into each other. A very easy rapport had been established between us. I had begun to enjoy him immensely and felt that the relaxing of his reserve had come about especially because of our kindred sense of humor, most of which we shared as we joked around at mealtimes. However, during work hours and in our daily meetings on patients or supplies, he was still very much "down to business."

He fingered his moustache as we sat on the piano bench. "Would you rather hear Mueller preach this morning? He's rather good at it." Ordinarily I would but, since our last talk on the historical Jesus, I had more unanswered questions than ever before—some on his trouble with the Church.

"If we may," I said, "I'd rather get back to *my* quest for the historical Schweitzer."

"All right," he smiled at my joke. Ali Silver was, as usual, annoyed by our bantering but Schweitzer was unfazed by her reaction. We continued from the previous session with the *Quest*. "You know, that first little pamphlet—and that's all it was," he began thoughtfully.

I interrupted. " 'Little pamphlet'—I've read how most of your 300-page books start out as 'little pamphlets'; and how one 400-page volume on Bach has been revised up to 800 pages."

Schweitzer, with an amused smile, explained that his first draft is always shorter by half than the second. "When I sit down to write, barely half of my ideas have been worked out. As I go along, new thoughts crowd in."

Anyway, that first pamphlet turned into a book he had been mulling over since he was a young student in theology. He had always been obsessed with the historic facts of Jesus' life and couldn't understand why the Church couldn't see them as he did; it was so clear to him. "Christianity had steered away from Christ." Later, even when he was initially proposed as a professor at the University of Strasbourg, some of the older professors opposed his appointment because of his ideas on the historical Jesus. They thought it would be too confusing to the theological students. "That is one of the main reasons I came to Africa, to show that I lived what I believed: my life would be my argument."

He shrugged. "Even if that book had weighed only a milligram, it still became as heavy a cross to me as the one Jesus carried to Calvary—or so I thought at the time.

"As I told you, I was turned down twice for a medical mission in Africa fifteen years after the *Quest for the Historical Jesus* was published. Imagine, those godly men letting the research of the heretofore relatively unresearched dogma interfere with the possibility of giving some relief to the multitude of the miserable in Africa." He shifted around on the piano bench.

At that time, about 1909, what he said in that "pamphlet" may have been the truth; yet he must have known that even then the Church, after some 1900 years of its own interpretation, wouldn't change overnight because of his research.

Perhaps he should have been more patient or not even have published then—he was so young. But there was more than one reason he did publish. First, there is no doubt he'd been a maverick, from childhood on, when it came to following a leader or a dogma. As he put it, "As a small boy, my father and uncle, whom I stayed with during most of my education, always encouraged me to pursue to the end what I thought was right. But even more, as I grew older, I realized that if one bent to every outside criticism, one could never reach a truth—especially a truth one knew was right from one's own research."

He nodded, pursing his lips. "One must have faith in one's work if it stands clear in the light of reason."

So he should have expected the hierarchy's reaction of "heresy." But he had naively reasoned, "Even simple people could understand simple truths (which the Church buried). The Church thought the rank and file must be led to it through fairy tales and ritual alone."

Then he got to the real heart of the matter of the Church's misconceptions. "Jesus never thought Himself a god. But it's more than that. As Christians, the Church just wouldn't admit the influence of the Old Testament on Jesus, for obvious reasons—the New Testament was their Bible; their very own Gospel. So, of course, they didn't take into account the Jewish milieu of thought that Jesus lived in. This was probably to break clear with any Judaic tradition and have their own as Christians." Schweitzer put his elbows back against the piano and, looking toward the ceiling, went on.

"I think I showed conclusively in my *Quest* that the words of two major Jewish prophets—Daniel and Isaiah—to whom Jesus constantly referred, were the forerunners of some of Christ's beliefs." (Dr. Friedman said that Schweitzer had also mentioned one other prophet in the Apocrypha, but Schweitzer later told me this was not true.) "Little of the Gospels other than Mark, Matthew, and part of Luke were authentic," he said. "This has been doubted for many years by theologic scholars and still is today. The other Gospels were Greek versions embellished to make Jesus more godlike and acceptable to the masses.

"For instance," he continued, "John's Gospel was obviously not from Jesus' words but what some other Christians had interpreted third-hand from His words years later—maybe a hundred years later."

As he spoke I wondered how the Church powers could call him a heretic if they had also read his medical school graduation thesis, *The Psychiatric Study of Jesus*. There, as a medical student, quite a bit after the publication of the *Quest*, he was defending Jesus as a great spiritual and ethical force. He defended Jesus' sanity then against a multinational group of modern (for those times, 1911) psychiatrists who had labeled Jesus a paranoid and a fanatic.

As he explained it, his anticlerical feelings surfaced. "The Church has a knack for selective reading. It always takes for granted any support of their existing beliefs but never seems to forget the questioning of another." Not only was Schweitzer severely criticized when the *Quest* first came out; later there was a pamphlet printed by Church "scholars" entitled, "Is Albert Schweitzer a Christian?"

"Anyway," he continued, chuckling, "I got my reward—a chicken coop Mission. I rationalized that if it was that bad—dilapidated and long vacant—maybe it better fitted my need."

This "need" was real for Schweitzer. He honestly felt especially anointed with his many talents; and he really had a *need* to redeem the many endowments of his birth and, not unlike Christ, to fulfill his responsibility to mankind.

Yet in a sense I felt that, in the aftershock of the *Quest*, the Church actually did him a great favor. I said, "You were not unlike an old friend of mine, a great Jesuit philosopher and co-discoverer of the Peking Man, Pierre Teilhard de Chardin. He once told me the Church, in its strictures, made God favor him. Teilhard, too, was not allowed to preach—to teach his type of scientific 'heresy' in Paris, just as the Church didn't want you to teach yours anywhere in Africa."

He interrupted, "How did you know Teilhard? I think I corresponded with him once. I knew that both of our lives were influenced by the dogma of the Church."

I told him that I'd become rather close to Teilhard during the last two years of my stint with the Marine Corps in Peking after World War II. "Speaking of godliness, never had I known a man with more innate goodness. He was one of the most creative Jesuit thinkers *and* the only Catholic cleric I knew of who attempted to get the Church to admit that the theories of Darwin should be encompassed by the Church, to its benefit."

The Catholic Church's handling of Teilhard, the Lutherans' giving Schweitzer the most dilapidated primitive Mission, did much for both men in many ways.

Other than giving Schweitzer the inner peace in fulfilling his responsibilities, later—probably two or three years—his aloneness gave him the time to write and play his music and, more, to think through in the perfect environment necessary to produce the Reverence for Life philosophy. Also, his sacrifice of the comforts of civilization to live in the jungle had caught the imagination of the world. That in itself gave him an almost deified popular image, which I think he enjoyed.

It's strange how chance works. Had he not gotten this Mission, he could probably have ended up somewhere in Africa in an urban church not too different from those in Strasbourg. Then there would have been the attendant social and personal distractions to learning about the essence of man through primitive patients and about nature and the preciousness of all animal life and the formulation of Reverence for Life.

Suddenly he asked mischievously, "Did you know I was once a soldier? It was long before the First World War. It wasn't by choice; yet it wasn't unenjoyable."

This surprised me since I had thought he was a total pacifist and abhorred the idea of armies in any sense.

He continued, "At that time, every able-bodied young

man in Europe had to serve a term in his nation's army. It was during peacetime and he could go home on weekends and even go to the university during the week at certain hours." Then, as if this had struck a chord in his memory, "Do you know it was in those same military barracks that I first worked out the *Quest*—between training and maneuvers? It was somewhere around 1895." I imagine Schweitzer was only twenty at the time and was already deep into this crucial theologic work.

I took the opportunity to get back to the original subject and asked, "Can you enlighten me as to what else the Church took umbrage at in the *Quest?*"

Turning his alert blue eyes on me, he said, "Are you sure you want all of those details?" Without waiting, he plunged right in, never faltering a moment. "In the eighteenth and nineteenth centuries, even the scholars were writing that Jesus thought He was the Messiah, the divine son of God, and was sent by God. It was clearly wrong. Jesus knew He was the son of Man—after all He was from the house of David. Also, from my interpretation of Mark and Matthew, it's apparent that Jesus believed deeply in the eschatology (the final days—the end of the world) of that day and that a supernatural world would take its place. The Church, trying to play down the supernatural, taught that Jesus' kingdom of heaven was only in the spiritual sense and what He was talking about was just a new moral world. Those scholars would not openly admit that Jesus was born and brought up as a Jew with Jewish traditions and a deep belief in the Old Testament prophets. My evidence showed that Jesus really thought that the material or natural world would end, and that the kingdom of heaven or the supernatural world actually would come, and that when it came He would then be announced as the Messiah.

His voice trailed off, then started again. "Jesus never

once mentioned in public that He *was* the Messiah, though He
believed He was. He told only the disciples this, and only
toward the end. Though the Church wouldn't admit it,
Christ's Jewishness had to have influenced His thinking. He
thought the kingdom of heaven was not some distant time off
but imminent. At one time, Jesus even changed His interpretation of the words of the prophets after certain things that
He predicted did not happen."

As if appalled, he continued, "The Church just
skipped over this. Jesus unquestionably was not just killed
but deliberately arranged His own death as a martyr. After
all, His reasons were to help avoid the tribulation His disciples were supposed to endure—according to the prophets—
also to redeem mankind and to fulfill the Old Testament
prophecies. He actually sought His own death on the cross; it
was not as the result of rank persecution, as Christian
doctrine contends."

Schweitzer grew adamant. "The hierarchy of Chris-
tiandom won't even accede to the fact that much of the Gospel
is only hearsay, embellished more and more over the years."

"Is there evidence for this?" I knew full well he had it.

"Of course," he said, slapping his knee sharply,
"reams of it, especially just recently. For instance, Jesus is
never quoted, in any reading I had ever seen, as saying He
was the son of God, only the son of man, just as the Messiah
was supposed to be in the book of Daniel."

He seemed to grow calmer. "Also, as the son of man,
Jesus didn't think He was divine, only divinely instigated. He
no doubt thought Himself the Messiah, which would only be
obvious when, as He believed, He came back to earth in a
supernatural state."

Just then, Pierre came in to remind Schweitzer that
two men from Lambarene were there for an appointment.

He acknowledged this with a cursory wave of his hand

and went on, "Jesus, as a devout believer in the prophets, naturally assumed that, as the Messiah, He would appear as predicted in the Old Testament. I interpreted it in that light because when Jesus sent the disciples out to different villages to preach His truths He told them that, according to the prophets, they would be abused and suffer. Also, that on their return the world would have ended and the kingdom of heaven would have come.

"This, of course, did not occur. They came back unsuffered and unabused, and there was no kingdom of heaven on their return. So Jesus retired to the mountains for a time.

"There," Schweitzer said with emphasis, "He surely contemplated chapter fifty-three of Isaiah, which intimated that the Messiah must suffer for His disciples and believers. He thought, then, that only through His suffering and death could He redeem mankind.

"Then came the Sermon on the Mount and the decision that He must 'force' the Sanhedrin and the Romans to persecute and kill Him to make the prophecy come true. Thus His belief that He is the Messiah—although He never said it Himself.

"After this episode, when He came back from the mountains to Jerusalem, Christ was still greeted by great crowds. The people did not desert Him then, as the Church maintains. No—He was followed by hordes of believers; but only the disciples knew what He was doing—that He was going to his worldly grave."

As he frequently did, Schweitzer got up, and, with head a bit bowed, began to pace the floor. Everyone had left the dining room. He spoke as he walked. "But as Jesus said, 'I will come back to a kingdom of heaven on a cloud, seated on the right hand of God, and there will be a judgment day, and you will be the judges.' The Church tried to interpret all of this in a worldly way with no supernatural element at all.

"But even with Jesus' supernatural ideas, what difference does it make as long as the new state of mind would be invested with His ethics—which were so new to those ignorant, semi-primitive, poverty-stricken people?"

Schweitzer brought up the Apocrypha and Jesus' following of the prophet Amos, who said that the disciples should give the word of God to all people not just the Jews, at which, of course, the Sanhedrin took offense. And which helped bring Isaiah's prophecy of martyrdom to fruition. He knew that His and His disciples' preaching to the Samaritans, for example, was certain to stir things up against Him.

I was now beginning to understand why the Church found Schweitzer's logic so upsetting. It was cutting the ground from under their thousands of years of teachings. He launched into still more evidence. "When John the Baptist's messenger from his prison asked, 'Are you the one?' it implied that John was Elijah come back to precede the Messiah, who was Jesus."

Schweitzer then quoted Jesus's enigmatic answer: " 'John would be the greatest of that from woman but less than the least in the kingdom of heaven.' " He went on to explain, "The Church thought this was derogatory of John, which it would have been were it an ethical kingdom in a natural world. But it was only that Jesus was comparing the best of natural man with the least of supernatural man."

We talked a while about Paul and Schweitzer's book, *The Mysticism of Paul the Apostle*, when, out of the blue, he asked me if I ever went to Hebrew school. When I said I had, he told me that Paul first knew of Jesus, as did most other non-Christians, in the most derogatory way. He learned this in a conventional Hebrew school in Greece. Even then it was taught that Jesus was a "pseudo Messiah," an imposter, not the one they all waited for.

"You know," I said, "I think I learned almost the same thing when I went to Hebrew school."

Schweitzer laughed, then hesitated as if he knew he had said it before and didn't want to repeat himself. "There is a spiritual evolution besides a physical evolution. And when man's true self evolves so does the goodness inside of him. But none of my interpretations were aired or studied in depth by the Church."

It saddened me that this still bothered him.

Later, I remembered that I had mentioned the word "divine" in relation to Jesus. He said, as if exasperated because he had told me before, "No, only God is divine; and we must not think of Christ as a god. Stop listening to the dogma; think more of His rational and ethical approach."

I'd asked if it is possible that the mystical and ethical, without the name of Jesus, could be a religion without worshipping a god.

We were really getting into his inmost thoughts, and, to my surprise, he really opened up as to his personal religion. "I have no god; no vision of heaven. I believe in the spirituality and ethics of and through Jesus. If, at that time, those Jews, even the ancient Essenes, through Jesus, had the secret, then they too had the spirit in their hearts. This had to come from somewhere, so let us say it was divine. But, whatever the source, His spirit and His ethics are my religion."

Then very slowly, word-by-word: "I need no churches, no dogma, and maybe no name (Jesus); I believe that action in life itself is religion, and this is what gives it harmony."

This was the key to what would shock the world of religion just a year or so later, when he was eighty-six or eighty-seven, and it was announced by the Unitarian Church that Schweitzer, as a "liberal Christian," had become a life member of that Church. In light of his writings and what he had always felt about the historical Jesus and the Church's intransigence in accepting his thesis, it should not have been a shock. But it was.

However, after what he had said to me and his previous denial of the Trinity, he was obviously more suited to the Unitarian than to the Lutheran Church to which he was born. As he said when he became a member, "I have always had a sympathy for your (Unitarians) affirmation of Christian freedom at a time when it resulted in persecution. I think faith in action is important."

But as a compromiser, which he usually was not, and as a gentleman, which he usually was, he gracefully said, "I am a Protestant but above all I am a scientist—the degree of which is questionable; and, as such, I can be on good terms with all Protestant churches." As to the question of the Trinity, which Unitarians deny, Schweitzer said, "Did Christ or Paul believe in it?"

Having revealed his true beliefs to me, he launched into a criticism of the formal Protestant Church. He questioned whether its stand was good for the people or was just to make sure of the maintenance and consistency of its own ancient dogma. "They stay with what's easy and has worked in the past, regardless of the fact that peoples and cultures change and the Church must change with it." His voice began to rise.

"The Church must lead by example and acknowledge the truth. The Church, for so many years, has had a certain perspective on Jesus; and it worked for a while but did it work for the so-called believers? Who in this modern world is going to believe what they're preaching? It has worked only minimally; otherwise, there would be much less strife today.

As a young man, I myself was struck by many doubts. From the little we know of Him, was there really evidence as to whether he was in fact God or man?"

Running his hand through his handsome, if unruly, mop of hair he grew more vehement. "Much of what is preached by the Church is myth. As I said, much of the later Gospels are highly questionable. Do you know that some theologians doubt Jesus' very existence? Some say Paul, in his fit on the way to Damascus, just saw and heard all of what Jesus should have said."

"But what made you so sure that you were right?"

"Why shouldn't I," he said, surprised. "My sources come from the same Gospel as the Church's but they took it as rote without trying to interpret it in the light of His time. What's more," he said confidently, "what I have written has not been scientifically refuted by theologians or scholars. It was always clear to me from my studies that Jesus' conceptions were astoundingly original for His time, yet still under the influence of the Jewish world in which he lived. And that was my main, and a most crucial, break with the Church's thoughts.

"Jesus was taken out of the context of His time, put into the Renaissance, and made a god—which was a terrible error. In the genre of the conventional thoughts of two thousand or more years ago, they could have simply acknowledged that a newfound message of love and truth was born," he said feelingly.

Just then, there was a knock on the dining room door and the Danish philosopher, Dr. Friss, who was to leave the next day, called in. Schweitzer went out to meet him; they talked for a few moments on the porch. Then I heard Schweitzer say, "I'll see you tomorrow before you leave."

By the time he came back and sat down, I was so full of his interpretation of the *Quest* that I doubted that I would be

À ma table de Lambaréné.

Au docteur Edgar Berman avec mes
bonnes pensées. Albert Schweitzer
Lambaréné 7. 12. 1960

In his room at his handmade desk

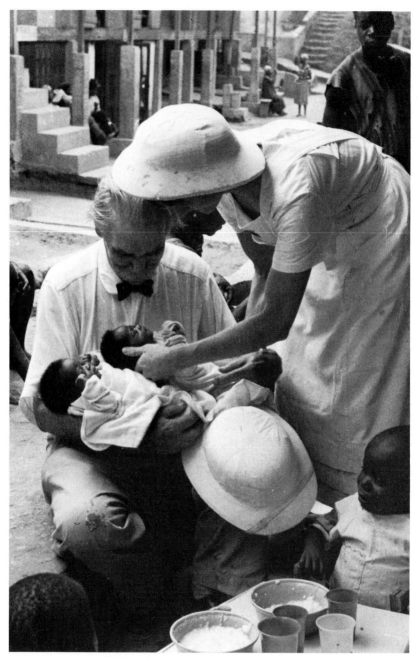

The birth of twins

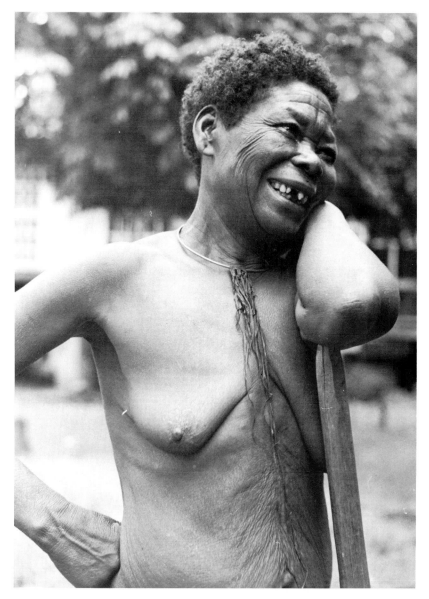

Mama San Nom—The Pygmy lady

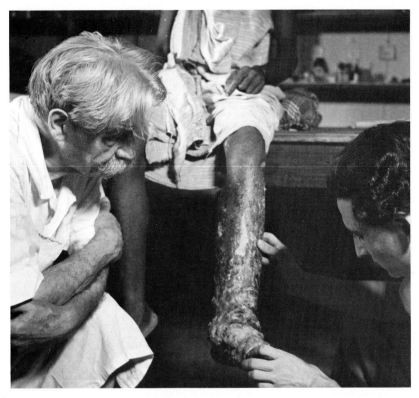

A jungle disease in a late stage

able to sort it all out later if he were to continue. I purpose-fully went off on another tangent. "Dr. Schweitzer, I've often wondered why you contacted Medico when you needed a surgeon and why it is the first and only organization of which you became a patron?"

I was surprised at his phenomenal memory. He cocked an eye at me. "I remember what you said about not being a 'do-gooder' but you and Dr. Dooley are sending doctors all over the world helping the poor and the ill; so, somewhere inside, you must have some of the same feelings I have."

"Well," I said, with some embarrassment, "people are always investing someone else with motives that they would like to believe. I'm not that modest and, I must protest, my motive was not so pure in coming here."

He looked into my eyes. Then, apparently disregard-ing what I said, he continued, "So, brothers that we are, that is why I accepted Medico's offer to be its patron." Then he smiled outright. "Maybe, unbeknownst to you and despite your original protest, you are more spiritual and less cynical than you think."

I began to squirm; he was wrong. He went on. "And, regardless of the reason you give yourself for being here, you must have a feeling or thought for your fellow man; and the spirit of Jesus is a part of you too." I was even more embarrassed.

As a defense reaction and to get him off the subject of me, I joked, "But I'm a non-believer in the Messiah. I'm a Jew. We're still waiting."

Opening his eyes wide, he cocked his head. "Surely, after all of our talks, you know he was also a Jew and not necessarily the Messiah."

By now Schweitzer, and certainly I, had obviously had enough of this conversation. "I must get down to my room. I have some people to see and some mail to finish," he said.

"But," I laughed, "this is the Sabbath—no work today."

"No one told my goat about that." His eyes twinkled. "You see this?" He pulled a sheaf of papers that had been protruding from his back pocket. One corner of most of the papers had been chewed off. "Yesterday, while I was giving instructions for the day, my sharp-toothed friend, who has no respect for civilization, nibbled at my back pocket without my knowing it. And it wasn't the first time. He digested a part of a chapter of the third volume of *The Philosophy of Civilization*; and I must replace it before I start my letters or I may forget my own words."

We moved toward the door. I said, "It's probably more than most people can digest anyway."

"They might but unless I repair the damage no one will have the chance," was his parting shot.

10

A NIGHT
TO REMEMBER

Nine p.m. was the usual hour for everyone to "retire" at the hospital. It was impossible to read for any length of time by the kerosene lanterns, and we were always dead tired from the hot, work-filled day. And then, as enervating as the heat was during the day, the night air, though a bit cooler, was heavy with moisture and much more uncomfortable. (The downpours of the rainy season were usually at night.) Our tiredness and the humidity made for long, tossing and turning, restless nights. At times, just turning over made drawing a breath somewhat labored.

On one particular evening the midnight lethargy was compounded by my continuous dehydration. Despite the care I'd taken with the drinking water, I suspected that I had finally contracted the more dangerous and endemic of the diarrheal diseases in Africa—amoebic dysentery.

About midnight, I became aware of a persistent

knocking on our screen door. My iron bedstead being only a few feet from the door I called out, "Who's there?"

Through the screen a voice answered, "It's me, Pierre." In his pidgeon French he shouted, "I'm sorry doctor, but Dr. Weisberg from the French Provincial Hospital downstream needs you for an emergency—a ruptured appendix. His *piroque* and paddlers are waiting for you."

Dr. Weisberg, a contract "surgeon" for the French government, was a good friend of Schweitzer's. He was a nice, kindly man; but, as I found out soon enough, not only grossly incompetent in surgery (a specialty I think he particularly abhorred) but also not too interested in the overall job he was supposed to be doing. As a Jewish refugee, he was working here in Africa—the end of the line—as a last resort, just to make a living.

Though Weisberg put on a rather worldly insouciant facade as both an intellectual Viennese and as a trained physician, he was basically a beaten and frightened man. I learned from Schweitzer that Weisberg had been thoroughly abused by the events of his times, first as a Jew in Austria and then as a Nazi prisoner. Now he was a Pernod-sipping refugee in an African jungle that he both loathed and feared.

His wife, a tiny emotional and social replica of him with a similar background and worse phobias, put on no such front. She was reticent and shy, hardly hiding her fright. She always looked so pale, and always on the verge of tears. She spent most of her time at an easel painting tiny primitive watercolors of jungle flowers as a means of occupying her mind against memories she couldn't abide. More than likely, she was deeply scarred by the terrors of her past and the anxiety of the present.

As I dressed, I aroused Phoebe enough to whisper where I was going. She whispered a sleepy reply. There was no moon that night, and I had to carefully follow the paddler's bobbing lantern to the dark river edge. As we walked down toward the landing, I began to wonder about Weisberg's patient. I remembered that during my first days at Lambarene Schweitzer had told me that he hadn't seen a case of appendicitis or cholecystitis (gall bladder disease) in forty years. That, plus the probability that Weisberg was deep in his cups at that time of the evening, made me doubt the diagnosis.

From my conversations with him, both on his visits to Schweitzer and as his guest in the Lambarene Provincial and Military hospital. I felt sure Weisberg viewed this episode of native illness as just another medical distraction interrupting his more pleasant alcoholic reveries. Yet, after being in Africa only a short time, I could empathize with him. I knew how much he must miss his now-long-past civilized existence as an upper-middle-class European physician with his prestige, his evenings at a vernissage or the Vienna Staatsoper.

For some unknown reason, possibly to save kerosene, the lanterns were extinguished as we stepped into the *pirogue*; and we paddled out into pitch blackness. Even the water we glided over was invisible, showing not a ripple of light. We arrived downstream at the village in about half an hour and walked up the path from the landing to the hospital.

An unsteady Dr. Weisberg waited and my prognosis of his condition wasn't too far off. Through his slurred, Austrian-French-accented English, frequently interspersed by his almost tic-like *n'est pas* for my assent, he explained his findings and diagnosis. Then he led me to the patient: a pretty fourteen-year-old girl clutching a polished piece of stone— probably a fetish given to her by her parents. She appeared very lethargic.

She already lay on the operating table. (It must be admitted that that operating room as well as the rest of hospital, unlike Schweitzer's, looked immaculate and up-to-date at first glance.) The moment I saw her I knew Schweitzer's contention was right: she had anything but a ruptured appendix.

She was obviously not flushed with the fever of peritonitis; instead, the deadly gray pallor of her dark skin pointed to internal bleeding. This was verified by the fact that her normally pink nail beds and conjunctiva (the mucous membrane of her eyelids) were a dead white from loss of blood. When I pressed her mushy soft abdomen, she screamed. It was this tell-tale sign of "rebound tenderness" (no reaction when pressing into the abdomen, but terrible pain when suddenly relieving the pressure), which told me there was blood in the belly. Though she was only fourteen, this was Africa. The diagnosis was most likely an ecotopic pregnancy (a pregnancy in the fallopian tube: as the fetus enlarges, it ruptures the tube and bleeds into the abdomen). Even at her tender age, many African children have gonorrhea, which can partly obstruct the tube, forcing the fertilized ovum to grow there instead of in the uterus.

As gently as possible, I confided my feelings to Weisberg who, without batting a heavy lid, vociferously agreed that there was no question about it.

There was, of course, no blood bank; so we immediately began giving her plasma from a military supply. It was the best blood substitute available and would at least give her some circulating fluid and protein to combat the complete shock she was certainly headed for.

I knew she would need blood during the operation; so we rigged up an open-ended laboratory bottle and fitted one end with some rubber tubing and a needle and the other end with a glass funnel to be stuffed with sterile gauze. I ordered it autoclaved (steam sterilized) as a package. The only way to save her was to scoop the blood out of her abdomen as soon as it was open and put it back in her veins. I would have to risk the danger of possible infection and clots. The gauze would strain out all but the finest clots. One saving grace: there was no need to type her blood; it was her own, therefore no danger of a mismatch.

As we prepared to scrub up, I was in the same clothes (chinos and T-shirt) I wore coming down. I added only the usual rubber apron. My assistant, Dr. Weisberg, still not too steady, showed me the extent of his instrument supply, of which there were not only few but of the most primitive kind. What there was of them were of the wide crushing type, hardly the delicate ones needed to cause a minimum of tissue trauma. Added to this, the only catgut he had was chromic number five, the heaviest made, which was probably sufficient to secure a *pirogue* to a mooring at flood tide. The rubber gloves would have had better use on the hands of an electrical lineman.

As we scrubbed and the instruments were being autoclaved in a rather modern sterilizer, a sudden commotion erupted in the O.R. There was great shouting, combined with whooping laughter. I poked my head in to see what was going on. The patient was gone from the operating table. I dropped my brush, tore off my mask, and ran outside. All the native *infirmiers* were standing on the porch jabbering, pointing into the darkness, watching the besheeted patient dash down the road toward the river. I began running after her; about fifty yards from the O.R. she faltered, then dropped to the ground. When I reached her, her pulse was rapid but still strong. After yelling for a stretcher, which Weisberg dispatched, we took her back to the O.R. She was unconscious.

The girl had obviously aroused from her semi-shock-like state, seen the powerful focussed O. R. lights pointing at her from above and those lethal-looking instruments all laid out before her. She must have been frightened out of her wits;

so she bolted out the door, tearing the plasma needle from her arm.

We lifted her back onto the table and started the plasma again. Outside the O.R., her family was in a frenzy, but her mother, a tall stately woman garbed in a bright yellow ankle-length African holiday dress and a beautiful yellow turban, was obviously the family leader and very intelligent. We explained everything to her through an interpreter. She was taken to the girl and soon placated her. Prior to that, the family hadn't even been told what was wrong and what we were preparing to do.

The girl then quieted down, seeming to understand. I gave her a stiff dose of morphine, partly for her pain but mostly to help put her under during the operation. At that time we had no one to give a general anesthesia and her pressure was too low to give her a spinal. I was compelled to operate after injecting only local anesthesia. I scrubbed up again, but, before preparing her abdomen and draping her, I talked to her in French just trying to relax her, though she understood nothing I had said. Strangely, she seemed more alert than before her sedation.

I called for another shot of morphine. By an instinctive quirk, or possibly by habit, I looked at the bottle from which the aide was filling the syringe. "Jesus Christ," I yelled, "not that, you fool." The aide, frightened, dropped the bottle and syringe and ran from the room. I was mad as hell, and losing my temper, screamed at Weisberg who was also quivering with fright. The bottle—the same one from which her first shot had come—contained adrenalin, which has the opposite effect of morphine. Weisberg was too shaken to be embarrassed; and, while garbling a gibberish of French apologies interspersed with his ubiquitous *n'est pas*, he roundly berated his black assistant. We then gave the patient a shot of

real morphine and waited for more than half an hour before
she began to drowse.

It was almost 3:30 a.m. when we started the surgery.
The girl's blood pressure was low (about 70 over 30) but I
noted with relief that she was not sweaty or cold—no true
shock yet. I quickly infiltrated the lower midline of her
abdomen (the line of incision) with novocaine and ordered
another small amount of morphine to drip in with the plasma.
Since we hadn't given her a general or spinal anesthesia, I
knew the patient would be squirming during most of the
operation, making it even more difficult to get in and out
quickly.

I tried to remain cool. After all that had happened in
just the last half-hour I knew that *I* had to be on top of
everything, to question everyone and everything that was
being prepared. This girl's life was going to depend on speed
and just one hitch could ruin it all, and I didn't care whose
toes I was stepping on, including Weisberg's. It was a very
delicate situation and I guess I was a bit nasty to some of those
helping.

When I thought all was ready, I made my incision
through the previously injected line of novocaine. I operated
as swiftly as I could but yet with no real feel of the tissues: the
thickness of those terrible gloves impeded my speed. I made a
quick if chancy decision and tore them off, further risking the
chance of infection, and did the rest of the procedure bare-
handed. I reflexively winced as I used the clumsy crushing
Kocher clamps, tying the bleeders off with the hauser-like
catgut. Still, I was into the peritoneal cavity in less than ten
minutes. Weisberg, swaying occasionally, was of little help,
except to hold the retractors.

As I suspected, the girl's abdomen was full of blood;
but, not bothering with that for the moment, I felt and

grasped her uterus, gently pulled it into the incision, and looked at the two fallopian tubes. Finding the pulsating artery spurting a thin stream of blood where the pregnancy had burst the tube, I immediately clamped and tied it and removed the damaged tube with the tiny fetus in it. Though strapped down, the girl groaned and writhed with every maneuver as I worked feverishly within her abdomen. We gave her more morphine.

Once the bleeding stopped, I ordered the blood contraption we had devised inserted into another vein. With my bare hands, I began scooping blood and clots out of her belly and into the gauze-filled funnel, watching as it went back into her veins.

After getting the greatest amount of blood we could from her abdomen and flushing it out with sterile saline water, I was ready to close. Weisberg offered to do the rest. Not wishing him to lose face in front of his staff, I began assisting him and we reversed sides. This didn't last long. With huge curved needle and heavy silk sutures, he started by going through all five layers—peritoneum, muscle, fascia, fat, and skin, pulling it all together in one lumpy mass. I stood there as long as I could endure it—which was only a few minutes. Then, as unobtrusively as possible, and from the wrong side of the table, I took over again, cut out his few all-encompassing stitches and sewed her up layer by layer, with him unhappily assisting.

When we finished the girl was still not entirely conscious, but her pressure was up to about 100/50, and she was beginning to look better. I, on the other hand, probably felt worse than she did. I was utterly bushed—mainly from the tension—bathed in sweat, and couldn't wait to get to an outhouse. Finally I then peeled off my soaked clothing, dried off with a towel, put my damp pants back on, and borrowed a clean, dry, orange-and-black striped turtleneck (it looked like an old soccer club shirt) from the doctor.

I wanted to get back to Schweitzer's and bed as soon as possible. Weisberg insisted we go over to his house for a few minutes. He roused his wife, who soon brought us wine and cookies. Even then he opted for the wine alone and had downed two glasses before I had finished one. The wine did help me relax but also made me very sleepy.

Later I realized my fatigue came from more than just the strain of the unusually harrowing conditions we were working under; it was more the minute-by-minute decisions I had had to make. It had been a continuous nerve-wracking tension every step of the way—from the time the girl disappeared off the operating table and ran down the road to the final closure of her abdomen.

Though Mrs. Weisberg offered the comforts of her nice government-built house to sleep in for the remainder of the morning (it was then about 5:30 a.m.), I declined. I had two major procedures to do back at Schweitzer's that day.

It was still very dark and I thought I'd sleep in the *pirogue* for the trip upstream. But as I sat there, I felt that somehow things didn't seem to be going right. Something bothered me that I couldn't quite figure out. Ordinarily, after a successful, if grueling operation, one has a good feeling, almost a sense of elation or satisfaction, even when almost exhausted. Everything should have seemed worthwhile, especially after a difficult job well done. Back in Baltimore, I would have quietly celebrated the night's work sitting around with the interns and unwinding with coffee and cigarettes. It was always a pleasant aftermath to a tough procedure, since it was impossible to sleep, right off, anyway.

This time it was unclear, different; I pondered the whole evening. Gradually my feelings became clearer and I finally pinned them down. It was the depressing futility of it all. I knew that of the two million people in metropolitan Baltimore, even if there were hundreds of emergencies on any one night, there was someone to take care of them all under the best of conditions.

Here I spent six hours on one case under the worst conditions. Throughout most of Africa there was no one to do even that. There was not even a Weisberg available in ninety-five percent of rural Africa south of the Sahara. There were thousands of terribly ill people who wouldn't even know what to do much less have a place to go for relief. There was no competent hospital within a hundred miles; and anyway, most of the people had no conception that pain could be alleviated or disease prevented or death averted.

For the first time since I had arrived I had a strong inclination to get back to civilization where the fruitlessness of it all wasn't so overwhelming. I had had somewhat similar experiences in other developing continents; but no matter how difficult conditions had been, a human life had a much better chance than this. I thought of all the children in Africa with simple fractures who would never walk again, of those thousands of people with ordinary infected lacerations who would die every night because six tiny pills were not available.

I felt an overwhelming frustration and wished that I weren't there.

In the blackness surrounding the *pirogue*, with just the grunting sounds of the oarsmen and the soft lapping of the paddles as they dipped in and out, I mulled over all of this and became even more depressed. I tried to think of other things but compulsively came back to it again and again. In spite of this one girl who I hoped may now have been saved (she was discharged in ten days) what about the thousands who would never have the chance?

Momentarily I exulted in the thought that soon I would be leaving this misery. Then I remembered the many people I still would have to see and treat in the weeks ahead: another old man with Filariasis (elephantiasis); the twitching of the unconscious sleeping sickness patients; the malnourished children, the huge number of women infected with gonorrhea (their children born blind), and the hundreds of others right there in the hospital dying off one after the other with Rubella or just plain diarrhea.

And those I would never see: a hundred miles from there, more masses of people whose suffering was taken as a normal part of life when they could so easily be cured. And so it was, on and on across the length and breadth of Africa other than in very isolated urban areas such as Lambarene or Libreville.

There was just so little chance of curing, much less preventing or stamping out, these and a hundred other diseases rampant in every other hut in this God-forsaken continent.

Tens of thousands of doctors were needed in Africa. And it would take tens of years to just educate the population that health care was available. And fifty years and billions of dollars to train doctors and assistants and build clinics and hospitals.

Even in the capital of this so-called nation, there was no chance of having a tubercular lung removed so as to prevent its spread and sure death; or the mitral valve in the heart stretched in thousands of rheumatic fever patients so that a young man or woman might once again walk a few yards without shortness of breath and fatigue. Monstrous disfigurements from scarring burns were everywhere, when simple plastic surgery could have done so much so easily.

The odds against it all were just appalling—you knew plain-out that you were not making the tiniest dent in this overwhelming tangle of suffering, and that the problems wouldn't be solved in a score of lifetimes by a thousand well-trained specialists, much less in one's own time by Schweitzer's simple efforts.

I knew then that even if I were younger than my forty-three years, aware of what I had learned since my arrival, I would never choose to come out here to practice medicine for even a year, much less a lifetime.

The experience in Lambarene had seemed to have had just the opposite effect on me than it would have had on the missionary doctors and the Schweitzers of our society. They would have said, "At least one human life was saved." And I guess they should be respected for that. For me the futility was too overwhelming.

As I glided along the dark waters immersed in my thoughts, suddenly, as if specifically to dispel my gloom, the blackness vanished and the sky exploded in light. As always on the equator, there was no gradual birth of dawn; it was instantaneous. Another day had begun.

We were not far from the hospital landing. The red tin roofs shone through the wetted greenery, their reflection shimmering on the waters. We docked about 6:30 and I went straight to my room. Phoebe was already awake, dressed in her spotless white, her curly hair shiny and neatly brushed and her fresh good looks ready for another day. I, by contrast, was thoroughly fatigued, sweaty, and depressed. I "showered" in our usual way with wash bowl and pitcher. While drying off and dressing for breakfast, I morosely detailed the experiences of my exhausting night. I asked Phoebe what she thought about leaving sooner. She didn't give me the direct answer she would have given me when we first arrived, especially on the day she found wrigglers in her drinking water. It was different now. Compassionate and intelligent as she was, she had gradually gotten caught up in the Schweitzerian ethic, in Schweitzer himself, and in the work of the hospital. She had also gotten attached to most of the children she attended in her daily duties in the *pouponniere*. Now she just put it off, saying we'd talk about it later.

We walked in silence up the hill to breakfast. Schweitzer was already eating, and the first thing he did was ask me about the night's case. I didn't know how he knew I was away, but I told him about it in minute detail. He could see my disconsolance and perceived the derogatory tone that crept into the description of my trials at Weisberg's and of Weisberg himself.

Schweitzer immediately said, "I know both the hospital and my friend; you must realize that he isn't here as I am. He is unhappy just being what he is."

As we finished breakfast and the others began to leave, Schweitzer beckoned me. I told him I was due in the O.R., but he disregarded this and indicated for me to sit on the piano bench. He sat beside me.

"Look at it this way: it will always be a terrible struggle for both of us; but, maybe in another hundred years, most physical and societal ills may be expunged from the earth if enough of us do our small share. Yet I know in my heart some will always be left suffering and uncured. Maybe some day enough of us will give our time, effort, and knowledge to do what is a doctor's real responsibility on earth."

"Dr. Schweitzer," I said glumly, "you are out of touch with the average physician. It does not seem a reality for now or even in a hundred years. It's just a vain hope." I continued bluntly, "The average doctor in our modern society, and that is where the vast preponderance of physicians are, is not concerned with man's responsibility to man but with his responsibility to himself and his family. I think I know the usual well-trained Western physician, and I can only say that your dream will only come with a Messiah."

He shrugged and saddened. "Mine had already come, but," he said, "realistically, yours . . ." he caught himself, ". . . our colleagues', Messiah, I'm not sure about; I don't know . . . you could be right . . . maybe never."

He got up wearily, as if I had reminded him of something he would rather not have had brought up. I was a little ashamed of how my last remark may have hurt him, as if all of his selflessness and hard life here was for nothing. I didn't know it would cut so deep, and I felt badly about it but I had to tell him what I thought.

COLONIALIST
OR PRAGMATIST

On our way to Lambarene, stopping off in other African
nations such as Kenya, Rhodesia (now called Zimbabwe),
South Africa, and the Congo (Zaire), we became confused as
to how Africans felt about Schweitzer. His reputation among
both black and white Africans was hardly flattering, compared to our impressions of him. He was not the celebrated
physician, philosopher, and humanitarian that he was pic-
tured in Western Europe and the United States. We, at first,
attributed this anti-Schweitzer grumbling mostly to the independence ferment that was moving through all of Africa,
especially among black Africans, in 1960. We figured it was
just the result of a generalized anti-white feeling that had
been smouldering there for a hundred years.

However, as we traveled, the accusations—especially
of colonialism—gradually accumulated. It made us apprehensive. In Kenya, despite the good he was doing, spleen was
vented on him because of his all-white staff and the purported

apartheid atmosphere pervading the hospital (which, of course, wasn't mentioned in South Africa). Rumors of his cavalier treatment of the natives were widespread.

On the other hand, in Rhodesia the complaints from white Africans were quite different, though no less vituperative. To them the hospital was not considered worthy of its name simply because of its lack of order and cleanliness. They also impugned the chaotic Schweitzerian family style in which the hospital was run.

Also, the Rhodesian and South African whites considered Schweitzer anti-Christ based on a different misconception—that promulgated by the Church and stemming from his *Quest for the Historical Jesus.* His religious "heresy" was brought up again and again, especially among the few clergy we met. In retrospect, however, even they didn't know exactly what they were talking about. Few of them had even read the book.

Strangely enough, in Rhodesia, though the native Blacks felt him antagonistic to them, the dominant Europeans who ran the government and just about everything else thought him anti-white and anti-capitalistic with pro-Communist leanings. There was even a small book concerning him: *Is Albert Schweitzer a Fraud?*

The more we heard the more we wondered what we had gotten ourselves into. We had come three-quarters of the way around the world primarily to get to know this eminent humanitarian, and here he was being severely criticized on all sides for the absence of that virtue.

Both Phoebe and I, from our readings of him and about him, were puzzled by this but we kept an open mind as we approached the hospital.

Later, through all of my conversations with Albert Schweitzer, during work or leisure, there was never any doubt in my mind as to his natural gentleness, his fairness, and his warm feelings toward the natives—especially the patients. Of course, he would scold or punish an *infirmier* who forgot to administer a medication or one who was lazy, dishonest, or ignored rules (like the one, who against specific orders, brought termites into the medical supply room).

But even today, twenty years after his death, one hears the accusation of colonialism when Schweitzer's name is brought up. Though he claimed it was of no moment to him, I did raise the subject with him more than once.

Considering Schweitzer's temper and his natural authoritarianism toward whites or Blacks in his own bailiwick, I think he treated people and animals proportionately better as they descended the social and phylogenetic scale. He was more apt to admonish a member of his staff than a native for mistakes.

Rumors of Schweitzer's colonialism were mentioned, *sotto voce* of course, right at the hospital by some of the more disenchanted of the staff. There was more than one reason for this. In my estimation, many of the white volunteers (just about all of the staff was volunteer) came to Lambarene expecting to give personal meaning to their lives or to find salvation either in the good work they did, the ascetic life they had to live, or most likely the proximity of the great man himself. "If they did," Schweitzer confided, "they came for the wrong reason." And for most, the reaction was disappointment in finding that the answer to their problems was only a man, not a god, and they found little of the redemption they sought. And what's more, this extraordinary man had such broad-ranging interests and talents that their lack of time alone with him made him seem distant and aloof.

Even those staff members without a hair-shirt mentality resented the fact that they could not get very close to

Schweitzer. It was terribly disillusioning to the ones who stuck it out for any period of time. The few who were there for a lifetime probably had no place else to go.

Most of the in-house dissidents who talked about Schweitzer's colonialism were not only disappointed but almost enraged. It was as if they had gone to Lourdes and found that the legendary miracles would not help them stand without their neurotic crutches. Maybe their disappointment was one reason most of them were grim even when Schweitzer was joking. Some used the "colonial" cliche as an excuse for leaving the demanding life at Lambarene, when in reality their reasons for departing were that the rewards expected were not forthcoming in that tropical "heaven."

Another source of the colonialist rumors about Schweitzer were the many short-term visitors who set themselves up as Schweitzer experts when they really had little substantive evidence of the man's feelings toward native, worker, or patient. From my personal questioning, these so-called experts all tended to rely on hearsay or incomplete and mistaken perceptions formed on visiting him for no more than a few days.

Some cited his authoritarian ways in berating a native worker for laziness or irresponsibility, knowing little of the real reasons for Schweitzer's anger and not having seen how he would treat his own medical staff for lesser mistakes or unheeded orders.

When the topic of his bias toward natives surfaces today, I always think back to the operating room my first day in Lambarene when Schweitzer, at eighty-five years of age, stood through my entire first operation to make absolutely certain that an unknown black patient received the best available medical treatment. In my estimation, Schweitzer's concern for that patient was one of the surest signs of his empathy for them. It proved to me that most of the gossip about Schweitzer's prejudice was false.

Whenever he was asked about his feelings toward his native workers and patients, he gave the same answer: "I feel for them like a brother, but like an older brother. The Negro"—Schweitzer frequently used that term (it was not then *declassé)*—"is a child in a primitive culture, and nothing can be done with children without authority." Then he'd go on to explain, "Their belief in white man's superiority has been founded on the magic of his technical skills, his miracles in medicine, in industry, and material things. They look up to anyone who is not African, who is rich, and above all who has the modern comforts of life."

But, as Schweitzer himself admitted, "The accusations against me as favoring colonialism are made primarily because I wanted to make independence a gradual process." The accusations were leveled mainly by some of the black African leaders who saw power and money for themselves in independence. Some of the more idealistic ones thought independence would, overnight, be the key to the promised land. Yet accusations also came from liberal white Westerners, most of whom had never been in Africa or had been there for a short visit and understood neither the culture nor the problems of independence on that continent.

As an outsider, before I went to Lambarene, I too was somewhat critical about Schweitzer's stand on independence. I knew little of the tyranny of tribal leaders who sold their own people to white lumbermen or miners to be exploited as cheap labor and encouraged in their alcoholic habits. And I knew less of the almost total illiteracy or the primitiveness of the people and their economy, unparalleled anywhere in the world. But once I had lived and worked with Schweitzer I saw that Africans had been irrevocably tied to white industry only at the most menial level. Knowing this, I could then conceive of the havoc, hunger, and misery that overnight independence might bring. As Schweitzer put it, "It may take a century—time is the crucial element."

Yet Schweitzer was classed by some with the European colonialists and with some Americans who lived in Africa and who continue the age-old system in the exploitative way it had always operated. Others called Schweitzer an anti-capitalist because he wanted to see the natives get a squarer deal and not be taken advantage of as they had been under the colonialists. He was even labeled a traitor to the white race because he preached and wrote that whites had exploited black Africa without giving enough in return.

Then, as if to prove his guilt, they put horns on the angel by bringing up an unrelated issue—his Christian heresy—which they knew about only from Church rumors. After being there only a short time, I realized how both sides were more against each other than against Schweitzer. He had honestly brought both the evils of colonialism and the problems of independence out into the open and was soundly condemned by both sides.

Schweitzer knew there was "a large shadow hovering over instant independence," and he was one of the few to say that it was mainly the result of how colonialism had been practiced. His prediction that after independence, overwhelming economic and social chaos would be caused by corruption and lack of leadership has certainly been borne out.

In explaining the difference between an evolving Africa and the evolving Europe of the eighteenth and nineteenth centuries, one fact to which he called attention was the snail-like pace of past African progress and Africa's continued primitiveness, which has continued for centuries. But it was related, according to Schweitzer, mainly to Africa's unstable economy. As he said, "Stability is usually nurtured by a long agricultural phase of society, which most civilized nations have gone through. Look at the backwardness of the world's nomads (Bedouins or Gypsies); stability of place is important in national progress. No society can go from the primeval directly to an industrial state without losing the leavening that time and an agricultural period allow."

Today, modern economists in Africa maintain, as Schweitzer did forty years ago, that agriculture is the only way to subsistence and true independence and industrial technology cannot be substituted. Schweitzer, who also preached the importance of the work ethic, especially in a family, showed how family agriculture on family-owned land espoused this value. But, as he said many times, "My job is not to bring this about. It is a political policy and I am not in Africa as a politician."

He also repeated over and over, "Education alone for primitive people is not enough. And it is certainly not for the purpose of making a new class distinction." Schweitzer cited one story with which I was familiar. It was about a young native male who was educated at the missionary school in Lambarene. One evening a boatload of supplies came in and only Schweitzer was there to meet it. Nearby was a young Black, and Schweitzer asked him to lend a hand. The young man replied with disdain, "I am an intellectual. I work with my brain, not with my hands."

"Someday I hope to attain that status," Schweitzer muttered as he began to unload the supplies by himself.

"No," he continued, "children of nature (which he frequently called the black native), as long as they can earn money from their labors for others, whether cutting timber or in mines, and just buy things and not produce them, will not progress, regardless of how well they can spell or write a complete sentence. Look at the native stores: they have few tools but are stocked with canned goods, perfumes, and fancy dress shirts. If these countries are to become a stable force, the natives must first gradually build their own agricultural system and family life and then their industry."

Schweitzer also cited the chicanery of the colonialists in using education. Sadly he cited, "They went about educating a loyal coterie of Blacks as a sop to getting their way with tribal chiefs, and eventually using them for their own purposes. The French were the greatest exploiters and the worst educators. Colonialization is not bad if the colonizer gradually helps to bring about a more meaningful social and political order."

Schweitzer admitted the situation could change. But he felt it would take more than just a few generations for Africans to attain stable self government.

Phoebe and I saw the turmoil in Africa ourselves, and independence was associated closely with arrogance and corruption. The new rulers were hardly better than the colonialists, if not a lot worse, especially the small educated class. With corruption at the top, the average breadwinner could only survive by indulging in corruption at the bottom.

Schweitzer, as far as I could see, was always fair in his dealings with natives. But I was also privy to his rage when his teachings and examples went for naught. One day, for example, a gendarme from Lambarene brought in one of the young native hospital help for stealing. Brandishing his fist, Schweitzer exploded at the young man; but then calmed down and just shrugged his shoulders, muttering, "Time, time," which to him was the major element to answer most of Africa's problems. When the policeman took the boy away, Schweitzer lamented about his frustrations but at the same time explained his practical philosophy. It was probably one of the reasons many of his detractors thought him aloof, as if he were holding himself above the average native.

"If I am to be their teacher," he said, "I cannot also have the comaraderie of a fellow student—which I would like. As their teacher I must earn their respect, but even before that I must have their attention and obedience. A child of nature doesn't respect us just because we know or can do so much. He also judges us on our moral standards, more than we ourselves do.

"Take that boy brought in for stealing. He knew from what I'd taught him that he should not have taken what he did. But ancient tribal customs and mores in the village affect all who live there. Usually, anything most natives find or find growing anywhere in or outside of the forest, and especially outside of their own village, can be taken when the owner is unknown. If someone is foolish enough to leave an object unattended, it suggests that the owner doesn't really care about having it. Would someone leave something they prized unattended? This boy had been caught expropriating a bushel of tomatoes for an important cause—a down-payment on a dowry to his intended father-in-law. Unfortunately, it just so happened to come from a remote and unguarded part of the garden of a white timber merchant.

"The natives take fairness and goodness on our part for granted. But if they find less than that in us, they will never bother to listen or obey. We can act superior to them, but we must see that our principles are at least equal to or better than theirs. But seeing our education and the apparent ease of our way of life, they soon replace their culture with ours and look down on their own. So even the best in us cannot be effective without some of the trappings and actions of authority."

Though many of Schweitzer's views as to authority, and his standoffishness, may have sounded colonial, Germanic, and rigid, the longer I stayed the more I saw how necessary and practical even the imagery was. Some of the strongest images Schweitzer used were the simplest and most obvious: The pith helmet; the white shirt; and, generally, the formality and similarity of the Western dress in relation to native dress were good examples. But he had either good reason, habit or precedent for all of these. Before I came, I never thought of those things as important; but, thinking back, I realize that even today the pith helmet brings to mind that old-fashioned memory of Africa.

No matter how out of date it is, this perception is still nurtured by TV shows and movies of the dark continent, from *The African Queen* to *The Snows of Kilimanjaro*. The pith helmet alone, usually worn by the British colonialists (whom Schweitzer thought were somewhat less officious than either the French or German), was construed as *the* symbol of white supremacy, even if it was the most practical head-dress. (Its cousin, the modern hard hat, is also a symbol—not as the badge of the uppercrust but of the blue-collar worker.) Yet besides its symbolism, the pith helmet had also a vital function: saving many from sunstroke (in whites), skull fractures, and frequently death. The majority of Blacks refused to wear them and took the consequences.

This is not to say that many white traders, lumbermen, soldiers, even the French Provincial doctors didn't wear the pith helmet for its symbolic value alone. But that couldn't have been further from Schweitzer's mind. As he confessed, he himself thought that that particular head covering had colonial connotations before he even got to Africa. "But after a while," he said, "I soon realized it was a much more practical matter. I learned through observing sunstroke and concussions that it was a necessity."

I don't know whether all of the reasons were valid, but I do know some were. A number of rather funny stories were told about chimpanzees and gorillas, from their treetop vantage points, lobbing heavy breadfruit and coconuts on human targets.

One day, when I asked Schweitzer about all the talk concerning the helmet and his colonialist image, he just shrugged and sighed as if he had been asked that question a thousand times and said, "As you are well aware, with or without the helmet, I have my critics. Yet I know my own warm feelings toward the people here, and I think I treat them in the context of those feelings. I've tried to imbue the Negroes with my values in relation to work, to kindness, to lying, and to stealing, just the same as I would if I were in Gunsbach. Some of it takes; some of it doesn't. Taboos and ancient cultures die hard."

The sniping at Schweitzer included an indictment of the hospital on the basis of its lack of cleanliness, its simplicity, and its lack of sophisticated equipment, and because it was only for natives. However, this was not so. By design, and for social and economic reasons, Schweitzer ran the hospital wards as if the patients and their families were living in their own village.

The Africans came to the hospital with their entire families, who cooked, fed, and lived with the patient. The way the hospital was run made practical and good sense. At first, without nurses, it was a necessity to have the family caring for the patient; later, it proved to work very well for both hospital and patient. For the patient and family it seemed especially reassuring mentally to be together in such strange surroundings. Though ill or having undergone surgery, a mother loved to see her family each day, eat the food she was used to, and be cared for by someone close to her. The patients also would not expect more than they could possibly hope for when they returned home to their own primitive surroundings, as they might from a more modern hospital.

As far as the maintenance of the hospital, it was kept as tidy as possible where it really counted. The operating room was kept as scrupulously clean as practicable in the simple rough building available. Of course, running water, available electricity, modern laboratory equipment, anesthesia, x-ray, and other up-to-date equipment would have advanced the medical treatment and more complicated procedures could have been done, but only with more experienced professionals. Also, for the predominantly simple and common diseases that were treated there, automatic beds and gleaming equipment, while comfortable and efficient, would have been more of a luxury than a necessity. Still and all, for the illnesses treated in Lambarene, the low mortality and morbidity was comparable to many plush urban hospitals in the United States.

There were, of course, other accusations leveled at Schweitzer, such as that the Blacks and the few whites were separated in the hospital wards. Schweitzer rightly gave as honest reasons that the cultures, the food, and the languages were too diverse for integration to be practical.

Another complaint was that natives were never involved in anything but menial or physical labor at the hospital. But where, within five hundred miles, could they get the necessary training; and who but the few would work for a pittance, as most of Schweitzer's staff did?

As I saw, each and every bright and ambitious Black who took responsibility in the hospital and wanted to learn was trained by Schweitzer or his doctors and nurses in the operating room and on the wards. I saw that, among his many chores, within the limitations of the time he could spare, Schweitzer was not only willing to help and train those who wanted to learn but would encourage them to go as high as their capacity, ability, and drive would allow. This also applied to their children. While I was in Lambarene, the son of Nyama, our native head of the operating room for twenty-five years, was studying in France at Schweitzer's behest for his doctorate in philosophy.

But there is much more proof of Schweitzer's interest in developing native talent. When I first went to Lambarene, I also had a special Medico project in mind that I wanted to ask his advice on. The program was to train, in America, the most educated Africans for a degree in medicine, on scholarship, with the proviso that they return to their native land to serve at least five years in the rural areas.

Schweitzer gave me a personal history lesson as to why it would never work. Slowly shaking his head, he said, "Most, if not all, of the Gabonese who trained in France—no different from other educated African doctors who trained in England, Germany, and the States—rarely came back to the Gabon." Wagging his finger, "If they did, they'd remain in Libreville, the capital city." I knew this pattern from my experiences with Medico in Asia and Kenya.

He went on, "Ten years before, I stopped encouraging bright Mission students to go to Europe to study (another among the accusations of his colonialism). Instead, I started a program for my own staff to train the brightest and more educated Gabonese for positions as male nurses. That was the highest training I could possibly give at Lambarene. Even some of *them* eventually migrated to the city."

I told Schweitzer that he had also been reproached for not integrating his Gabonese male nurses' aides into the staff. He shook his head negatively. "That is sheer nonsense; it was always left up to the Gabonese as to whom they would rather eat with or live with. But it's true I always encouraged them to remain tribal in culture, which they did." One of the reasons for this, though rarely expressed, was that he was not so sure that our Western "civilization," morally and ethically, was any great improvement on theirs. After all, the decay of European civilization was one of the reasons, if a lesser one, why he himself was in Africa.

12

BACH: HIS SPIRITUAL CATALYST

It was an experience never to be forgotten—a musical one. It could have been staged by Bergman; orchestrated and conducted by Toscanini. It had the mystique, the sensitivity, and the drama that could be produced only by theatrical genius; yet it was totally spontaneous.

The setting could not have been more natural: first, the multicolored and multishaped jungle backdrop that changed to blackness with the suddenness found only at the equator. Two leading musical virtuosos met by sound alone yet separated by space, the wide flowing river and, even more, by culture. The performance melded the most primitive of rhythms with the most sophisticated, intellectual, and spiritual of compositions. During it, time was suspended. No one was sure, when it was over, whether it had lasted two minutes or ten.

This musical epoch took place on a Saturday evening at twilight. The end of the work week was always sort of festive. Phoebe wore a colorful blouse and I a blue polo shirt. We lit our kerosene lanterns to take with us to dinner (darkness usually fell quickly while we were on our way). It was still light outside as we came out of the door. We shooed off a few of the waiting chimpanzees who slinked about, enamored with Phoebe. We went down the few steps to the narrow path bordered by jungle plants of various sizes, colors, and hues of green separated from the path by rocks. This passageway converged with the main one leading up the hill to the dining hall. Many others of our colleagues were in front and in back of us going up to dinner. The woods were alive, full of sounds, monkeys calling and tree frogs chirping.

As we were ascending the hill, the curtain of black night suddenly dropped, blotting out the shapes and colors of the jungle shrubs. The yellow and orange jungle flowers around us lasted the longest, as if the lights in a huge theater had gone down. There was neither moon nor stars that night, and all we could see were the bouncing lights of lanterns carried by unseen colleagues.

Into the nightly hubbub of insects with their din of mating twitterings and the animal barks and calls from the massive intertwined growth around us came the sounds of the scales of Schweitzer's piano-organ. It poured out stronger and stronger. Suddenly a percussion section of drum beats in a rising crescendo joined in from a nearby village, as if they, too, were tuning up. These more rhythmic sounds traveled toward us across the river to meet the waves of sound from the organ. As the sounds met in syncopation, every tiny moving light up and down the path stopped simultaneously, suspended in mid-air as if the curtain had just gone up.

Somewhere the conductor must have raised his baton for quiet, as all practice sounds from the two musicians and their instruments stopped. The entire audience, including the crickets, tree frogs, and the howling monkeys, was now expectantly still. Even the gentle whispering of the branches and leaves of the giant trees and shrubs seemed hushed so as not to interfere. Below us, the tiny flickering lights of the audience in the orchestra section and the lights from the balcony higher up on the hill remained motionless.

Abruptly, as if the conductor of the symphony had given his downbeat, the organ and the drums started again. And then, as we listened in a trancelike state, there seemed to be some kind of auditory hallucination. For as the organ music and the drums swelled, each seemed to harmonize with the other; gradually, any musical disparity between them vanished and they played as one.

It was a Bach prelude and fugue in all of its eloquence coming from Schweitzer's homemade organ, with the drummer (also on a primitively-made instrument) playing in unison. They played as if they were a practiced duet. I envisioned them seated side by side: Schweitzer, his eyes closed, his shaggy head thrown back and pointing upward, his arms stretched across the keyboard with his feet and hands moving coordinately as if in time to the drums. Beside him, resting cross-legged on the floor, an elderly black man hunched over a colorfully decorated drum hollowed out of a tree trunk, the fingers and heels of his hands beating out resonance on the tautly stretched animal skin.

Reality returned only when, by some ethereal coincidence, the duet ended on a simultaneous note. It was as if the phantom conductor had flipped the last page of his score and twirled his baton in a final flourish.

For a brief moment all was eerily quiet; then the jungle noises resumed, swelling to a rousing applause. Like a firefly, a single flickering light above us began to bob again.

Immediately, others followed, guiding us up the path to dinner. This prelude to the Saturday night meal somehow had a sobering effect on all of us, quieting the usual end-of-the-week conviviality and gaiety.

The magic of that evening brought to mind what I had read about Schweitzer's love for, involvement with, and preeminence on the organ and in particular the music of Bach. So, the next morning after breakfast, when he motioned me over to the piano bench and seated me beside him to talk about a problem he was having with some of his staff, I found the opportunity to talk about his music. When we finished discussing hospital business, I brought up the previous night's concert. I told him that we were all entranced by the duet.

"What duet?"

"Didn't you know you were accompanied by drums from across the river?" I described the drama of that experience.

His eyes widened, "No, I didn't know that," he said, surprised. "Yet I've heard those drummers since my first night here, and maybe their rhythms have seeped into my brain."

"Have you ever met the drummer?"

"I may have," he shrugged, "but it may have been different ones over the decades. But I doubt that they hear me. It's probably just a coincidence anyway. Some natives take my music with indifference and some very mystically. But," he paused, "they like to see how the notes and bars are arranged. They don't understand that it is written music; they're just fascinated by the design. They used to steal my scores—I think only for decoration—so now I have them carefully put away." He chuckled just thinking about it.

Which reminded me that not one of his staff had ever

talked about his music to me or, as I later learned, to him. Yet it was so much a part of him, especially relating to his spirituality. I asked him if he ever gave a concert here.

"I play or practice almost every day after lunch or before dinner and on Sundays, and everyone can listen. Playing a serious concert at my age takes too much out of me. But," he said, "would you like to come over this morning while I practice?"

I immediately agreed and went back to my room to get Phoebe. We knocked at his screened door and he waved us into his little alcove off the main room, just like ours, still cluttered with books and paper. Neither the fawn nor the owl seemed to be around. He was seated on his crudely-carved long piano bench in front of his zinc-lined "organ." We sat near him on rough rattan chairs.

There was sheet music already on the ancient rack. He was soon explaining the mechanics of the organ to us: "After the key is struck there is no aftersound and one can play two octaves at once. One can play the bass with the left foot and the melody with the hands, which is twice as difficult as with most organs. That is why the old French and German organs are so superior and why their organists, too, are the best."

Then, as usual, either from his experience or his Germanophilia, he added, "Though the great Charles-Marie Widor was one of my teachers, ordinarily the French are too undisciplined to be great all-round musicians, especially in orchestras or in choruses. It seems the French cannot control themselves long enough to become part of a whole, not only in music but in their social life as well. It's part of the French mentality. On the other hand, Germans are disciplined and can cooperate as part of something."

Though I had heard Schweitzer's special disdain and bias against the French in general, one couldn't discount anything he said about their organs or organists. Almost every musical authority, French and otherwise, acknowl-edged his absolute superiority in organ music, from building an organ to training an organist.

I understood little of this technical knowledge and told him so. He then began to play—first Bach, then Mendels-sohn, and finally Cèsar Franck.

As he played he seemed to metamorphose back to his youth. He seemed fresher and his skin pinker. After a while he was almost flushed—as if the music were stimulating, renewing him.

Phoebe sat fixed, entranced by him, her soft features becoming almost as suffused as his, her hands clenched in her lap. Once when he paused she asked him if he ever thought of composing.

"Yes," he said. "But after I researched and wrote the first two volumes of my interpretation of Bach I fully realized no one could ever do as well. Interpreting is challenge enough for me."

I had read somewhere that, at the age of seven or before, Schweitzer was a poor student because he hated to practice; he wouldn't read notes because he was constantly improvising, creating, and dramatizing. Yet, now, he seemed to love to practice. Also, though he said he couldn't compose, I wondered why. He had certainly created much in theology and in philosophy. I asked him about it.

"Music is different; it's not thinking in your head; it's feeling in your heart—and there is a world of difference."

"Have you ever played twelve-tone music?" Phoebe quietly asked.

"No," he said, "I haven't. Listening was as far as I got because I thought Schoenberg's music was not real—it was not architectural. All great music is architecturally based, and one should be able to build on it. And one couldn't build on Schoenberg's tones."

Probing further, Phoebe asked, "Do you enjoy abstract painting?" She mentioned Wassily Kandinsky, a Russian, but a longtime emigré in Germany. Schweitzer swung all the way around to face her and looked directly into her eyes. "If you are taught to like and respond to abstract painting, you can possibly enjoy atonal music," she continued.

But then, as if to lighten the conversation, he said, smiling, "You know I play jazz," and he reeled off a few bars of Gershwin.

As abruptly as he changed the conversation, so did Phoebe. "You know. Dr. Schweitzer, I'm a palmist. Let me see your hands." He laughed and held them out to her, then changed his mind. Looking at me, he said, "Examine my right hand." I knew exactly what the firm, cordlike fibrous tendon in his palm was as soon as I felt it.

"It feels like a Dupytrens Contracture," I said, "but without the usual contraction." This benign disease is rather common. The palm tendons, leading to the third, fourth, and little fingers, contract and produce a clawing of those fingers.

Schweitzer said, "My father had the same thing."

"It is known to be inheritable," I said, "but, you have no contracture, just the fibrosis of the tendon. It's probably because of your years of organ playing and practice."

He nodded. That was probably so.

Then swinging around and facing Phoebe again, he held out his beautiful, thin, long-fingered hands to her, palms up, and winked to me over her shoulder. Phoebe studied them for a while and he followed her gaze. She traced lines, flexing and squinting more closely. "I could tell you a lot about yourself," she said confidently.

He laughed. "After some eighty-five years, more than I already know?"

"Maybe," she said. He threw his head back again in a hearty laugh.

"You don't think much of my science," Phoebe said

half jokingly, putting his hands down. "A month or so before we came here, I read the hand of a leading psychiatrist. He wanted me to come out to his hospital and read patients' palms, and possibly coordinate my findings with their histories and their diseases."

"Well," Schweitzer said, cocking his head sideways, "I don't doubt that with a psychiatrist." I wondered why he frequently sounded as if he didn't take psychiatry very seriously.

Giving up on her palm reading, Phoebe changed the subject. "You know, Dr. Schweitzer, we may be related."

He opened his eyes wide in mock surprise. "How?"

"My mother's maiden name was Schweitzer, and my grandfather was Albert."

"With a *tz?*"

"Of course."

He then went into the genealogy of the Schweitzers. All the Schweitzers with *tz*, he said, were from the Swiss cantonment of Schweitz; during the Reformation they were driven west by the Roman Catholics. His family was mostly teachers; and, at that particular time, education was growing in Alsace and they needed teachers badly. And that is why his great-great-grandparents stopped there.

Turning back to Phoebe he asked, "Was your father a teacher?"

"No," she answered, "he was a farmer in Pennsylvania."

He took her hand and with a chuckle kissed it, murmuring, "My newfound cousin."

Turning back to his organ he played Bach again. At one point, he went over one passage again and again until he got it just the way he wanted it. At eighty-five, he still wouldn't allow himself one small imperfection in his interpretation.

When he finished, almost as if he guessed our

thoughts, he turned and said, "When you play Bach it is a sin to play it badly because it is pure and comes from the purity and the genius of a great religious spirit." I felt, when he mentioned the word pure, he virtually implied things German. He equated only one other composer with the "purity" of Bach, and that was Richard Wagner.

In passing, he mentioned that the simplicity of Bach's music was important in pulling all the various Germanic oligarchies together into one nation during the nineteenth century—not unlike the operas of Verdi which did the same for Italy then.

He mused on the greatness of simplicity. "You must realize that Bach himself lived and preached the simple life." He looked out into space. "The simpler one remains and the closer to nature one is, the less complicated life one pursues and he is more peaceful and productive. It prevents the cluttering of the mind, and the preoccupation with trivia."

As he frequently did when we talked about his convictions, he gave analogies or stories. In this instance, he cited the Bach family and told how it was a large, closely-knit, and loving family that lived among themselves with very little outside influences.

"I think from Bach's spiritual sensitivity and his deep belief in Christ that everything he created was flawless, devout, and came from the Gospel. All of Bach's manuscripts had inscribed on them, 'To God alone the glory'. Only someone so simply—so purely—inspired in his heart could compose as prodigiously as he. Bach's life shows, I'm sure, that he not only didn't fear death but almost yearned for the peace and glory of the kingdom of heaven."

I interrupted. "Wouldn't you call this rather fanatical? Isn't this the negation rather than the affirmation of Christian life that you teach?"

Patiently, he said, "No, it isn't. Few could live up to

the spirituality of Bach. He had a rather calm life yet a few worldly rewards came his way. His posts at Weimar and Cöthen, for example. It may sound fanatical, but the music he produced was truly inspired by Christ. Imagine composing almost perfect pieces of religious music weekly."

Then he compared his life with Bach's. Schweitzer thought it impossible in his own mode of life with "the lack of simplicity" he lived by, as he said. I was stunned. But he went on to explain, "I have too many involvements besides music."

Leaning back, his hands behind his neck, Schweitzer stretched and went on into the overwhelming spiritual core of Bach's genius. "He never realized his music would ever be enjoyed by a secular society." Then he said, "Music, and primarily Bach, *was* deeply responsible for or closely related to my own spiritual feelings and maybe even my thoughts on the reverence for life."

Schweitzer had said to me once before that if he had to choose the one discipline that gave him the greatest pleasure he would pick music. "I've often wondered why I enjoy it as much as I do. It may be a show of divine grace because it seems to have been born in me. I've often questioned how I became so enamored of Bach. I know one of my first teachers, Dr. Eugene Munch, had a large influence on me; but I vividly remember the first organ concert I was taken to as a child. It was an overwhelming experience for me, which to this day I remember clearly."

He then admitted that Bach's music seriously influenced his spiritual life. "Music is abstract, but it is a powerful mover of spirit and the emotions."

"After you came here, didn't you think you'd have to give up playing Bach and didn't you miss playing on some of the greatest organs of the world?" I asked.

"Of course, I thought it would be lost to me. But when the Paris Bach Society sent me the zinc-lined piano organ, I realized how I had missed my music." He continued, "Yet as much as I've loved music, it was basically too abstract—not in Phoebe's terms of abstract (this was the first time he called her by her first name; he never dropped his formality with me)—and too distant from the suffering of people for it to fulfill my other obligations." He furrowed his brow, as if in sadness. "I needed a more direct and tangible contact, rather than one carried on the waves of sound.

"Music was not only my first love; it also turned out to be another handmaiden to allow me to fulfill myself spiritually." His voice quickened. "Even as a young man my concerts while in gymnasium allowed me to earn the money for most of my later schooling—even for medical school—and, for the past fifty years, enabled me to build and supply this hospital. But it was not just Bach and the organ; it was both together."

Then I repeated something I had heard or read somewhere: that, through Bach, Schweitzer was a mediator between God and man.

This seemed to get him very excited. "No, no, it's the music and the instrument, not me," he answered vehemently. "It's just that each would be less without the other, and both somehow tie in with the spirit of man. I cannot adequately express in words the marvel of the organ—the most complex and expressive instrument man has ever played. In fact," he went on, "the only test of a great organ is by the music of Bach; and the test of the music is the spirit it invokes. Yet each great organ has its own personality."

Schweitzer talked at great length about the great organs of the world, most of which he had played while still a teenaged virtuoso. He spoke of his unstinting pilgrimages all over Europe to try to save the classic instruments that were being torn out to make way for newer ones. As he pointed out, it was almost criminal because the sounds of some of them could never be reproduced.

He seemed to know every screw, nut, bellows, and pipe and what they contributed to the organ's sound. I asked him if he actually examined them. "I have probably spent more time in old dusty organ lofts than I have at the organs themselves and enjoyed myself just as much." Which again launched him into berating those who were still destroying the old organs of Europe.

Schweitzer always referred back to the instruments in Notre Dame and St. Sulpice in Paris, on which he had played often, as the most incomparable organs in the world, "which more organ architects should have copied but didn't."

Schweitzer ascribed his leaning toward music to that gene inherited from his great-grandfathers on both sides, but not to his father, who he said played the organ but not so well. "Still, at three and four, I was enthralled for hours listening to him practice." At the age of nine, Schweitzer had substituted for the regular organist in the village church.

He talked of his Grandfather Schweitzer, a great organist. He also spoke of his first great instructor, Eugene Munch, and how that family had a long history of organ musicians. As an aside, he told how he would take his teacher's nephew, Charles Munch, for walks as a child. He gradually came back to Bach and creativity.

"You must read more about Bach," he stated. "He was virtually self-taught, yet he knew the great music of every nation—not only of Germany. He transcribed most of it into German and even added to some of it. But his creative genius in music was only the end-point of his many talents. He was a poet, a theologian, a particularly lucid writer, a logician, a painter; and he had mathematical and architectural skills beyond one's imagination. He could go into a church, hear the organ, and tell you exactly where to stand to hear it best: it was as if he were solving a difficult architectural equation.

"Many people think I know every aspect of the inner workings of the organ, but I am only a dilettante by comparison." Bach, Schweitzer said, was an intensely practical man, who thought that a fine organ was a symbol of perfection and that the music that poured from it had to be perfect because that is what comes from mystical perfection. "Bach in music could only be compared to Michaelangelo in the graphic arts or to Leonardo in his many talents." (Schweitzer himself had been compared to the latter.)

"Yet," he admitted, "as great a teacher as Bach was, he produced not one great artist; in fact, only mediocre ones, and not one composer."

It seemed that Schweitzer could not give too much credit to the tremendous influence that Bach had on both his intellectual and spiritual lives. He couldn't decide whether his own innate spirit was attracted to Bach; or whether, by Bach's music, all of Schweitzer's philosophic beliefs in the reverence for life and his beliefs in Jesus came about.

"It's another secret that I'll never solve, but it doesn't bother me. And I hope I've paid him (Bach) back a tithe. A few years ago, I finished writing the *Organ Works of Bach*; it took about fifty years to be fully published. Yet," he went on sadly, "there are still many other things musical that I've always wanted to study and know about that I'll never have time for."

Our conversation ended on that note. At eighty-five, and apparently healthy, he still had so much to give but no idea how much longer he could. It was painful to think that such a man as he should be allowed to die.

The following morning Phoebe and I found a handprinted genealogy chart of the Schweitzer family going back to the seventeenth century pinned to the door of our cubicle. He must have worked it up after we left. Surprised, we saw that Jean Paul Sartre was his first cousin.

13

VILLAGE LIFE—
ANOTHER TALK

One Sunday I was awakened about 5:00 a.m. by a mournful chanting from the tuberculosis ward just below our room. A young mother had died the night before. The chant seemed to be coming in waves which reached a wailing crescendo then started all over again. It was still dark, and, after lighting our green-bowled kerosene lantern, I washed and dressed and used the time to make notes from days before in my diary.

Finally the breakfast bell rang. After the meal, Schweitzer told me he had promised to visit an old friend, a village chief, across the river that afternoon and asked if Phoebe and I would be interested in going along. At the chief's request, he was to baptize the chief's infant daughter.

Schweitzer, though more than glad to help convert the natives, believed, "It must not only be voluntary; it must be their seeking out the Christian way because they are convinced it's good." He had seen too many superficial conversions revert after confusion and schisms with the tribal culture.

I was sure, also, that the pressure from the Protestant Mission in Paris for a more aggressive approach to conversions was another reason—besides his heretical *Quest*—why Schweitzer wanted to be free of Church restrictions.

Phoebe and I were eager to see another village. Other than Lambarene, which we'd usually visit on Saturday or Sunday for a European type meal and a shower, we had seen only two other tiny clusters of mud huts near the hospital.

After breakfast, with nothing to do until ward rounds, Phoebe and I leisurely walked down to the hospital square where Dr. Adler was preaching. The number of natives in the square listening to the sermon was more than three times that on any other day, and much less noisy and active. Mothers continued to nurse their babies, cook under the eaves of the ward; the men, as was usual on Sundays, were conspicuous by their absence.

The goats and chimpanzees, of course, roamed the area as they pleased, totally unaware of the sabbath but seemingly interested in the gathering. Dr. Adler spoke about Job: Pierre translated into what I think was Fang, and Joseph into Galoas. The assembled mass listened indifferently.

After the services, the doctors made rounds. Some of us passed the rest of the morning relaxing near the river wall just talking. Lunch was the usual midday meal, with a rather mushy type of soup and powdered potatoes. Beer was served, as a Sunday treat, as was papaya and mango for dessert.

Soon after lunch, those going with Schweitzer met at the landing. There were five of us for each of the two *pirogues*. Our first stop was down river at Lambarene, where Schweitzer had some business to attend to.

Lambarene was a ramshackle tin-can town on a dusty,

orange dirt road along the Ogowe River. All rivers in Africa seem to be in a skein that tie the whole continent together. For the average native, it was the only sure means of transportation other than paths. Vendors of all sorts, from butcher to knife sharpener, sat cross-legged on the banks, turbaned because of the dust, plying their trade in a hawking sing-song cadence. Their boats were beached at the water's edge.

Other barges piled high with lumber were seen being towed downstream to Libreville by tugs.

Lambarene's unpaved main street was composed of a row of rickety shacks where just about anything could be purchased, including American cigarettes, locally-made clothing, clogs made of old rubber tires and all sorts of pots and pans. As Schweitzer wryly said, "everything except tools to work with." We looked in on the biggest trading post in Lambarene, Hatton and Cookson. It was in a large run-down wooden warehouse building which was first operated by the famous Trader Horn. It also sold everything the natives needed least—from patent leather shoes to French perfume.

Every American schoolboy connects the name Trader Horn with African adventure. In Lambarene, his reputation was among the worst. Schweitzer once called him a great African scoundrel. Hatton and Cookson was probably the crux of one of the natives' greatest problems—alcoholism. The shop sold the cheapest whiskey, and, on that Sunday, as on probably every Sunday, the main street looked like skid row.

Sitting on a well-worn cushioned chair leaning back against the wall near the door of Hatton and Cookson was the reputed director of "Gun Running Incorporated." We were introduced as Americans and he as a "gun broker." He was a large, pot-bellied Frenchman, whose belt fell below his huge stomach. He didn't bother to get up. He had a bottle of Jack

Daniel's by his side and offered us a drink. His red, bulbous nose attested to the constancy of the bottled friend within easy reach.

I asked him, "Who in the devil do you sell guns to here? I've only seen spears and bows and arrows for hunting." He made no apologies about his business. "Who says I sell guns for hunting? The gun is a means to independence for the exploited African." He shrugged and winked cynically, knowing that we knew full well he cared little about either independence or the exploited. He was one of many typical unabashed white scoundrels in the area.

Nearby was the old three-story, thirty-room Hotel Relais on a rise overlooking the river. Every white for miles around congregated in the lobby, bar, and dining room on Sundays. There were no Blacks except for the waiters. The crowd was predominately French, with a smattering of Germans, mostly involved in lumbering, trading, and mining. Uranium and oil were bringing the entrepreneurial Europeans to Gabon.

After an hour or so we all met back by the *pirogues*; and continued on about four miles up and across the river to the village we were to visit.

Like most African villages, it was built near the river bank, not only for the convenience of itinerant merchants but so that water, despite the sewage and garbage dumped there daily, could be available for drinking and bathing. Typically, it had neither a well nor a septic tank.

We walked around the thatched mud and bamboo huts—there were about twenty-five of them arranged rather haphazardly—which were about twelve by twelve feet, with dirt floors and circles of stones in the centers for cooking fires. In each hut, half a dozen straw mats were scattered around the floor.

Children ran around stark naked. There were some

children as old as four or five still being nursed. (The women had probably learned that as long as they nursed they would rarely get pregnant). Outside the huts there were additional small cooking fires. On the dirt floors were decorated wooden bowls and heaped manioc, plantain, and banana, and some salted fish, the main staples of the village diet. Mixed in with this were different kinds of wild animal meat, usually rancid and smelling to the high heavens. With the lack of refrigeration, it was not unusual for the natives to eat putrid meat. And in many huts, salted and smoked monkey and buffalo meat hung from the ceiling. That particular day everyone seemed to be cooking monkey meat.

There is a very close brotherhood within each tribe, but rarely between different ones. The peaceful Galoas tribe—about two hundred people—inhabited this village. The main commercial product was manioc root, which grew in knobby sticks about two feet long and about an inch or two in diameter. The women of the village planted and cultivated the crop. Men, especially the chief, did the merchandising and bargaining. They sold to our hospitals and to merchants in Lambarene. It brought in about 24,000 African francs (about $95) a month total.

It was a Christian village. An itinerant preacher came weekly. He preached in a small thatch and bamboo structure with a carved wooden cross over the front entrance. Inside, facing a wide altar, were two rows of about twenty rickety handmade stools. Looking in through the window frame—there weren't any panes—we could see two goats tethered on one side of the altar. Near the church stood a small thatched building, a Mission school, which was conducted by a local black schoolmaster who taught in a French patois. He had been trained at the Mission where Schweitzer's first hospital had been located. About thirty pupils attended.

At about 4:00 p.m., the drums started up in one part

of the village and everyone gathered around. In addition to the three drummers, each of whom had a hollow log over which a skin was stretched, two natives were beating bamboo sticks together. The natives were in all sorts of colorful hand-dyed garb. Some of the men were in partly Western dress; the women's dresses were ankle-length. Some men had only pants and vest, others wore shorts, dress coats, and leopard hats.

This was a special day and a special celebration: a girl had been born and this was as good as money in the bank for the parents. Dowries were probably the most lucrative business for any family. If the newborn had been a boy it would have been just another Sunday.

The ritual dancing began with the entry of the evil spirit—a non-Christian priest in a weird headdress with horns and white and green stripes painted on his face. Here, as in most of these villages, Christian and pagan rites went on side by side and frequently meshed. In one hut to which we were invited, a crucifix hung on a wall right above a fetish amulet.

The evil spirit went into a slow, shuffling, stomping dance; then, as he began to whirl faster and faster, almost everyone around took up the beat and danced with increasing frenzy. As the dancing progressed, the evil spirit disappeared and returned in a more benign mask and headdress which seemed to be made of a reddish wood with a very serious mien—obviously the good spirit. The dancing slowed perceptibly and finally came to an exhausted halt.

Phoebe and I weren't at the baptism, but we did meet the chief later. He was seated in what looked like a store-bought lounge chair in front of his hut which was, of course, one of the largest. He was a rather small, very black, heavy-set man with quick black eyes and almost Caucasian features. We were not introduced to any of his wives; he reportedly had four.

Around 5:00 p.m. Schweitzer informed us it was time to leave. This village was near a swamp and was known for its high rate of malaria; he didn't want to be caught there in the dark when the anopheles mosquito was doing its dirty work. We got back into our *pirogues*. As we approached the hospital, we saw the family of the woman who had died the night before loading her body on their *pirogue* to take it back to their village. They were still wailing and chanting.

That evening we had a typical Sunday dinner of canned cold cuts, some cheese, and cold buffalo meat. The latter was as tough as shoe leather with a very peculiar taste—not exactly gamey, but peculiar. Schweitzer, who was in a particularly jovial and talkative mood, got something special from the cook: fried liver—from what animal I did not know, nor did I want to know. As was his whimsey, he passed some over to Phoebe, saying with naive humor, "This is for females only." Phoebe ate it. From the partly hidden grimace on her face it was not very appetizing.

Then he gave her some radishes—considered a delicacy. Phoebe offered a few to her neighbor, Marie Louise Cullum (the American volunteer), but Schweitzer admonished her, "No, there are certain things one cannot do with gifts, and one is give them away." Phoebe asked him why; and he said, with a wrinkled smile, "That is another chapter which you may get to know if you stay here for five years."

Phoebe asked jokingly, "Why, do I have to get a Schweitzer diploma first?"

Schweitzer, who had gotten so many of them, answered, "I put no faith in diplomas and give none. Once there was a nurse who applied for a job here and started to show me all her certificates. I stopped her and asked, 'Do you have a sense of humor?' She said yes. 'Then you're hired,' I told her."

After dinner we had our usual ritual culminating in a

biblical interpretation. Schweitzer talked warmly about Isaiah, pointing out that the first mention of the Messiah was around the time of Zarathustra. He also talked of how Jesus had told, according to Luke, that three days after His death there would be the kingdom of heaven and then His resurrection. Schweitzer stated that since there was not the former there could not have been the latter. "But," he explained, "we know Luke wrote this maybe one or two hundred years after Christ died and it may be fictitious." He explained that many Greek followers of Christianity embellished the Gospel to help substantiate Jesus's predictions and thus "prove" His supernatural powers.

Schweitzer spoke of other books in the Bible, that, like Luke, had been embellished. Then he put a hand flat on the table for emphasis and said, "The most inconsistent and obviously nonhistorical is the book of John.

"And this is an example of the myth, not the truth, in Christianity. The truth of the matter is that we have been taken by dogma not truth. Even primitive people seem to have a sort of Christian spirit in their hearts, which cultured people have lost because of the misguided Church. We have lost it because of our lost values or our materialistic life-style or our selfishness. However, much of the loss is the Church's ethical fault."

He was getting emotional about his subject. He rapped the table with his knuckles as he continued. "Natives appear to grasp this idea of an ethical God easier than most Europeans—they are not burdened with dogma. Even before they are aware of Christ, they usually adhere to the simple religious ethics they already have. Faith may begin in the heart, but must be developed in the brain."

He got up and began to pace. "The village we just came from. You saw how simply those people live, how close to the earth. In Africa, being away from the land is perverted and unnatural. Most earn only enough to live by and are strict in obeying their man-made laws, their priests, and even their taboos. Without ever having read a book the chief is logical and firmly believes in Jesus."

Later, alone with Schweitzer, I asked him, "Wasn't it rather complicated for the chief to live with four women?"

Schweitzer laughed, "I always thought so, but who am I to differ with Solomon?"

"But how do you approach it when you're teaching Christian morals?"

He laughed again. "Well, I don't endorse it, and neither did Jesus, but neither of us had condemned it. Western man must just face different cultures and customs, especially in this African male world.

"Polygamy is part of the economic system. Dowries are important for the well-being of the family of the bride, and the sold bride is important as the breadwinner of the new family. After a young man puts his down payment on a wife— and he'd better keep up his payments—his job is merely to clear a patch for her to work in. After that, his working days are over. His only job then is to sit around the village square and palaver for a second wife, and later on haggle over his best cash crop (his daughters)—if he's lucky.

"Meanwhile, the wives are plowing, planting, weeding, and harvesting the crops year after year until that patch is infertile. They then move to a more fertile spot, where the man again builds another hut and clears another patch for one, or perhaps two or more, wives. His job is then finished again for a time. When he acquires more wives, the second helps the first, and the third helps the second. But the big bonus is the many wives producing many daughters."

"But don't you tell them it's not the Christian way?" I goaded him.

"History—not religion—has taken care of that since

biblical times. As soon as the nomads settled down to an agricultural life and began to own land, men then became the workhorses and monogamy began. This hasn't happened here yet."

Knowing that the village was at least part Christian, I asked Schweitzer if he thought these primitive people really thought through the Christian ideas—something he was always admonishing me about.

He ran his hand through his shaggy mane. "Some of the ethics that these natives live by cultured societies seem to have lost. For instance, when a child is orphaned or abandoned, the village usually takes it in. They consider all children as partly theirs."

This was borne out when Phoebe had taken to a set of orphan twins in the *pouponniere* (Phoebe was a twin). She had helped bring them to good health and was enchanted with them. Tentatively, she had asked Schweitzer about bringing them to the United States. But, as he had explained, "After about two years at the hospital, all orphan infants are taken back and taken care of by the villages."

And, in fact, that evening his conversation seemed to be directed mostly at Phoebe. She gazed at him affectionately. We both had become very attached to him and couldn't wait for these conversations.

After everyone (including Phoebe) left the dining room, Schweitzer took off his bow-tie and seemed to want to continue to talk. We talked especially about the Gabon and the possibility of building a middle class with their new-found independence. He explained its practical weakness. "Even doctors, like even the best of the native leaders, are insecure and become selfish and greedy. They want to get all they can before the bubble bursts—especially after becoming accustomed to the ease and material things of city life. This is one of the many reasons I wanted independence to occur slowly. Now it is already leading to corruption and chaos."

Thinking about my work in Asia and my three years as an administrator of health for the Alliance for Progress in Latin America during the Kennedy years, I later saw the truth in what he said. Many Latin American doctors who trained in America, went back, then sent their children to private American schools and were usually disinterested in helping the hinterlands—even in health.

"But," I asked him flatly, "why didn't you educate more bush natives in your hospital if you thought the doctors would never stay in the villages?"

He remonstrated coolly, "I could educate only a few at first, especially with my own problem of barely surviving. And though at one time I had started courses in nursing, the language barrier, especially with so many dialects, was particularly difficult. But many more natives learned to speak a French patois so I started the course again: And it still didn't work out well."

Schweitzer's mood had saddened from his dinnertime levity during our talk. Now he sat silently and just gazed. "Dr. Schweitzer," I interrupted, "I wish I had more time with you because I am just beginning to learn what I'd come here for."

He looked up and, with a softness in his eyes, said, "Stay as long as you wish, if you'll work as hard as you have." Then, "I hope I've kept up my part of the bargain, but I must say I didn't have to try hard to do it." He paused. "Not with the way you were always probing me," he added with a jaunty laugh.

"Come on," I jibed, "Dr. Schweitzer, you weren't so difficult to probe. But there is one question I almost forgot. You once told me that you go directly over the top of the mountain, while Teilhard went slowly around its base, but you both meet at the same point. Yet from speaking with you personally, I find you are not really that direct."

"I was speaking then," he said quietly, "only in a spiritual metaphor. Teilhard was steeped in Catholicism and its absolute dogma, and he adhered to much of it. Maybe I should have used some of his diplomacy and adherence to regulations. But I had no bent for circumventing. I try to go straight ahead." And he thrust his big fist forward.

Then he abruptly changed the subject. "I forgot I wanted to apologize to 'my dear cousin'. I wasn't very nice to her yesterday." I knew what he was talking about. The previous day Phoebe and Marie-Louise Cullum, who managed the *pouponniere*, decided to clean it. They took everything and every child out and, using buckets of soapy water, scrubbed the place down. When they had just about finished and gotten all the babies back on their nice clean shelves, Schweitzer just happened to go into the supply room below the poop. Phoebe said he came out positively apoplectic (luckily she didn't understand his German expletives). Apparently, the soapy water had run down through the floor and wet everything beneath it. He had stalked off angry: some of the supplies had been soaked.

"I know she did it with good intentions," he told me.

He looked very tired as he put his hands on the table and pushed himself up very shakily. He rubbed his eyes and said, "Let's go, I have a large stack of correspondence to finish."

We lit our lanterns and walked down the hill together. Around midnight I had a call: a small child with severe pneumonia was having a breathing problem and I had to aspirate the phlegm from her throat. As I made my way back to my room, I noticed the light in his room still on.

THE POLITICAL
SCHWEITZER

It seemed out of character for a man as spiritual, as musical, and as learned as Albert Schweitzer to be both politically oriented and politically active. But he was. Though we never had specific conversations on politics, references to political issues, such as peace, nuclear arms, and certain personalities, surfaced at various times when we were in the midst of talks on other subjects.

The first inkling I had of this side of him occurred when he told me of his gambit to obtain a missionary post in Africa after the publication of his first writings on Jesus. He shrewdly refused to come before a plenary session of the Church's tribunal to be "burned as a heretic," as he put it, because it meant certain rejection of his application. Instead, not unlike politicians such as Lyndon Johnson or Franklin Roosevelt, he arranged to meet and arm-twist each member of the tribunal individually. In this way, he convinced a large majority of them that he was serious and a true Christian;

and so got the Church to allow him the benighted opportunity to work in Lambarene.

Even in 1960, some twenty years before the nuclear freeze hysteria of the eighties, he had already perceived the dangers of nuclear war's annihilative powers and had written and spoken out about a political solution to nuclear war.

Though he had a natural political mind, I would imagine it had been nurtured in the ambience of his native Alsace, where as a boy he was pulled one way and then the other as France and Germany alternately overran and ruled that border province. Through this experience, he must have had to learn the fine art of being politically flexible to survive. At times, he seemed terribly naive about politics; and, not infrequently, he seemed opinionated and slanted on the subject of Germany. Of course, during his jungle years, his insulation and the lack of up-to-date news, obtained superficially and only occasionally by radio, limited his knowledge of the current political scene.

But just considering his thesis on Reverence for Life, one must recognize his political bent. Those philosophic principles of "reverence" may seem remote from the average local or national means by which we organize society, but good politics on a grand scale (or certainly at its very roots) is essentially a reverence for life. It's an attempt to create a system whereby all men can live in peace under any form of government which guarantees a free and secure life. Isn't that the ideal of all enlightened voters? The spiritual reverence theory in its respect for all living things is only a means of notifying man that he is just one part of a whole. If he would think of the well-being of a mosquito or an alligator then, at least, he would certainly think of the welfare of his human brothers.

In an everyday sense, Schweitzer's political sensitivities were much more practical and less philosophic or religious than I would have guessed prior to meeting him. I remember the warm deference he showed the local officials, even gendarmes, when they came to the hospital for various reasons. The higher the official's level, the warmer was his welcome. As much of a celebrity and as admired as he was in that province and in that nation, he still played the political game knowing that ultimately he was there only at their pleasure. He understood the value of personal rapport with the politically influential.

In our on-and-off discussions of politics, he never seemed partisan to any political ideology because he would in a word or phrase even-handedly give the other side its due. At times, he seemed very pro-American. He praised the Marshall Plan, which had enabled his beloved Europe to get on its feet again. But, knowing the psychology of international politics, he ruefully prophesied, "You will see what you are already seeing in France and Japan; your AID programs will go down in history as the most unappreciated gesture of friendship ever offered to broken nations."

At other times his talk was very anti-American, especially when he discussed the concept of keeping China out of the United Nations. "If it's a place to negotiate problems among nations, then how can one possibly leave one nation— or dozens of nations—out, especially one which is potentially so very powerful? America considers China an antagonistic nation because of its military aid to North Korea; and China considers America imperialistic. But if an antagonist to America is not even allowed in, how can their differences be resolved?"

He hadn't heard yet that one of his previous visitors, Adlai Stevenson, was made ambassador to the United Nations by the President-elect John Kennedy. However, more importantly with regard to China, Dean Rusk would be America's next Secretary of State.

"But," he said, "China will be in the U.N. anyway within two years." (He was wrong by ten). "However, a bad feeling has been left with the Chinese because of their past rejection."

"No worse a feeling than has been left in America by China's intervention in the Korean war," I countered, looking him right in the eye.

Then, as was his method, gently, with a rueful smile and in a relatively conciliatory tone, he said, "There are really no bad nations, only inadequate political leaders and groups—parties—that influence people in the most insidious, inflammatory, and demogogic ways." He then brought up the American Secretary of State, John Foster Dulles, as an example. "His method of brinkmanship is dangerous. This type of man should not make policy. They are spellbinders who infiltrate people's minds and put fear in them, or tempt them with the impossible visions of a better world by their system alone. Then everyone chooses sides. Take your Senator McCarthy, how he had every American afraid that America was being taken over by Communists."

"No, Dr. Schweitzer," I objected, "I'm afraid you're wrong. In the beginning, when he was waving papers around, supposedly with well-known public names on them, many liberal professors and political figures knew they could be ruined by this madman of a Senator—and many were. He used this formula of intimidation and, admittedly, produced a mass hysteria; but it didn't last long. As soon as he exposed himself on television, all Americans knew that he was a fraud and were revolted by him."

"But that was only after he was sick," he said, narrowing his eyes.

"No," I said, "it was years before he became ill with his alcoholism."

Schweitzer brought his political debating skills into play. "Your great Nobel scientist, Linus Pauling. Look how he's been crucified as a Communist for his anti-war and his anti-nuclear position." Schweitzer had already given me hints regarding his special pro-Soviet bias when I first told him I had just been to Russia in 1958.

I was getting annoyed. I corrected him on Pauling. "Though accusations against him have been made by the right wing, he had continued to teach freely at a great university, work in his laboratory, even with the aid of United States government grants. What's more he can say and do what he wants, and can travel anywhere in the world at any time." I contrasted Pauling with Russia's Boris Pasternak. "Pasternak received the Nobel Prize for literature by portraying the early Soviet Union as it really was in his *Dr. Zhivago*. Then he was persecuted by the *Pravda*, humiliated, made to recant, and was not allowed to accept the prize. He died a broken man."

Schweitzer looked troubled: he was not happy with my comparison of Pauling and Pasternak. "I do not know Linus Pauling personally, but I have corresponded with him. He is a gifted but unhappy man—"

I then interrupted again. "He may be an unhappy man but it was certainly not because of political persecution. Do you think that you could have openly corresponded with Pasternak in Russia as you did with Pauling in America? Could Pasternak get a letter past Russian censors if he were complaining of his unhappy status?"

I then tried to assure him, "When our new President, John Kennedy, takes over, he is going to cancel all nuclear testing until next year."

He retorted, "It will make little difference since the Pentagon has insisted to President Eisenhower that the United States must test."

"But Kennedy is not an Eisenhower, and the Pentagon will not rule."

He shrewdly came back with the fact that Red China

was now making the bomb and that those Chinese scientists were trained in America.

I said, maybe too bluntly, "You were trained in France and Germany; and, from what I've seen, those countries could never control your thoughts or your creativity." I couldn't resist adding a little dig. "Even the Church couldn't."

There was a long pause. He had his head in his hands.

I continued, "You know, we have this new, young, intelligent President and you should write directly to him. I'm sure, with your prestige, what you have to say would be taken seriously." (I knew he had had correspondence with President Eisenhower, and later I heard that President John Kennedy did write to him about a nuclear pact.)

He looked up. "I'd never presume to interfere with a man's or a nation's thinking without being asked."

Then he threw a bombshell and, at the same time, showed a politically naive side. "There is only one thing your President can do for peace: pull your troops out of Germany and leave both East Germany and West Germany as is—two separate states. East Germany is ethnically different from West Germany, and Germany should not be united again." His eyes went steely.

I was aghast. "But, Dr. Schweitzer, you must know that, if the President did that, the Soviets would fill the void in twenty-four hours. Look at their most recent invasion of Hungary." (This, of course, was over twenty years before Afghanistan or Poland.)

He didn't answer but went on, with a touch of irascibility, "America has wasted a lot of money in Germany already." Schweitzer was vehemently opposed to Adenauer and almost equally opposed to Ehrhart. He then intimated, "Under Willi Brandt maybe your money would go to a better cause." (Willi Brandt resigned in 1978 under a political cloud.)

Fighting a little unfairly, I asked, "Wouldn't a plebiscite between East and West Germany be a good way to resolve this?" I knew that he must know the Soviets would never allow a plebiscite because they'd surely lose East Germany.

He did not answer again but went on gruffly, "East Germany is not influenced by the Soviets. The Russian army pulled out long ago. East and West Germany started as separate states, and if they remained separate there would be peace."

I couldn't believe what he was saying. "Dr. Schweitzer, everyone knows that if the Soviets pulled back they didn't pull back far and they were certainly not maintaining the separation for ethnic but simply for political reasons." We both remained committed to our opinions.

During another talk, he abruptly asked me how long I'd been in Russia. I told him I was there for a month on a Soviet invitation relative to my experimental work on the transplantation of hearts.

Seemingly indifferent to why I went, he said, "Visitors to Russia told me that religion was increasing and would increase even more. That the churches were crowded."

Both Phoebe and I knew differently.

"Dr. Schweitzer, I don't know where your information comes from, but we saw with our own eyes that only a few churches were still open. The others had been converted for other uses, such as offices or nursery schools. There was one church that had even been converted into an anti-religious museum encompassing and embellishing every wrong the Church had ever perpetrated. The Soviets don't even hide their feelings about the Christian Church. And you must have heard of the century of pogroms against the Jews.

"There were some few church-going people," I admitted, "but not droves, and few of these people were under the age of fifty. What's more, it was rare to see teenagers in church even when accompanied by their parents. You know you don't go far in the party if you're a church-goer."

He didn't give up. "There are baptisms, so there must be young Christians," he answered fervently.

Arguing back fiercely, "The baptismal ceremony may have made them nominal Christians at birth; but the holy water could hardly counteract the everyday anti-religious propaganda they hear from the age of three on in the schools and in the media. Dr. Schweitzer, I saw it. I heard it."

He nodded, reluctantly admitting this. I felt just then he was playing the American baiter rather than the Soviet advocate.

"Not only that," I added, not giving an inch, "the churchgoers are watched like other dissidents. If you're a believer in anything non-Sovietized you're considered a dissident and are denied material advantages.

"Do you think a country such as Russia, with only a 'philosophy' of spiritual and ethical teachings but without a spiritual being such as Jesus, could progress to the happiness you feel in your religion?"

Clasping his hands together decisively, he affirmed, "Of course, didn't they have Tolstoy with a spiritual and ethical message?"

He semi-scolded, "You Americans are constantly worrying about *Communism* when Communism doesn't worry about you."

Phoebe said angrily, "The Soviets worry about us all right. And, if they wouldn't be constantly overrunning free nations we wouldn't worry about *them!* Has any nation in our time, other than Hitler's Germany, been so blatant in their grabs for land?"

At this, he veered off. "Poor nations, like India, need a socialistic state with a government owning most industries."

As the conversation wound down, he relented a bit. "I

don't say that all people in Communist countries are so happy with their form of government."

But then he came back to my Russian visit. "When you were in Russia, didn't you see happy, secure people? I've heard that the people there feel as free as Americans."

Then Phoebe really pitched in. "Dr. Schweitzer, that's a long way from the truth. They wouldn't choose that way of life today nor would you. When a nation is surrounded by barbed wire and machine guns pointed in, not out, to prevent the people from leaving, there's something wrong with the system. We saw this; it's not hearsay. When we left Czechoslovakia by car to go into Austria, it was that way all along the border. Most of them, I think, lead a sad, drab life. If they had the freedom to leave, there would be few people left except for those in the Kremlin."

I interrupted at this point. "Dr. Schweitzer, you once wrote in a book on human rights that there must be freedom to emigrate—freedom to circulate at will. Do you think Soviet citizens have that freedom?"

He admitted that he did write that but, instead of defending it, he again went off on another tangent. "Look how much the Soviets give their people—just about everything. Take, for example, education: the youngsters go right through college 'free,' while in America the child cannot even go to high school without paying."

"Dr. Schweitzer, I'm shocked: I can't believe you are so unknowing of the American system." When I showed such disbelief, he said that he was unsure of this but an American had told him so.

Then Phoebe asked him point blank, "Doesn't democracy and a representative government with all its faults have it all over any dictatorship? Do you know of one totalitarian government that is not oppressive and do you really think the satellite countries are happy?"

He didn't answer immediately. In the pause that followed, she asked another question. "Dr. Schweitzer, do you really believe what you said before that the Soviets would have no influence on Germany if the United States pulled out?"

"East Germany is perfectly satisfied," he observed. Then he brightened, "There are some East German professors coming here right after New Year's. Why not stay and ask them yourselves?" He took Phoebe's hand—as if to make up with her. I think that he was more interested in Phoebe staying than her learning more about East Germany.

"Dr. Schweitzer," I broke in, "when we were in East Berlin in 1954 the people we met were most dissatisfied. After all, there are about four thousand East German refugees a day who are fleeing, some even dying, to get into West Berlin." (This, of course, was before the Berlin Wall was built.)

He countered, "They were very bad off economically in 1954, but it's different now."

"How about the abortive revolt then?" I asked.

He shrugged it off, "Just a small economic episode."

It seemed that our political discussions often concerned Soviet-American relations. But once he brought up the situation in Hungary. "A professor friend in Budapest, with whom I correspond, thought that there was no major dissatisfaction in that country either. After all, that 1956 affair was only a student rebellion."

(When Phoebe and I discussed it later, we both thought that Schweitzer must have known better but was just drawing us out.)

Sometime later, I tried to pin him down while we were discussing academic freedom. "Dr. Schweitzer, you know of the repression in the arts and in the sciences that Stalin and the Russian system have imposed. I'm sure you're aware of the Lysenko Affair, where the government supported the

His greatest joy

Lambarene village on market day

Reverence for a small friend

Le Grand Docteur in the midst of construction

long-outmoded theory that acquired characteristics can be inherited only because it fits into their political theories. We've already talked about Pasternak. You also know there is no free expression in the graphic arts; if artists won't paint social realism, their work is banned. Now, do you really feel that your creative work, disregarding your religious writings, could have possibly been published under the eyes of a commissar? From what I've read of you, when it comes to truth, whether it be music or philosophy, you're more a revolutionary than they are. I doubt if you'd last long in that society."

He didn't answer.

Another time, I brought up a subject which had been bothering me since we first heard him extolling the virtues of the German people and their sensitive and disciplined mentality. He had spoken of their superiority over the French in music, their belief in hard work, their insistence on quality, and their perfectionism. During a discussion about the great German surgeon, Sauerbruch, and his work for the Nazis in human experimentation, the subject of Thomas Mann came up. I asked Schweitzer if he had known Mann.

"I knew him very well," he said, "but from what I've heard, Mann was very unhappy in his later years" (his refugee years in the United States).

"Why?" Phoebe asked, and Schweitzer's rigid pro-German sympathies came out again.

"Any man who speaks out against his native land must be unhappy because it is a traitorous act," he said emotionally.

"You mean, 'my nation right or wrong,' " Phoebe flared, her eyes widening. Outspoken as she was, she tempered her words with the affection she felt for him. "From my knowledge of Mann's writing, he showed every aspect of German life and, from his books, seemed to be German to the core." Then, unwilling to be less than frank, she said decisively, "Yet he was objective; and Nazi Germany to him, as to most of the world, was monstrous. I understand that as he went on in America he not only enjoyed his freedom but was a very happy man there."

Schweitzer closed his eyes tightly, put a hand to his forehead, and was silent for a while. He knew what we were driving at. "You know that Hitler got into power through a presidential election," he said defensively. "The German people elected Hindenberg thinking he was a nice old man, and that with his experience he could lead them out of the mess the Allies had put them in at Versailles. Actually, he was too old and too weak." Schweitzer's face was grim. "Hitler completely bullied him, and from then on everything Hitler did was rubber-stamped by a stupid Reichstag. Then the people could do nothing."

But Phoebe interjected, her temper rising again, "In practically any other nation the people would not have tolerated a Hitler. They would never have allowed the repression and genocide—the extent of which the world had never before witnessed." She went on caustically, "Only Stalin came close with *his* own people."

Schweitzer suddenly looked frail and defenseless. At this, Phoebe melted and took his hands in hers. In a low voice he continued, "Well, they were powerless anyway; it's a subject I hate to discuss." In all of our talks he had said not one word against Hitler, the death camps, or the megalomania and murderousness of the man. I'm not sure whether it was just the idea, as with Mann, of "talking against his native land," but I doubt it. I'm sure part of it was a deep shame for a people and a country he loved and respected so much. He just couldn't comprehend this behavior because of the high regard he felt for the German mentality. Then he made one small admission, "I never stepped foot in Germany during the

Hitler regime." This, of course, could have been for a number of reasons, such as because he had been in Africa during most of that era. For another, he had a Jewish wife.

I pushed on. Maybe I shouldn't have, but I had to. "But you have constantly praised the German people and their culture. Is it this culture, their discipline, and their sense of superiority that is at fault? Is it this that allows them to be led by just anyone preaching the 'master race' and 'Deutchland über Alles'? What I am saying, Dr. Schweitzer, is that it recurs so frequently in Germany."

He just shook his head sadly. "Yes," he agreed, "it was a terrible thing." He went on, "I'm sure you have heard of my friend, Reverend Martin Niemoeller, a loyal German patriot. In the shape Germany was in, he was, at first, a supporter of National Socialism. He couldn't have known what it would become after 1933. After Hitler came to power, he saw what it really was and he preached vehemently against it." He was intimating that the good Germans knew little in the beginning, until all Germany was burying its head in the rubble.

"But, Dr. Schweitzer," I interjected, "he only started preaching against Nazism because they were interfering in Church affairs. He never came out against book burning or the other obvious atrocities occurring right in Germany very early."

"That was the overt reason, but he was against many of their actions," he pressed on glumly.

I let the subject drop.

Germanophilia was a peculiar quirk in his otherwise magnificent mentality. He could philosophize on his reverence for life as a means to peace and security, and he could also politically fight to ban the bomb as an extinctive process, but he could not condemn outright—at least to me— the suffering and death caused during World War II by the country and the people he loved.

Although those particular conversations involving the Soviets and Germany had become very heated, I soon learned that Schweitzer hated a personal confrontation of any sort. Usually, when he saw it coming, he would either remain quiet or change the subject. Later he admitted to me he learned this kind of discipline by traumatic experiences as an argumentative child in a Germanic household. But he didn't mind expressing himself in no uncertain terms in his writings or in his preachings when there was no vocal opposition.

Once in the dining room on a rainy Saturday morning, Schweitzer brought up a rather humorous political story. He asked me if I had ever heard of Eugene Debs. I said I had and that I thought he had run for President on the Socialist ticket sometime during the twenties.

"Yes, in 1920, but he didn't get many votes." Then, laughingly, Schweitzer added, "He was a cousin of mine; my mother's nephew. I think he overstayed his leave in politics. We corresponded for a while until he died. But about thirty years ago, an American sculptor came here to do my head. I don't know why," Schweitzer said, breaking into a grin, "they always want to sculpt my head." (In Gunsbach in 1983 we saw, stashed in a closet, about twenty sculpted heads of Schweitzer in every conceivable medium.) "Anyway, this artist said, 'I have a feeling I've done you before.' Finally, he asked me if I knew Eugene Debs. He had done a portrait of Debs while Debs was in jail."

He continued, "I once asked a very bright music student, an American I had met in France in the early twenties, when I was back in Europe, the same question I asked you. 'Did you know of Debs?' The student castigated Debs in no uncertain terms; and, when I told this student that Debs was my cousin, he was appalled at his *faux pax*." Schweitzer chuckled. "I told him, 'this will teach you a lesson. If anyone asks you again about your views on a person, always ask first whether he is a member of the questioner's family.' "

I broke in, "Maybe the seeds of socialism, as with Debs and Sartre, run in your family; maybe they're inherited," I referred jokingly to his pro-Russian feeling.

He shook his head and pointed at Phoebe. "She's in my family; is she a socialist?"

The rain had ended and that ended our morning interchange.

Another time, in his room, I asked him why and how a man with so many interests could become involved with politics.

"I can only tell you," he said thoughtfully, "that whatever interest I have in politics could not have come from my father, whose whole life was his family and his job as a preacher and a moralist. His world was limited to the Gospel and Gunsbach. But it was different with my mother, who was intensely interested in more worldly things. I remember that she would be upset if the newspaper was a day or so late because she would miss the latest reports on political events in the world. As you probably realize, Gunsbach had no newspaper, so the one we received daily was already a day or so late."

"Did your mother ever discuss politics with you?"

"No, I was too young then; but I often heard her discuss the situation in Alsace (with friends or neighbors). Alsace was a hotbed of politics. But my real political interests came in my later years and it was never my principal one. I always considered it part and parcel of philosophy, just as most Greek philosophers did. It's the basis of how man can live together in the most peaceful and productive way. My mother always thought that."

Mentioning his mother must have brought back powerful memories because Schweitzer's whole mood seemed to change. His face darkened and he held his hands up to his temples as if to ward off some thoughts saddening to him— maybe thoughts of her and how he finally had gone to Africa without her blessings.

When he got up he seemed more stooped and older than usual. Without looking at us he uttered his usual *a travaux* ("to work") and we left, feeling very uneasy.

15

REVERENCE
FOR LIFE

It is ironic that often, in the popular media, Schweitzer's greatest contribution to peace of mind and peace on earth is brought down to the lowest common denominator—the humorous and ridiculous level: that of not swatting a fly or stepping on a bug. That his reverence for life—one of mankind's greatest thoughts—should be considered in such pejorative terms, rather than in the most lofty, is in itself a dark reflection on the human intellect and the difficulty of gaining universal human acceptance of Schweitzer's way of life. As I learned at Lambarene, the real core of the idea involves man in his totality in the universe—his relation to all other living things, his mystical and religious side, and even the security of his everyday life.

In reality it is an understandable, simple, noncomplicated idea of life, living with all other life. Schweitzer himself felt intensely about all of its many facets. He also lived it. I saw him take pains to free a wasp caught by chance within the screening of his room as if he were freeing a slave, and I saw him avoid stepping on an ant as if it were the most precious of lives. To him this was the essence of Christianity.

Schweitzer put it very simply. "I have attempted to associate Christianity to the holiness of all life while the Church tries to confine it only to human life. Jesus spoke in a universal language; why limit His words to the human form alone?"

If I had any doubts about Schweitzer's true reverence and feelings for all of life there was a touching episode among the many quintessential and spontaneous examples I observed that is as vivid today as it was in 1960, when it happened.

It happened on a Saturday when work was usually scheduled only until noon. That particular morning there was a larger operating load than usual. Just as we were about to leave the breakfast table to begin work, a shriveled, kindly old native man of about seventy dressed in tattered clothes came onto the porch of the dining room and begged one of the *infirmiers* to see "Oganga." The *infirmiers*, like all the native help who worked with Schweitzer and who associated themselves with his fame and "magic," considered themselves above their fellow natives. They wouldn't let this man in. But he would not be turned away, and the commotion that ensued at the door prompted Schweitzer and a few of us to see what was going on.

The old man was barefoot, his hair was matted, and tears streaked his sweat-begrimed face. He looked totally worn out, as if he had been through a rigorous physical labor. He obsequiously and repeatedly bowed as he saw and recognized Schweitzer. Joseph then interpreted and told us how this man lived about forty miles downstream. It must have taken him two days by *pirogue* to get to the hospital.

In a choked voice, the man said, "I've brought my

oldest friend up to see you, *Oganga*, because I feared my friend would die. Everyone in my village had told me that only the white doctor's magic could make my friend well, that Dr. Schweitzer was my only hope." His friends had put food and water in his *pirogue* and sent him off.

Schweitzer was silent until the man had finished and then asked, "Where is your friend?"

The old man pointed to a large woven-reed mat lying near the door. Schweitzer, surprised, turned to the mat. As we looked closely, we saw the nose of a dog protruding from one end. The straw mat was the means by which the old man had carried his pet and protected it from the hot sun. The man gently opened the mat, revealing a large dog of unknown lineage or vintage which weighed sixty or seventy pounds and was cushioned by a worn blanket—probably the old man's only one. The blanket was encrusted with blood. The dog was very sick. His dry tongue hung from the side of his mouth, his eyes were glazed, and he was gasping for breath. The old man turned from Schweitzer for a moment and knelt beside his friend. He lovingly wet the dog's parched tongue with a damp cloth that he dipped into a bottle of water he carried. All the while, he was telling how some hunters had accidentally shot the dog. "They didn't mean to," he murmured.

Schweitzer tenderly turned the dog on its back to examine it. The dog was obviously in his last throes, and incontinent. There was a large gaping wound in the upper abdomen that glistened with the lustrous sheen of busy flies and the wriggling of white maggots.

As stenchful as it was, Schweitzer felt no aversion to carefully examining the dog. He then ordered some paper napkins from the dining room to keep the flies from the wound. He told two *infirmiers*, "Transfer the dog to a stretcher and take him immediately to the O.R." He put his hand on the man's shoulder, and, his eyes glistening, said,

"Your friend is very sick but we'll try to save him." The man threw himself at Schweitzer's feet, held onto his legs, and tried to kiss his hands.

Schweitzer was visibly moved by the whole affair, as all of us were. This anguished old man had used all of his waning strength to paddle two days against the rushing current. We also thought how that old, withered body had borne his sick "friend" off the boat and carried the heavy load up the steep hill to the dining room.

Schweitzer helped the old man up, keeping a hand on his shoulder. He seemed to want to clasp the man to him. Almost as if to hide his feelings, he quickly turned to one of the younger doctors who was scheduled to go to the O.R. and ordered him to get things ready and prepare to operate on the dog. "I'll be down," he said.

The doctor remonstrated that it would be an hour or two. First, he had to repair a recto-vaginal fistula of a woman patient.

For about the third time in a few weeks, I saw Schweitzer's well-publicized anger. The two other times were when the gendarme had brought in a boy who had stolen, and another time when Schweitzer returned from a trip and found his native laborers all drunk.

This time his ire was aimed at one of his own staff. He remained quiet for a moment, trying to control himself. Then, giving the young doctor an ice-cold glare, he asked how long the woman had had her fistula. "Two years," the doctor replied.

Schweitzer exploded. "She can wait another two hours; this man's friend can't!" He turned away.

As I strode down the hill toward the operating room with Schweitzer, I heard the generator go on. "We've done so many operations on animals here," Schweitzer said, "but they usually die of pneumonia. I think it's from the anesthesia." (Though highly flammable and dangerous in that heat, ether poured over a nose cone was frequently used.)

I followed him into the O.R. The young surgeon was now not only ashamed but also contrite and would not look either of us in the eye. It always appeared to me that whenever Schweitzer showed his displeasure to one of his European helpers, they immediately became overtly and overly solicitous about their patients. But even more evident was their repentant attitudes toward Schweitzer—as if they were disciples who had in some way spiritually failed their Christ.

We watched the young doctor begin to operate; but almost before he began to debride (surgically clean) the wound, the dog gave his last gasp. The dog had not only been depleted from loss of blood but was also terribly dehydrated. Though he was given intravenous fluids, the heat and the two-day boat ride were too much. The bullet, which judging from the size of the wound, must have been a large calibre, had penetrated the side of the chest then went through the diaphragm and liver and out, leaving that gaping and festering area.

When the dog stopped breathing Schweitzer turned and went outside. His brow furrowed, shoulders hunched in sadness, he went over to the waiting native and took him to a bench. Sitting with him, he sadly explained, through Joseph, that they had done everything possible but had failed. His friend was no more.

Schweitzer then spent about twenty minutes telling the old man how much he admired the man's love for a friend, but that he must immediately begin a new relationship with another friend.

"I understand your grief," Schweitzer said, "but go home to your village. We will give him a proper burial." Schweitzer, with an arm around the old man's shoulder, helped the man, now sobbing like a child, to where his *pirogue* was tied up, We soon had him provisioned with food and water and wished him well.

I followed Schweitzer back into the operating room. He wanted to tell the *infirmiers* where to bury the remains. As we walked in, everything was just about cleaned up; and the young surgeon was getting into dry chinos.

"Where is the man's friend?" Schweitzer asked. Since that morning, he had not mentioned the animal as anything other than "the man's friend." Pierre, another *infirmier*, pointed diffidently to a trash can containing all of the post-operative soiled sheets, bloody sponges, and empty bottles piled in it.

Schweitzer's eyes grew wide, his teeth clenched, and he exploded into a roar. "How could you degrade that body?" he shouted at the young doctor. "Haven't you learned yet that there is as much dignity of the spirit in death as in the spirit of life—in any life—even this poor animal's?"

The young doctor and all the *infirmiers* were actually cringing. Schweitzer went on, waving his arms and pointing his fingers, saying, "Never will I hear of this again, or you can all leave." He repeated himself. "Have you learned nothing? Do you still have so little feeling even for the spirit of the friendship between this dead animal and that old man?" Trying to calm himself, he added, abruptly, "Give him a decent burial." He mentioned a place on a hill where other pets were buried. Slowly, he turned and left.

This emotional experience had taken a lot out of him. Weary to the point of exhaustion, his head sagging to his chest and his feet almost too heavy to lift, he slowly shuffled down toward a favorite place on a stone wall next to the river. He usually could be seen there in the early evening, petting one of his many animal friends—a deer, a pelican, a chimp.

Today he sat alone, as if he had been beaten, as if he had failed someone.

The whole incident seemed a sorry reflection of what Schweitzer and I had recently been talking about—the possibility of even educated men from good backgrounds—let alone natives—having a reverence for life. After all of Schweitzer's teachings of the ethics of Christ, his biblical interpretations, his everyday examples, and his nightly philosophic reading, he still had to contend daily with the average human attitude toward the suffering of others.

It must have been devastating to realize that what he believed could not even be transmitted to one well-schooled adult—the young doctor. To Schweitzer, that primitive old man's love for his animal was not only an exemplary grace but should have evoked a heartfelt reaction and been an inspiration to most everyone.

The young doctor was almost catatonic, and in no mental state to do any surgery. He canceled the procedure he had planned. I took advantage of the time and performed some simple surgery which had been pending. When I came out of the O.R., an hour or so later, Schweitzer was still sitting on the wall. He was absentmindedly fondling a fawn which had come over and was nuzzling him, as if it knew and was trying to assuage his human friend's anger and dejection.

He didn't show up for lunch that day.

This episode flushed from my mind any remnant of rumor questioning his compassion or his rapport with Blacks. It scotched the loose talk that he lived differently from what he thought and wrote. That meeting between an ordinary primitive tribesman with his sick dog and this sophisticated philosopher, musician, and physician reflected a melding of Schweitzer's deep spirit of life, his religious beliefs and his concern for his fellow man. Now, twenty-five years later, on reading over my long lost diary, I still feel its powerful emotional impact and every detail stands out clearly.

It also brought to mind an early autobiography I had read in which Schweitzer had mentioned that at the age of six or so he was considered peculiar by his young friends as well as by his parents because he wouldn't go to a zoo or circus. He couldn't stand the sight of life being caged. Even at that age the contempt with which some people treated animals and even each other made him miserable. His feeling for all life, I think, was innate. Even at the age of nine, he added to those he prayed for, "and to everything on earth that has breath." It was "Reverence for Life" in the making.

At first, some of his "reverence" philosophy was difficult for me to comprehend. The phrase itself was, of course, its superficial attraction, and I knew that the true meaning must be much more involved. I could sympathize with the compassion he felt for all life. But from what I had heard, it was not comprehended by many others either.

That evening after dinner, I was surprised when Schweitzer asked me to join him in his quarters. When I got there, Dr. Friedman was already there making out some forms.

With the dog incident fresh in my mind, I posed a rather blunt practical question: Did he think that the natives or even his own doctors and nurses here really comprehended his painstaking effort in freeing that wasp or understood the meaning of that old man and his dog?

He shrugged, his eyes became troubled, and I realized that the experiences with the man and his "friend" must have given his hopes of the masses ever taking up his philosophy quite a setback. He sadly allowed, "Most of man's feelings and reactions are similar, but if they'd only think about it for just a moment their whole outlook might change."

He knew that human reflexes had priority over thought. He knew that every evening tens of millions of wasps were being swatted or purposefully stepped on all over the world. He admitted that even as a child there is an average learned response to every possible pain or injury. But if the child was constantly shown by example that a bee or wasp does not sting unless provoked—which is true of most animal life—he or she might respond differently.

Yet, as he pointed out, there was also more to revering life than just the absence of fear. If the human is taught early that he is only a tiny part of the living universe—and not too far removed from his tiny brother the wasp—he may get a feeling for all life. "Who knows," he said somewhat ironically, "he might even start thinking kindly of his fellow man. That to me is Christianity."

As we talked he got up to stretch and then sat back at his desk with his hands behind his head. "A wasp could even be as dangerous as man," he said, again showing his satirical side. Then, more seriously, "But humans through thought are allowed priorities.

"The question in our minds should be, do we truly have to kill even when protecting ourselves from an animal or kill to prevent starvation?" He brought up the less violent options available. "Can't we avoid confrontation in one case and in the other eat less than our friendly domesticated animals? Thinking before doing an act of violence to any living thing should always be the humane man's creed." As he had said many times before, even the feeling for God shouldn't be taken on blind faith. "And isn't the act of thinking, not just for yourself but applying the Golden Rule to all life, the way to personal peace?"

He sat bolt upright. "Isn't the act of thinking supposedly the major differentiation between man and other animals? Isn't the brain the instrument man uses to cooperate with other men to get along, to survive—if only for his own security?

"Do not forget that animals too have their own 'civilization,' hunting in groups and protecting and feeding their young.

"If we have a responsibility to the miracle of life itself—all life—it includes an ant or a wasp. We are all part and parcel of the same family," he said forcefully.

He relaxed somewhat as he added dryly, "If you believe in evolution, how can you kill your own ancestors, except in self defense? Yet, we, as individuals or even nations, are suspicious and on the alert for what we might think are unfriendly gestures, even if they aren't. But we do not immediately attack an opponent without seriously thinking it over and trying to talk it over. We should be above that. So why should we not, at least, apply this logic to all living things?"

There was a prolonged silence. Then, more gently, Schweitzer allowed, "We might eventually bring ourselves to think that way, for that is the spiritual essence of 'reverence.' Anyway it's my interpretation of the spirit of Christ and of a civilized life. His message might then truly provide an on-earth kingdom of heaven—a peace for everyone."

In pondering all of this, a trivial though cogent thought passed through my mind. On the basis of priorities in killing or not killing, how about the cow and the chicken that we must destroy in order to eat? Why didn't he take up vegetarianism?

His thinking on this was logical and human, if not quite humane. In fact, I felt he rationalized as he spoke about millions of years of man as a hunter and the animal as a food on which man thrived. He allowed that it was logical but radical for man to change his diet and pointed out the almost overwhelming discipline necessary to deny his taste buds. Also, though there are other sources of animal protein, he spoke of the necessity for that type of protein. However, he did agree that, in time, with a strong personal philosophy of reverence, we might also temper our instincts even as our diet.

Pausing for a moment, he said, "Today to take any life unnecessarily or, even worse, purposely, such as killing a harmless elephant for a trophy or a butterfly just to pin it to a board—even if it gives some people pleasure, which it obviously does—is *grievous*."

As Schweitzer talked he seemed fidgety. He walked around the room, doing small chores, stacking papers, putting out letters that he wanted to answer immediately. He had a sense of defeat in his tone but also a tinge of open cynicism which I'd heard before.

Then I pursued his thought perhaps further than I should have. "When you speak of 'Christian,' by your definition few of us are. War is certainly not humane and 'Christians' have been some of the greatest instigators of war in the Western world for most of their history. Certainly there is nothing rational about war. And since wars come about usually on the basis of high principles, such as loyalty to a cause or even an ideology, aren't these principles and ideologies brought about by thought? In that mode of thinking, how can there be reverence for anything but a political belief? Speaking about thinking and violence, there have been five or so major and at least fifty minor wars just since World War Two.

"Now even in our daily living, everyone is becoming so fearful of one another, with mugging, murder, and rape in cities all over the world." This was just at the very beginning of the worldwide problem of terrorism. "It seems that there is even less reverence for life today. Wouldn't you say that, all in all, thinking and religion have taken us backward, not forward?"

"But," he reiterated, "man is just in his infancy, and peace within him won't come easily or soon." Then, ruminating, "If we can only hold on."

As I considered this I thought how farfetched the idea of Reverence for Life really was. "Dr. Schweitzer, you know that most of mankind doesn't think at all, much less rationally. They live by their reflexes just like cats—only more violently. A man thinks mainly of feeding himself—just like a cat. And he even competes, yet with probably less cause than a cat. He is too busy to think. He awakens; he breakfasts; he works; he comes home; he eats; reads a newspaper or watches television; fornicates; goes to bed; and repeats it all over again the next day. He is not that far removed from his ancestral cat cousins as far as his thinking goes."

Schweitzer walked over to his desk and took something from a stack of papers. Then he said quietly, "Don't think about the *least* of men. Even if the *least* are in the majority, they can be led by the *best* and then they could become the *most* of men. So there is hope that, in time, the least may become the best, and then become the most. Having faith cannot just take the place of Christianity and love; it must be founded on it."

Pursuing this, I asked bluntly, "Do you really think man's brain will evolve fast enough to save him? His upright stance and his agile thumb each took millions of years to evolve. You spoke out early on the possibility of man destroying himself with nuclear weapons. If you see this as a possibility now, how do you expect him to contain himself until the twenty-first century, much less for a thousand years?"

Without answering my question, he went off on a tangent as he frequently did when he sought time to think. It was usually a logical tangent, and many times reverted to the "truths of Jesus."

"Average man, when he is not emotionally instigated, seeks to live in peace. We must count on this as Christ did. And even two thousand years of war have not yet destroyed us."

Schweitzer must have known better. We neither had the power nor the means to do a really thorough job of destruction until now—in the nuclear age. Now we have the most evil of weapons—the nuclear bomb. And this weapon was fabricated by man's partly evolved brain, in which Schweitzer seemed to place so much faith.

I couldn't resist coming back with, "Today, even the man with a full stomach will kill on the basis of his civilized brain and his national ideology. We have seen your Germany commit murder and genocide on a scale never before perpetrated, and now it's the same with yet another worldwide ideology. Are we going forward or backward with our great brains?"

He winced at any comment bringing up recent German history. Sadly, he admitted that annihilation by his own hand could be man's fate. "I think we are still learning that if each human could affirm life and promote ethics, which most everyone wants for himself, no H-bomb will ever be used," he said tiredly.

I brought the conversation around to the killing that seems to be constantly increasing in a more "thinking" educated world. "We may be more learned today," I commented, "but it seems that the more sophisticated we get the less feeling we have for any life. We kill leopards, mink, and baby seals for fur coats; and we kill each other by the millions for what each of us feels is the best way of life. Is life itself to be held in less esteem than a way of life—such as democracy or Communism?"

I added, "It seems to me that as we fabricate more

civilized ways of obtaining peace, such as the United Nations, we have more and more wars. The twentieth century has been more grim than the dark ages—in religious wars alone. Look at the religious factions in Ireland killing each other's children in the name of Christ. How much could they have learned about His teachings or your ethics? If Luther had never lived, the Catholics and Protestants in Ireland would at least have had one less reason to bomb and shoot each other. Then there is the Middle East and their religious wars. Where is there hope?"

By now we were only repeating ourselves. My mention of the United Nations reminded me of a joke so applicable to man helping his brother, especially here in Africa. It was a crazy thought, but I asked him if he would like to hear a bad joke about international aid and our jungle friends. He nodded and smiled, seeming to enjoy a reprise.

"There was this meeting of cannibal elders gathered in a thatched hut sitting around a fire at a high-level conference. The chief spokesman, in typical cartoon style with a bone through his nose said, 'You all know how kind the white man is and how he wants to aid us underdeveloped people. Well, here's the plan. We let out the word we're in a state of political flux. The Russians hear about it and they send a delegation to arrange help and aid. Then the United States sends a delegation to make sure Russia doesn't get the edge and offers us more and better help and aid. Then when they're all here, we'll eat them.' "

Schweitzer didn't quite understand the joke; Dr. Friedman explained it in German. Schweitzer let out a roar of laughter that could be heard across the compound.

The seriousness of the conversation was broken by this, but not my contention on the impossibility of man persisting to his state of grace. Schweitzer again raised the importance of rearing children as thoughtful beings. Not to upset him, I said as gently as possible, "Dr. Schweitzer, you must realize that too few humans feel as sensitively as you do for animal life, especially at the age of four or five. Most children at that age are busy tearing the wings off butterflies and feeling the squish of stepping on a beetle or tying a can to a dog's tail."

"Youth equates an outward show of feeling or sensitivity with weakness," he retorted abruptly. Leaning back and closing his eyes, he said, "That may only be a matter of conditioning. I remember I was ashamed to tell my friends that I got sick watching a fish as it tried to free itself from a fishhook. But without conditioning, I could never understand the callousness of my friends, but then I didn't want to lose them as friends. However, I eventually learned that you can't fight your basic feelings forever.

"I once saw a vendor in Gunsbach beat his old horse because it was getting dark and he wanted to go home. I had nightmares about it but I kept it to myself for years.

"Nevertheless, I soon freed myself from the criticism of others and was not so swayed by their opinions, especially as to my feelings about other people or animals." (Some have equated this with rank stubbornness.) "But right now in our society, most hide their better sentiments—just as I did as a child."

"Well," I confessed, "whether it's innate or not I know that most butterfly-wing rippers are still there as adults. And I feel too it's not only innate cruelty but learned. White children learn by family and peer example to hate Blacks, and vice versa; and there is still hate between Christians and Jews as well as among different sects of Christians themselves."

Schweitzer kept nodding as I talked. But Schweitzer was a most rare breed—a mutant. And as we know, only the rarest of mutants persist and become the majority. I had read, for example, that he couldn't tolerate going to school with a warm coat when so many of his classmates came in rags, whereas most kids today can't wait to show new things off, even to their most raggedy classmates.

Trying to be humorous, I broke in, "Now I know why you had such great respect for Goethe. You're a modern-day Dr. Faustus trading off your happiness with the outside world for an inner satisfaction with your many talents."

"No, it's not Faustian," Schweitzer chided me. "How could I make a deal with the devil at such a tender age?" With a droll sidelong glance, he referred to a remark made by the press: "Some people put me up with the angels; now you put me down with the devil."

"No, I didn't mean it that way." I tried to explain but he guided the conversation toward a discussion of his strong feeling of free will against my thought that it was the strength of the gene in reference to those who might acquire a "reverence for life." As an aside, I mentioned the newly-discovered gene structure substance, DNA, which supposedly programmed almost every thought and action that man has—maybe even his will—which would indicate that today's experiments in sociobiology prove even more that almost every move and thought that we have is pre-programmed.

Schweitzer was very skeptical about our basic genes programming our thoughts even though he'd read about DNA. Fumbling through some papers as if he didn't want to look me squarely in the eye, he inquired, "What are your personal feelings about reverence for life?"

I answered evasively. "I'm not sure that deep down, even with your teachings, I could go against my instincts. I may have a great reverence for man's life. I have fought in a war; and though I didn't kill I certainly could have and probably without thought at that—just like so many others that did the same.

I rambled, "Other than the ordinary pleasures that most of us get out of life, whether material, sexual, the lust for power, or just achieving, I must confess I rarely think of any life other than my own, my family's, or friends'. A nuclear holocaust may destroy us all and with it will go our will—much before your reverence for life could ever catch on in our world."

With a hint of a smile lurking at the corners of his mouth, he asked, winking, "Don't you think the spirit could live on unembodied?"

More seriously, he continued, "All we know now is that the world exists with the human on its pinnacle. But that is only so far. One can't discount the fact that even some of our close brothers—other hominids—ape men—are now extinct. But if we disappear by our own scientific hand, it's only because man is not practicing the ethical life. However, I think we will go on."

Pondering for a moment, his fingers suddenly playing the edge of his desk, he gestured toward his pet deer at his feet. "Do you see this fawn? I've been close enough to her to know that she thinks. I've seen her make choices and decisions, just as I've seen my dog make decisions, even complex ones. With eons of time she has evolved from the amphibian to the mammal, from a primitive thinking beast into a more thinking one. It took their will to live, but always with time. Then, take the chimpanzee, an even higher animal, which makes some profound decisions. It's not like the reflex of an amoeba or an earthworm. They have a developed brain, and weigh the pros and cons of a situation and make choices. Who knows how much further we have to go?

"There is no doubt in my mind that animals at each level have different thought processes; it's just a matter of degree. So, instinctively, by the will to live, they have evolved. As your friend Teilhard has pointed out, most organisms have a nervous system that became more developed as man came up the animal scale. But as the brain enlarges it develops a forebrain which could control instinct. That doesn't say we are not still influenced by our older reflexes and instincts."

He brought up a criterion of distinguishing the thought process of man from animal. As he had said many times, "Man knows but he knows that he knows. Animals know but it is doubtful whether they know that they know. This puts them out of the realm of possible feeling for their fellow animal other than family, and so they are not able to revere life other than by instinct.

"Teilhard may be right," Schweitzer nodded, "man may be unconsciously seeking evolvement into a better being just by longevity and reproduction. Therefore, with time given to evolution, if we act as real Christians, it would naturally insure not only our survival but possibly further mental development and attainment of reverence for life."

I then posed a question I had long wanted to ask him. "Can you be a Christian and still a scientist and experiment with life? We use vaccines and medications on humans, all derived from testing them on animals and even on other humans."

I didn't get a chance to go on with that thought: it was then about midnight. We had talked a long time and both of us were tired. Admitting his tiredness, he broke our conversation off rather abruptly and we parted.

Walking back to my room, with my lantern lighting the way, I thought about our long conversation. One thing that he said particularly stuck with me: many humans think in reverent terms; but their lives are so filled with their daily efforts to survive, to make ends meet, to deal with other humans that they rarely think about, much less act as reverently toward, life as they should or would even like to.

16

MAN, ANIMAL, AND SCHWEITZER

Before I went to Lambarene I had pored through much of what I could find on Schweitzer's "Reverence for Life" theory. After being there a while I was both convinced that Albert Schweitzer enjoyed and suffered both with and for animal as well as human life.

The love he exhibited for his pets—his fawn, his dogs, his owl, and the chimpanzees—was, of course, evident. But the incident of the old man and his sick dog convinced me beyond a doubt that Schweitzer's feelings for animals were as tender as those for all life.

Though I had seen Schweitzer in many moods—preoccupied writing at his desk; off in the clouds at his piano-organ; and, on occasion, red-faced in anger at the disobedience or laziness of a worker—I had never seen him so saddened and depressed as he was that day of the dog's death.

That episode said much about Schweitzer's inner thoughts and feelings on man and man's relationship to animals. It also said much for my argument to Schweitzer: the impossibility of his "Reverence for Life" philosophy ever attaining popular belief. It was not so much the death of that particular animal or the sadness of its master, but the automatic indifference and abject callousness toward a living creature of his closest students—professional and native. If *they* weren't affected by his philosophy, then how could one expect the less educated with no direct teachings to espouse it?

Schweitzer's depression at the incident was temporary because he would never allow himself to think nonaffirmatively about man for any length of time. He always made allowances for the words of human beings and their actions toward each other and other creatures.

And, generally, he tried to explain man's fear of the undomesticated animal. As he said, other than the rare rogue, an animal would never stalk or hurt man unless the animal itself was in danger, suddenly frightened, or extremely hungry. It was nature and her eco-system at work. "It's only the fear and ignorance of each other's ways and the lack of self-security of both 'wild' animal and man that makes them so mutually suspicious and defensive. But as we see a hungry animal hunting for food, so we understand man in his own environment killing to sustain life. Yet other than for food or in self-defense, killing is still a way of life with man— not only against animal but even against his fellow man."

These feelings which he came by early in life, were the base on which his Reverence for Life philosophy had been built. And, I must confess, as pessimistic as I was about the relationship of man to animal, the ever-increasing worldwide movement for the prevention of cruelty to and the preservation of animal life leads me to believe that perhaps there is an innate if submerged feeling in many people for "reverence" which could be a promise of the future, albeit a very long-range one.

Schweitzer had a closeness with the animals on the hospital compound beyond that of most of us with our pets. It was evident in his teasing of his pet turkey; undoubtedly, the meanest bird I had ever met. Once I was ten minutes late to the operating room when I met him on the path. He wouldn't give an inch, pecking and flapping his huge wings at my every move.

I'm not sure whether it was by chance or choice that the most numerous "wild" animals on the place were the chimpanzees and the monkeys—the ones so very close to man on the phylogenetic tree. Usually these were baby primates taken in after being found starving when their mothers had died or had been killed by the natives for food. (Since the smaller primates were the least wild and the most trusting, they were also the easiest to hunt and be eaten by both other animals and the natives.) At the hospital, the baby chimpanzees were raised on a bottle until adulthood and, of course, fed and petted by everyone, although each was usually adopted by one particular person.

All of the animals roamed free. Schweitzer would allow no animal to be caged. Yet the various species of animals seemed to have a mutual respect for each other while on the hospital grounds: each hardly noticed the presence of the others and each kept its distance. Each was free to go back into the jungle at any time. They rarely did.

With one exception, they were no danger to anyone. Only the mature Great Apes could be dangerous if suddenly frightened. Yet even they would not go back into the forest when grown. Once, as a last resort, against Schweitzer's protest, one had to be shipped to a zoo.

The chimpanzees were no doubt the most charming,

though hardly the cleanest, of the animals roaming around. Phoebe took a great liking to them. She walked hand-in-hand with whichever one was around at the time and carried the younger ones and played with them—at least for the first few weeks. Then the strangest thing happened. I don't know if it was the usual male-female attraction or a son-mother relationship; but one male developed a strong attachment to her. He and a group of his chimpanzee playmates began hanging around outside our room.

They didn't bother with me very much, but they all seemed to enjoy Phoebe—particularly that one. When we got up in the morning we could see him peering in through the screen with his hands cupped over his soft brown eyes watching for her to waken. When I arose he never moved, but as soon as Phoebe got up he'd start chattering, showing his teeth, and slapping on the screen.

This affair soon became too involved. Not long after we came, Phoebe washed out some uniforms, hose, and undergarments, and hung them out to dry overnight under the porch roof. The next morning when I got out of bed I saw our little friend in his customary place looking in and waiting for Phoebe. He seemed to be wearing a hat, which surprised me. I forgot about it while dressing. When we came out the door to go to breakfast, the first thing we ran into was Phoebe's laundry. It was filthy with mud, and strewn all over the place; some was even hanging from jungle bushes a dozen yards away. As Phoebe began picking up the pieces, mumbling angrily under her breath, her little friend came over behind her and tugged at her shirt. As she turned in his direction to scold him, she burst out laughing. There he was with her stockings tied securely around his neck, as if a scarf, and her brassiere looped over one ear and over his head like a granny cap.

Soon after this, other chimp problems arose. At times

the chimps were prone to roll in the mud and even play with their own excreta. The romance between Phoebe and her primate admirer ended one morning when she came out, spic and span, in her white uniform on her way to the *pouponniere*, and her friend, unusually happy to see her, leaped into her arms. She was soon a disheveled and smeared mess from head to foot.

After that morning, I would go out first and shoo the waiting chimps away to give Phoebe a chance to dash for the safety of the nursery.

Not all of the animals were as friendly as the chimpanzees. The turkey was a mottled brown and black variety with a mean eye and a blood-red wattle. He was huge, fat, and aggressive, unlike the average scrawny fowl in the tropics. Everyone in the compound, especially the whites, were constantly on the lookout for him. If any white came too close by accident, or when Schweitzer was feeding him, the bird attacked—squawking, wings flapping, and head pecking.

I once asked Schweitzer, with all due respect, why he kept such a vicious bird around. "We understand each other," he chuckled. "He thinks he's the boss of the hospital and I think I am; so we respect each other, with no confrontation. Neither of us wants to disturb the other's ideas of preeminence."

The pet pelican, whom Schweitzer called "Monsieur le Pelican," was not vicious, though it certainly wasn't friendly, especially when someone tried to approach Schweitzer's room when he was not there. A beautiful snow white with a huge yellowish gullet, it roosted nightly under the porch eaves, and early in the morning would regularly swoop down to the river's edge where he'd scoop up schools of small fish as his reddish beady eyes spotted them coming close to shore. At the end of the day, when Schweitzer sat on the stone wall near the river bank, the bird, also finished with his day's work, would look for his friend and come up to perch near him, and enjoy the quiet and the view of the river.

I never got to know Schweitzer's owl very well, no matter how hard I tried to bribe him off his rafter. However, after several evenings with Schweitzer, I at least could pet his fawn just as he did when we were talking.

After dinner Schweitzer always brought food back to his room for his housemates. His pet pig, well fed and well housed on his porch, was a particular source of enjoyment to Schweitzer. Though I never heard it, Schweitzer said that the pig always accompanied him with grunts whenever he played Brahms. Schweitzer also claimed that his pig friend was the ultimate gentleman. Someone brought the pig a girlfriend and he would never lie down in his bed on the porch until his girlfriend had first made herself comfortable.

And, of course, the dogs on the place would bay and howl whenever the dinner bell was sounded, especially on Saturday night when both the bells—one by Dr. Friedman and the other in the Leper Village by Dr. Takahashi—rang together. Maybe the dogs knew that those two bells rung together signified the end of the work week.

One Sunday afternoon, we all dressed up to go to a special dedication ceremony of a new house for the school-teacher a few miles down the river. It was at the Mission where Schweitzer had first set up his clinic in 1913. We went down in a parade of *pirogues*. Schweitzer was dressed not only with a special white shirt and bow tie but also with a coat (which looked like a busboy's jacket) and his beat-up felt "European" hat.

As we climbed the hill to the old house where the teacher lived, Schweitzer suddenly came to a halt, holding both arms out from his sides, palms turned backward, to stop us. There in front of him was a broad band of ants, about six

abreast in three or four enfildades, marching across the path.
He began a dissertation on this particular specie, first pointing out the special channels that they so intelligently dug to
make themselves invisible when they came out from the cover
of jungle growth to cross a path. As he explained it, this was a
battalion of Traveler Ants on one of their migrations. These
occurred usually at the beginning and end of the dry season,
and the reason for them a mystery. Most likely they were
looking for a new nesting place. Schweitzer bent down to
examine them more closely, then motioned us over and
continued his homily.

"This is unusual because they generally march at
night. This column might be a mile long." He showed us how
organized they were and pointed out the various divisions of
labor. The warrior ants guarded the procession by facing
outward, just as the secret service men do with a president.
As Schweitzer pointed at one group, then another, we saw
worker ants marching as if they were carrying shovels and
farmer ants who, as soon as they settled, would be tending
their livestock of aphids.

At the point at which they emerged from the jungle,
Schweitzer's head almost touched the ground. He pointed out
the large jaws of the warrior ants open and ready to protect
the columns of the "baby sitter" ants carrying the larvae. As
he explained to us, the warriors were disciplined to stay in
place as long as the procession lasted.

Suddenly, as if by command, the column broke up.
Apparently it was mealtime. They seemed to go berserk,
spreading over yards of ground and up the trees and bushes
like an undulating blanket, as we all moved back. Everything
in their way, both plant and animal life, was devastated.
Schweitzer told us, "Once when I lived right here in my first
hospital, the ants moved through my chicken coop one night

and killed most of my laying hens by penetrating their beaks and nostrils, suffocating them, then eating their fill down to the bones."

He abhorred those ants as much as he did the termites that would get into his rice supply, his wood pile, and even into his bandages and ruin them before he knew they were there. He said that for this ant species moving and foraging was usual and instinctual for its survival. "They too have the right to live."

"Look," he grimaced, "they're killing everything in their path." He spotted something a yard or so away where there were two groups in an absolute frenzy. "Come over here." There on the ground was a perfectly normal worm and a beetle, both struggling to get away as the ants tore them apart. "Do they not act like a modern army on the move— killing and devastating everything in their way, whether necessary or not? Is it not like a mob action? Each of them in a hurry to kill, eat, and move on. So don't step on your brothers under the skin," he joked.

I didn't mention his contradiction as he warned, "Don't step on them, they're doing this to live; their instinct guides them no differently than ours. But if they attack us or our means of survival, we must do what we have to do."

Then, as if an example were in order, Schweitzer slapped at his pant leg as an ant bit him. They also got to one of two others of us. He pulled down his sock and showed the dead insect. Then, by attempting to pull it off, he demonstrated how the jaws stayed gripped on his skin like a vise. Both parts of the mandible had to be extracted separately.

Earlier during our stay, Phoebe and I had had our own experience with ants, which had occurred on a Saturday afternoon as we took a walk in the jungle with one of the native workers. Off the path, the foliage was impenetrable on both sides, with heavy bushes and large trees with huge roots extending in every direction. There were heavy spiny bushes of every shade of green, some with huge red berries. Then there were the vines as thick as a man's wrist hanging from many of the trees.

Within an hour we'd seen all manner of wild animals and colorful birds—one of which was the weaver bird which hangs its nest from the delicate, outermost branches of trees as a means of protection, knowing that these branches would not hold the weight of egg-hungry, tree climbing snakes. Occasionally, a multi-hued parrot fluttered past. Each of these birds and beasts seemed to have its own language and twittered and chattered constantly in a raucous din.

One Great Ape sat high in a tree. It was very serious looking and never took its eyes off us until we disappeared from view around a bend. Dozens of monkeys and chimpanzees of various kinds did their circus-like acrobatics and chattering away as they dove, swung, and chased each other.

At one point on the trail Phoebe and I froze. We had come face to face with a long thin, green snake hanging from a tree at about face level. It was an evil-looking animal with shiny scales, a flat head, deadly slit pupils, and a constantly flicking forked tongue. It was most likely poisonous, as most of the snakes at Lambarene were said to be. Our guide matter-of-factly motioned us to stand back. With no benevolence aforethought, nor reverence for life, he whacked the head of that snake off in one swish of the machete. Hardly missing a step, the native continued to lead us on as if nothing had happened.

When we returned by another route, the omnipresent ants appeared. Not too far from the hospital we happened across a jungle-style architectural marvel of aesthetic delight. It was a cone-shaped mound of earth about two feet high with warty excrescences the size of golf balls, everywhere stippled by tiny holes. It appeared to be an abandoned ant hill which obviously belonged to a species other than the Traveler Ant.

It looked exactly like the famed architectural master-pieces in Barcelona, designed by the world-renowned Spanish architect Gaudi. (Gaudi, by the way, was an admired friend of Schweitzer's. The doctor once asked me if I'd ever seen any of Gaudi's buildings. I'd said I had. He then told me he had asked Gaudi, through an interpreter, how they could under-stand each other since neither knew the language spoken by the other. Gaudi responded, "If you like my work we'll get along.")

Phoebe gasped with pleasure—so taken with the beauty of the abandoned colony. She turned to the guide, "Would you help me carry it back to our porch?" The guide looked at her as if she were mad. We didn't know why, for in testing it, we found that it was easily movable and not very heavy. After much protest, it was carried back without incident and set on our porch.

At dinner, she proudly told Schweitzer of her Gaudi acquisition. He gave her an enigmatic smile and said, "Yes, they are beautiful. I hope you still enjoy it tomorrow." This was rather cryptic, but we thought little more about it until the following morning.

When we awakened the next morning the floor was alive with what appeared to be a million huge ants, each three times the size of the Traveler Ant, coming in droves through the door, climbing the screens, and exploring every nook and cranny of our room. It took us an hour just to get rid of the source—the not-so-abandoned ant hill—and sweep and slosh our room clean, revering the life of not one of them. We only wondered why they didn't show up on the jostling trip from the jungle.

We asked Schweitzer at breakfast about our ant invasion. Phoebe wagged her finger at him knowing he knew what would happen when we told him about our acquisition the night before. He laughed and just offered that it wasn't so difficult to understand. As usual, he explained it in very practical and human terms. "What would any of us do if our home was attacked and uprooted by some giant and then moved? We'd hide and be as quiet as possible. Then gradually, we'd come out to see what had happened.

"But," he said, "haven't we already talked so much about doing without thinking first?" I pointed to Phoebe, and Schweitzer smiled mischievously. Phoebe gave me a sharp kick under the table. In mock seriousness, he turned to her and admonished her for appropriating and moving someone else's home.

Our conversation on animals and man did not end with the ant episode. One of the nurses had come in with some problems relating to the laundry. When Schweitzer returned, we resumed our talk about animals but in an entirely different vein.

17

THE TRIAGE
OF REVERENCE

That morning's talk, on man's relationship to animals, had continued after lunch that same afternoon, on the piano bench in the dining room. Both Schweitzer and I skipped our daily siesta that day.

I brought up the beheading of the snake on our walk.

Schweitzer was relaxed and seemed to want to talk. He agreed that the reptile was probably of the viper family and very poisonous but should certainly have been avoided, not necessarily killed. He was sure it was not intent on eating or poisoning us. "After all, you are not on his diet; so it wasn't a kill or be killed situation. Why could you not have just prodded it with a long stick or gone around it? If one gives an animal a chance to avoid conflict, it will." He sighed.

I sat tensely, drawing my thoughts together, then brought up a most serious question left unasked the night we had finished so late. It had nothing to do with killing a snake, but the priorities of killing life as a scientist when one is also a

Christian. As he had said, if one doesn't really revere all life one can't be a true Christian.

With few preliminaries, I got right to the point. "We use vaccines, antibiotics, and other medications to kill bacteria or parasites that are harmful to us, or we experiment and kill higher animals such as rabbits and dogs; yet they are also only trying to survive. The microbes don't purposely try to invade and kill. They get into our bodies by chance, not by design."

Schweitzer leaned forward. "In every species the instinct for survival is to protect its own," he explained. "Killing the species that is detrimental to the survival of your own is part of the survival system. Though there are laws of nature that we consider beautiful and grand, remember nature is not always benign. She can be cruel."

Schweitzer always considered nature in the female gender.

He continued earnestly, "All life lives at the expense of other life. But man is the only one with the judgment and the compassion to spare other species, which may even be his undoing at some later time."

Nurse Maria, tall, thin and very kind, was with us that morning, interpreting when necessary, but otherwise very quiet. From the almost blank expression on her face, it was obvious she did not understand nor did she seem interested in what he was saying. But she wasn't the only one disinterested. Only after I talked with some of the others about Schweitzer's philosophy did I realize how little interest most of them had in his thoughts on religion or "reverence." As to religion, they seemed only involved with the conventional thinking and rituals of Christianity: the hymns, the sermons, and the more formal aspects of prayer. As to "reverence," they thought only of the killing of animals, not what it meant spiritually or its other applications to the welfare of society.

Schweitzer continued, his voice strong and clear, "Nature being what she is, the highest form of life, the human, which we as Christians exalt, may easily be overcome by the lowest form. An innocent child is assaulted, suffers and dies from the thoughtless tubercle bacillus or the unthinking trypanasome of sleeping sickness. There was no malice intended, but that is the terrible contradiction in nature." As he put it, "It produces life in the trillions every day and yet destroys life in the trillions, and causes much suffering in the process. In this balance, nature is guilty by instinct, yet innocent by design, and we are part of it. Frequently, man must be cruel and defend himself as a first priority."

But he was quick to point out, forcefully, "Only man is different. Unlike the bacteria or the snake, we cannot be at the same time innocent and guilty because we have the facility to judge, with the will to do or not to do. If we destroy just what is absolutely necessary to maintain our own lives and survive, we are only then showing by our humanity and judgment why we are superior."

He paused for a moment, as if expressing his next thought was of critical importance. Pacing back and forth, he continued, "The lowest form of animal, the amoeba, will shy away from intense heat; therefore, it must have the capacity to suffer. It also may have an instinct for friendliness, or even love, in that it also seems to agglomerate with other amoebae. This may all be just a chemical reaction, but so may be all of our thought processes. Then, with no malice, they reproduce themselves and by pure chance congregate in the human body and, unconscious of their destructiveness, kill a human with amoebic dysentery. But with our brain and education we have become aware that they may be in our drinking water. So, in self defense, we may boil our water or use drugs to kill them before they kill us."

Schweitzer meditated. There was another long silence

then he went on, "So only man, with the fullest thought process—and I must always qualify this with 'as far as we know'—has that God-given privilege of reverence for life—all life. Yet sadly enough, having that privilege, we rarely exercise it."

Schweitzer paused again and then brought up the interesting point, "We do harbor and live in symbiosis with the colon bacillus in our intestines. At one time they may have been harmful to us. So possibly we could even make peace with other bacteria as time goes on."

We got around to scientific experiments on higher animals, such as dogs and cats. As I thought of this I could not but think of the animals Schweitzer absolutely loved: his cat, which sat on top of his desk in the pharmacy as he wrote; and his somewhat moth-eaten-looking mongrel dog, the only animal he allowed to wander around in the dining room. (Later that dog had to be destroyed because of a rabies epidemic. The anxiety and sadness Schweitzer must have gone through in ordering its death must have been hard for him to bear.)

I shook my head. "We breed gentle and innocent rabbits, which never harm any other animal species. We give them diseases, and the suffering that goes along with those diseases, so that we might some day not suffer from them."

I blurted out, "Is that a priority for reverence or is that an arrogance because they are so weak and peaceful and can be handled so easily with no harm to us?"

Schweitzer's eyes narrowed as if in pain. "That is a most difficult question and I'm always torn by it. But in our natural state of life fighting life, we are not so different from the animal—we instinctively consider ourselves first. I have thought of this many times when I had an amoeba under the microscope and knew it would kill or be killed by our drugs."

"But," I protested, "Those amoebae were also one of

our ancestors and now they are trying to survive, as you say, wherever and in whomever they can. Yet just because we are fortunate enough to have a brain to experiment with them and destroy them, don't we flout God's will?"

There was no answer. Instead, he brought up Teilhard again. "Maybe it's by design, not luck. For according to your Jesuit friend, God put organic life on earth from the beginning with a nervous system, albeit a very primitive one. Then the culmination, so far, of God's will is that very discerning brain that has evolved only in us. In that sense, God must also have done that in His wisdom and by the same token let other species go to their reward."

In speaking to him on animal experimentation in relation to "reverence," I began to reflect unhappily on how much of it I had done. Though, I must say, it also bothered me before I came to Lambarene, my feelings were intensified here.

I remembered how, in 1957, after my experimentation with heart transplantation, I was invited to the Soviet Union to work in the transplantation unit of the Lenin Institute in Moscow. There I saw hundreds of man's best friends fastened to boards on their backs, their innards exposed to test certain drugs, until they died. There were monkeys whose arms had been amputated then reimplanted on reverse sides of the body to see if limb transplantation would be feasible. But those were just a few of the millions and millions of animals suffering like this in laboratories all over the world and eventually killed. Doctors, supposedly the most humane among us, are the worst offenders.

On that sweltering day in December twenty-five years ago in Lambarene, Schweitzer made an unusual admission. "I preach that we must all answer with our minds; yet I still tend to do it with my heart." It opposed much of what his "reverence" stood for. He continued, "It hurts to be reminded of it when I should be looking at priorities objectively. But even priorities include cruelty. I admit my personal answer explains nothing. My answer should be intellectual not emotional." Then he bent forward a bit and said, "In nature, life is not all at one level; and one level of life must compete with other levels of life unreasonably. But we hope more reasonably by those endowed with brain power." He looked out of the window, his deep eyes searching.

I pondered this complicated answer; for I knew we gassed cats and dogs by the millions with even less reason, if any at all, under the excusable "humane" societies, but in reality because they are too numerous, are a nuisance. Yet they are no threat. Sure they may starve, but I wondered why not let them compete just like humans do, and leave it to chance whether some might survive.

The conversation was getting too heavy and Schweitzer didn't seem to be enjoying it. But I felt compelled to go just one large step further.

"Dr. Schweitzer, there is one other terrible moral problem that crops up here. It concerns some closer cousins, not just bacteria and ants. Suppose I posed the problem of experimentation with human life?"

"Human life!" he jerked his head up, shocked.

Talking as fast as I could before he could stop me, I said, "You know scientists experiment with primates such as your beloved chimpanzees. And that scientists choose the animal that is closest to the human on the phylogenetic scale because their psyche, soma, and physiology are most similar to ours and thus give us the most valid results. Yet we also know that the higher animals with more advanced brains think more and suffer more."

He nodded.

I then went into *his* special definition of "humans"—

that humans do know that they know, and animals may or may not know that they know. (In the seventies, social and educational experiments at the Yerkes Laboratory in North Carolina and the work of Jane Goodall in Africa proved that chimpanzees not only know but can even point out human errors in certain tests, producing questions and answers of a cognitive nature.)

Schweitzer, looking pained, said almost in a whisper, "Yes, I often think chimpanzees and apes may to a degree 'know that they know.' We had a baby Great Ape here which was so very intelligent." Then he interrupted himself, "Did you really mean experimentation with humans?" It was as if he wanted me to get on with what I was driving at.

"Yes," my voice was strained. "I bring it up only on the basis of your 'reverence' logic and its priorities in making a choice for experimentation. Why should we experiment with and make suffer a chimpanzee or monkey when there are some humans who we are positive have less probability of knowing or feeling anything? Some have no I.Q. and may not react at all, may have less ability to suffer than the ape. It is certainly true of the severely retarded, the brain damaged, or the hydrocephalic, and other congenital tragedies with no chance in life. Yet we nurture them until they die. From my personal experience, they have less ability to love or even know that they are loved."

I then recited my experiences with retarded children. "I've played with them daily in the wards; yet when I would leave for a weekend or a month there was neither a reaction of sadness when I left nor happiness when I returned. There was just an emotional void—an unknowingness. The nurses who fed and bathed them every day got the same nonreaction. These children seem, at times, really almost-inert matter.

"On the other hand, as soon as Phoebe and I pack our bags at home, our dogs know we're leaving and are not only saddened but depressed. The people who take care of them while we're away tell us they mope around for weeks. When we return they jump all over us. Under similar circumstances, I'd think a chimpanzee would react even more morosely when a friend leaves and happier when he returns. So wouldn't you then say, in all compassion and for the best results, we ought to choose the retarded human for experimentation over either the dog or the chimp?"

I paused, waiting. When Schweitzer answered, it was very slowly.

"The decision to kill anything is crucial; yet I know in order to preserve life we must destroy life. But to kill another human for whatever reason is impossible for me. The death penalty, even for the worst criminals, is debated every day in most civilized societies. But I tell you frankly the question you pose is difficult for the 'reverence' philosophy. So what can I say about experimenting with one of our closest ancestors much less another human? Yet," he said thoughtfully, "with all of the family travail of a congenitally malformed child with few human traits, a mother frequently becomes most attached to and showers more love on him or her than on her normal ones." He paused again. We began to speak of other aspects of "reverence," and the conversation brought to mind one of the many physicians who performed experiments on humans and whom I thought Schweitzer had told me he knew. "Dr. Schweitzer, didn't you tell me that you knew Professor Sauerbruch, Germany's foremost surgeon, at one time?"

"Yes, I knew him well."

"There is a new book about him . . ." Before I could say more, as if he knew what I would say, Schweitzer said,

"I've heard the rumor of his experimentation on Jews. But, in his defense, I must say that in Sauerbruch's last years he was senile and demented."

"Yet," I answered, "according to this rather authoritative book, he was not senile when he condoned murder and was part of human experimentation."

Schweitzer's face sagged; he suddenly looked frail and old and I was sorry I brought it up. Supporting his contention of Sauerbruch's senility, he said, "I think he *was* senile, for it was said he did many fatal operations because he would forget what he was doing or even where he was. It was said that at times he would leave in the middle of a surgical procedure and his assistants would have to cover up for him." (This is too horrible to contemplate; but, even in today's modern surgical world, it happens with alcoholic or drug-addicted surgeons.)

"Dr. Schweitzer," I objected, "the book stated that Sauerbruch did human experiments in 1942 before his senility. And what about the other German doctors, like Mengele, who performed experiments on the inmates in concentration camps?"

"I can't visualize," he said murmuring morosely, "the circumstances under which any human, much less a doctor, could do this."

Not wanting to push these harsh personal memories, I switched to another aspect of this subject. Could he possibly think of letting the life support of food, drink, or medication be discontinued on a terminal cancer patient who is in terrible pain? I also brought up the many monster-type children—blind, deaf and dumb, some with hardly any brains at all. "Right now in many hospitals, we quietly let these babies die by withholding nutrition and medication."

Still disturbed, Schweitzer said between compressed lips, "Yes, I know that happens. And it may be more merciful and even more ethical to let a life expire," he sighed, "but I couldn't let life just expire."

Though Schweitzer's philosophy of Reverence for Life depended on intellectual decisions, here he was again using his emotions not his intellect. But as he said, "When we make a life and death sentence decision for God's highest creation, even in the most ethical terms, emotions intrude."

I wondered aloud, "Would Jesus, with His heartfelt empathy, have dealt with the suffering humans who had no chance of survival? Would you think that if He lived today His compassion would be deep enough for Him to relieve human suffering by cutting off life support, if a patient requested it?"

At first he evaded a direct answer by saying, "Jesus performed miracles, so why should He allow a human life to end if there is a possibility of a miracle?"

"Dr. Schweitzer, as a scientist, you don't really believe in miracles?"

He confessed, "No, there are no organic miracles that can be explained but some so-called miracles may be because of something we do not know. We've both seen deathly ill patients survive. The miracle of Jesus' time may have been mainly allegorical or even imbued by a hysterical fervor or self-hypnosis; but, as my work on Christ showed, we must judge a man only in the milieu of his times."

He then answered my question directly. "Maybe if Jesus were alive today, with His compassion for mankind, it might possibly encompass the limits of human life itself. But today it is a terrible decision for a physician and for the State."

Here, Schweitzer showed his prescience. He anticipated the furor, the moral, and legal questions mercy killing posed. Should the family's wishes or the government's wishes prevail over an infant microcephalic such as Baby Jane Doe with an open spinal cord, bladder, and bowel dysfunction, and with practically no chance to ever live a normal life? Should surgery be done on that child to extend its life for a year or two when the family and physician, in their judgment, were taking the compassionate, if not the legal or moral way by withholding treatment?

This entire conversation must have bothered Schweitzer, because a few nights before Phoebe and I left he brought the subject up again in another vein.

18

REMEMBRANCES
AND COMPARISONS

It was a sodden hot Saturday; the weather fluctuated between sudden downpours, lasting no more than minutes, and a blazing sun and breathtaking heat beating through the ever-present fluffy white clouds. Everywhere steam rose, from the earth, the river, and even from the concrete gutters where the open sewage flowed through the hospital compound. That afternoon, at 4:00, there was to be a dedication of a new Schweitzer building at the old Mission. We were all going to the site of the house in which Schweitzer had lived his first few years in Lambarene.

At 2:30, sixteen of us assembled near the landing and arranged ourselves, for balance, in four large *pirogues* plus one small one that Siegfried, the intellectual handyman, had built for himself. The large *pirogues* were each manned by three black oarsmen, all standing, one in front and two in back. As Schweitzer came down the hill in his usual rush—he was always late—I noticed that he was not wearing his pith helmet, which was highly unusual. Instead, he had on his old beat-up felt hat. He called it his European hat and wore it at a very rakish angle; it was the one he was buried in.

The poorly fitted, wrinkled, tan cotton coat he wore for special events hung open; however, the outfit was formalized by a white shirt and his black clip-on bow tie. I must say, though Schweitzer's clothes were completely disheveled, he was a handsome sight. It reminded me of an anecdote he had once told in which he'd told someone who was going to introduce him on a stage in Europe to "just say, 'he is the one on the end that looks like an unclipped Russian wolfhound.' "

Schweitzer took over as soon as he reached the landing, counted all who were waiting, seemed satisfied, and with a brisk *allons* got into the lead *pirogue*.

The trip downriver to the Mission, which stood alone in a cleared area of jungle, took about forty minutes.

The white pastor, a mousey, balding little man, his wife, a few neighboring whites, and many more black natives met us as we pulled up to the landing. The Blacks were spic and span and sported Western dress, coats, and ties and wore patent leather shoes. Two of them had cut a goodly portion out of the leather from over the small toe to alleviate the painful pinching of their feet, splayed by twenty or so years of walking barefoot.

There was also a group of about thirty native adolescents, all scrubbed and smiling but in less formal dress and barefoot—not having reached the sophisticated state of higher education calling for shod feet. There was yet another group of ten or so younger natives on the lawn above us who killed time by playing soccer. The school taught about 120 native children, from grade school through gymnasium (high school). Some of the upper classmen were twenty-five to thirty years old because many did not start school until they could be spared from the "hut" (home). They were all converted Christians of sorts.

The old church, by the shore of the Ogowe River, looked New Englandish except that the steeple and bell tower were sheathed in a ghastly mauve asbestos shingle. The main part of the building, with its wooden, Gothic window frames (with no panes) and one central Gothic door jamb (with no door) was shabbily peeling down to the bare wood. Inside were plain, wooden, backless benches and a central aisle. At the far end stood a simple altar with a handmade wooden cross behind it.

When we reached the new house, Schweitzer went all through it. He tested some of its supports, looked closely at the workmanship, and finally nodded his approval. The pastor made a speech from the top of the porch steps. Then all the black students, standing below with the whites, sang a song they had composed. It was about Schweitzer and his hardships in the early days of the Mission, some forty-seven years before. The ceremony concluded with Schweitzer cutting a French tricolor ribbon.

After the ceremony I stood looking out over the river, and Schweitzer beckoned me to a side porch and gestured toward a fragile-looking delapidated small building about twenty feet away. It was made partly of decayed wood and rough concrete, with patched corrugated iron sides, and a thatch roof that was almost gone. The foundation was a greenish, crudely chisled rock. This was Schweitzer's first hospital.

His eyes glistened just looking at it. His voice quavered, "The day I arrived at this Mission there were dozens of patients with their families already waiting for me. News had been spread by drum and word of mouth that a white doctor was coming. I couldn't disappoint them. I was the only doctor within a thousand square miles, so I had to put the filthy old shack to immediate use."

Schweitzer leaned over the balustrade and, smiling to himself, reminisced. "Over there on the side of the house was a deserted bamboo and thatch hut, an addition to a kitchen. We cleaned it out and used it for a diagnostic and admitting clinic. There were no other out-buildings except the one used as a chicken coop by our predecessor. We needed something for a pharmacy and operating room, so Helene and I immediately began to clear out and convert the old roofless coop into a surgery and treatment area. We put up shelving, storage bins, and even built the stove. In one corner, over the brick stove with an iron grate, over an open fire, my wife Helene sterilized my instruments and dressings."

As he talked, Schweitzer drummed his long fingers along the railing. Then he was quiet, as if a flood of memories were swirling through his head. He pointed out how he had divided the little chicken shanty into three rooms (see drawing). The stove was in the room that became the O.R.; the rest of the shack was divided into two smaller rooms for a dispensary and pharmacy and for a place to store drugs.

"I don't know quite how I survived that first year," he mused. "I had few instruments, only simple drugs for dysentery and malaria, some iodine and Gentian Violet for wounds, and hardly enough dressings. My quinine, aspirin, bromides, and ointments were almost out before the next shipment was due to arrive. What paper I had brought for record keeping was eaten by termites and lasted barely two months."

(When I visited Gunsbach in early 1983, Ali Silver had a batch of his old records, including some of the original ones. Every scrap of paper or cardboard with white space on it was used. One patient's record was on the back of one of Schweitzer's 1913 wedding announcements.)

Turning his back on the little hospital, he murmured

feelingly, "I remember the first night we slept here under netting. There were all kinds of flying life, from large bats to huge mosquitoes and what looked like immense dragonflies. But we couldn't be bothered with those annoyances; there were so many patients needing treatment and not enough room inside to examine them." He shook his head. "We had to do that over here, outside." Turning back he pointed to one side of the tiny building. "When it rained, there wasn't any place that most of the patients could go, so they just got soaked.

"Looking back, I still can't believe that, with only my wife giving the crude anesthetic and a helper who had some dispensary experience, I did a strangulated hernia in the little chicken coop that first week." He continued, shaking his head and staring at the broken-down shack, "Without antibiotics and with hardly any shelter, that patient went home in a few weeks. I was so grateful and so proud of that case."

I remembered reading that so sparse were his resources during those early days that he ordered that when the pills or elixirs were given out the small bottles or tins (other containers wouldn't last a week) had to be returned before the patient could be treated again. Even then, Schweitzer worked from 8:00 in the morning to 6:00 in the evening every day except Sunday. I suddenly had a deep feeling of empathy.

He continued, "We held simple services on Sunday for anyone who wanted to come. The natives called me *Oganga* ("white fetisher"); and I guess, with what I had to work with, I was probably more a fetisher than a medical doctor. Thinking back on how I coped with leprosy, malaria, sleeping sickness, and tropical sores, among a hundred other diseases, plus my own difficulties of getting used to the climate, I can only conclude that God must have been with me."

Taking me by the arm, he guided me down the steps and around the back of his one-room hospital to a clearing.

"During the First World War, I grew tomatoes there," he pointed to a small overgrown patch of weeds. "You didn't know I was a dangerous enemy. See down there," he pointed to what was left of a wooden hut. "This is where the soldiers stayed who guarded me as a prisoner of war. Alsace was part of Germany at the time, and the French had me under house arrest. They wouldn't even let me treat my patients—that is, until some of their officers got sick and their doctor sent them to me because he had no knowledge of tropical diseases. Also, the native chiefs complained to the French commandant about their sick people."

I said, in passing, "This old chicken coop hospital might be fixed up as something historic."

I couldn't believe his reaction. He grasped my arm firmly and asked it I really thought that could be done; his eyes sparkled, expressing hope and delight at the idea.

As we walked back around to the new buildings, and talked to some of the young students, Schweitzer suddenly looked at the sky. "We have to go; a storm is coming up." The sky looked no different to me, but Schweitzer had a peculiar knack for predicting storms. With the others, we gathered at the landing and hurried into our *pirogues*.

Schweitzer asked me to join him in his *pirogue*, and the two of us sat in the rear, two others took the front seat and, sculling in his homemade boat, Siegfried led the way. Schweitzer, still exuberant, wanted to continue our talk. I was seated in front of him and had to turn half around as we talked.

The sky was darkening as we shoved off. As we smelled the ozone of a coming storm, the jungle noises seemed louder than usual and were interspersed with the grunts, chants, and shouts of the oarsmen. The huge kapoc tree branches towered menacingly over the shorter, greener foliage; and the river grew darker. Suddenly a cloud of white birds appeared, in tight formation, alongside us, only inches off the river. They were a flock of herons that kept to a rigid schedule of flying down the river at 6:00 a.m. and back up around 5:00 p.m. As we progressed up the river, the Saturday night drums began to throb on the opposite bank.

Rather offhandedly, Schweitzer commented, "I finished the review you gave me of Teilhard's book, *The Divine Milieu*. Have you read the book?"

"No," I said, "I just bought it a few weeks before I left and I haven't gotten into it yet."

"Have you read his other books?"

"Some of them." Then I told him that I had seen the draft forms of the manuscripts in Teilhard's quarters in Peking; he wrote in longhand. Back in Paris the Jesuit Order had forbidden the publishing of any of his theories, expecially those related to evolution. Teilhard, though a very flexible man, seemed to still live by the strict Jesuit code of obedience, chastity, and poverty, which, from what I've seen, not many do. (In New York in 1985 an elderly female philosopher at Columbia surprised me by revealing that Teilhard had had a mistress in New York for twenty-two years.)

Back in 1946, Teilhard had told me he was going to send copies of each manuscript to Paris to an old nun friend of his, Jeanne Mortier, for safekeeping. "Who knows," he said, "maybe someday the Vatican might see their value."

I related to Schweitzer, "After Teilhard's death I tracked the nun down, and we spent an afternoon talking in her austere little cell in a cloister right in the center of Paris. She must have then been around seventy-five; she was small and a bit heavy but still very feisty. She told me that Teilhard had had no notion that his works would ever be printed. She said rather bitterly, 'He did more for the Church than they ever did for him.' She felt he had too many important things to say for those manuscripts to be buried and his name forgotten."

Schweitzer leaned toward me, intensely interested; he undoubtedly compared Teilhard's problems to his own with the Church. Schweitzer and Teilhard have frequently been compared by many who knew both or knew of their trials with the Church. Their similarities were not only in the irrational treatment by their respective Churches but in their creative works, their attempts to change the outlook of their Churches, in their broad liberal concepts of what religion should be and in the many professional facets in which each of them excelled. They were both also great devotees of Darwin.

Anxious to hear how the Church responded, he urged, "What did the Church do when they were published?"

"What could they do?" I declared shrugging, "He was dead and she was retired."

For me, that wasn't the end of the story. In 1967, I went to Rome with Vice President Humphrey on an official trip. We had an audience with Pope Paul VI for nearly half an hour. Pope Paul and Humphrey were old friends.

Near the end of the audience, disregarding Vatican protocol that questions come only from the Pontiff, I said, "Your Eminence, I know it's not proper for me to question you, but something has been bothering me for years; it's about a great Jesuit." The State Department people who were with us were aghast; but the Pope waved his hand as if to say, "Don't mind the protocol," and indicated that I was to proceed. "I knew Pierre Teilhard de Chardin in Peking, China, back in 1946," I said, "and I thought that the goodness of that man couldn't but be realized by anyone who knew him." The Pope nodded his head and I continued. "It's been so many years now, and the Church still has not acknowledged his writings."

"I knew him," the Pope said. "He was not only a good man but a good priest; I am familiar with his work." Then he took my hand in his and said gently, "My friend, don't worry, we are studying him and his works now. It won't be long."

Today, nineteen years later, I have not yet heard any announcement about Teilhard from the Church.

By this time our *pirogues* had arrived back at our dock. It was pitch dark and there were occasional flashes of lightning and the rumble of thunder. As it began to rain, Schweitzer got out first and an oarsman handed him a lantern. Without looking back, he waved; and, in the glow from his lantern, I could see him tugging at his clip-on tie and opening his collar as he headed toward his room.

We had been served cold cuts and wine at the dedication, so dinner that night was very light and late. Afterward, Schweitzer still seemed intrigued by Teilhard and the Church. After the others, except for Dr. Adler, had left, Schweitzer and I stayed at the table and talked.

Taking up where we left off, Schweitzer said rather touchingly, "Teilhard must have had a miserable life (implying that it was the Church's fault); but he was a great thinker and could have brought the Church out of the dark ages, especially in relation to science and evolution. Sometimes I feel like a brother to him." Then, ruminating almost to himself, and shaking his head sadly, "Can one believe that in our age that a Church wouldn't have accepted Darwin?"

"Dr. Schweitzer, I don't think Teilhard was miserable but he didn't do as you did and press his convictions," I interjected. "Teilhard had told me once in a very kindly manner, 'They sent me from Paris to Africa so that the students would not be tainted by my scientific heresy. And yet that is where I learned so much about Darwin. It was through study of early man and his relationship to his animal ancestry.' " The exile, which the Church had imposed on him as punishment, had given him time to think and formulate his theories relating to evolution and the holy spirit—just what the Church had forbidden. Unfortunately, on his return from Africa it became known that he was again teaching his students his "heresy."

Soon thereafter, the Church leaders ordered him to China, where in his anthropologic work he was fortunate in having the time to help find the Peking Man—which disappeared when Japan invaded China. Teilhard had shown me four unpublished manuscripts which later evoked such controversy. What Teilhard had done was simply to explain how a true rapprochement between science (evolution), the Church, the mind, and the spirit could accrue to the Church's benefit.

Schweitzer came back to the review he had read. "Teilhard had a vision of God, and that is the difference between us; I have none." Then, continuing the comparison, in an even tone, "It's the spirit of God, not the vision; and I'm sure that's how Teilhard also found his peace.

"Did Teilhard ever show the anguish that the Church had caused him?" Schweitzer asked, concernedly.

"Never by word—maybe occasionally by his eyes. We had many chance meetings either in the city or when he visited at the Peiping Union Medical College, which I administered. But we had dinner together every Thursday night. It was during those evenings that he told me so much, but he never said an unkind word about his Church." (Neither had Schweitzer, publicly.)

We used to meet at the French embassy; they had a weekly soiree, attended by important military officers and Peking socialites, with cocktails, talk, and cards. We would

skip the cards and go to a small Italian restaurant near the
Chien Mein Gate and talk until very late. He was most
relaxed then. He was a delightful dinner companion and
seemed at peace with himself and his Church. I learned much
from him.

Returning to Schweitzer's use of the phrase "vision of
God," I said, "I don't think Teilhard meant his 'vision'
literally; but, if he did, keep in mind that he was brought up
from childhood deep in the Church."

"So was I," Schweitzer responded firmly.

"But he was a Jesuit," I argued. "Though by far the
most intellectual order, they are still the most rigid in their
discipline. In other words, *he was not totally free.*"

Schweitzer laughed, his eyes twinkling, "I don't know
how free they are, but I'm glad I was never a Jesuit. I guess
they wouldn't have kept me in the order for very long. As I've
said, he and I crossed a mountain in different ways. He went
around the base; I crossed directly over the peak. But we
invariably met on the other side. But I think he believed in
Jesus more conventionally than I."

"Maybe," I said, "but regardless of how Teilhard
believed, he had his own rational thoughts about man's place
in the universe, not unlike you. Also, like your work, his
could have freed the Church from reflex dogmas."

Schweitzer was still comparing himself with Teilhard.
"I also may be different from Teilhard in that I really don't
try to solve secrets of nature—" Then this most creative man
astonished me "—even through science. I don't really create.
I try to interpret correctly. That's all I did with the historical
Jesus and with Paul, and I've been personally happy with
living by the ethics of what I've found."

This was a direct contradiction to what he once told
me: "I have never had a completely happy day in my life."
With his antennae so supersensitive to human and animal

misery, I could believe this earlier statement more readily. I reminded him of the contradiction, but he didn't explain the change.

Bluntly, I went on, "You know this is not the only opinion you've altered. You once said a man must find in life, aside from truth and love, his place in the universe. Haven't you found yours? I can understand what a tiny percentage of the people of the world down through the ages—even now—even wonder, much less think, about who and why they are. If so, how can one spread truth or love—much less explain why man is on earth—which you said you expect when people are almost totally concerned only with self?"

Schweitzer turned the subject on me. "You are a rank pessimist."

"Dr. Schweitzer, in some of your writings, you have voiced more skepticism than I. Haven't you written of the moral and spiritual corruption of modern man? Isn't that one of the basic reasons you left, as you've put it, 'the moral decay of Europe'?"

"Yes," he said, but then playing with semantics, "that is skepticism, not cynicism."

"No," I went on, "in general, humans abhor thinking, especially about abstract ideas such as the spirit. Most people need something tangible to see with their mind's eye—God, Heaven, Peter at the Gates, even Hell and the Devil. If they have faith, it is blind and usually by dogma; it's easy and I think it works."

Schweitzer argued, spiritedly, "That's one of the Church's problems, they've given up on the rational. Of course, dogma is easier, but it doesn't stand up to scrutiny with a faith that would be lasting and lived by."

"But, Dr. Schweitzer, are you really surprised that the Church balked at your 'thinking man's faith'? I read a review by a Mr. Laurenfelder of one of your books, and he was defending you as *not* being an atheist. Did the Church accuse you of that?"

"Not with that word explicitly," Schweitzer explained pensively, "but by implication. If I didn't believe in Jesus the way they did I was not a believer. But since when does rationality and historical fact preclude mysticism or piety." Then he repeated his religious creed once again. "People can be stimulated to think out their faith."

"Most cannot think it out as deeply as you would like but perhaps blind faith is better than none. Even going to Church once a week does some good," I reiterated.

He defended his stand. "People cannot feel the spirit of Jesus blindly and that is mainly the Church's fault." He wound up by again calling me a rank pessimist.

Suddenly the intense odor of ozone filled the air. It had stopped raining but it was about to start again. A tremendous clap of thunder struck, whereupon Schweitzer got up, handed his Bible to Dr. Adler, took his lantern, and headed for the door calling out *vite* ("quickly"). Before he was halfway down the steps, with Adler and me close behind him, the deluge began. I was soaked to the skin by the time I got to my room. Phoebe was already asleep. I dried off and fell into bed exhausted. It had been a long day; and, despite the persistent drumming of the rain on the corrugated iron roof, I was asleep in minutes.

19

JESUS: MESSIAH OR PARANOIAC?

After a time at Lambarene, I was usually able to recognize many of Schweitzer's moods and habits. I came to know when he wanted and didn't want a break from his many chores. Throughout the day, nurses, doctors, and various workmen stopped by his desk in the pharmacy. If he didn't want to be bothered, he'd look up for a moment and answer the question or he would just keep writing and only wave his pen as a sign of recognition. But when he swiveled all the way around in his chair and encased the nib of his glass pen in its piece of rubber tubing, and said "So," I would sit down and we'd talk.

The day after Friedman's episode with the violent mental patient, Schweitzer motioned for me, as I passed his desk, to sit down. It seemed that the problem of psychiatric patients, which I had brought up before, was on his mind.

Our conversation this time began with an admission of

shame over the violent patients who suffered in locked airless cells without much light, water, or toilet facilities. "I've always thought it was a crime to cage animals, so why humans? But what else can we do with the violent patients who must be separated from the others? The psychiatric wards and treatment in Libreville are no better. We badly need new buildings." Schweitzer's voice was strained. "If I were up to it, I would make one last concert tour to raise money for a new psychiatric ward."

It was the first time that I had ever heard him mention, even in a casual way, his health, his lack of strength, or his travel limitations. He always put up such a vigorous and vibrant front.

As an afterthought he mused, "I've never made a concert tour in America, but I did play before a few small groups during my stay for the Aspen Lectures. Maybe I will now." (Unfortunately, Schweitzer never made the tour. In fact, he never left Lambarene between 1961 and his final days in 1965.)

Schweitzer mentioned that mental illness was a terrible problem in Africa. He had once gone to the Cameroons, and the Mission doctor there told him that they had many demented patients but no doctors equipped to treat them. "There are few enough general physicians of any kind, much less psychiatrists, who will come here from the cities," he said.

I questioned, "Why should there be such a prevalence of mental disease in Africa? Why should this be, with such a simple life in the bush and with so few of the stresses common to modern society?"

Schweitzer spoke lingeringly of his "Children of Nature" who may not have the problems commonly brought on by the speed and tension of life in New York or Paris. "But," he said, gesturing with his hands, "other than their psychoses, they still have ambitions, frustrations, the difficulty of family life, plus the problem of the men being uprooted and separated from their families when they had to travel a hundred miles to work in lumbering or in the mines. Added to this were also the superstitions, taboos, and the fears inculcated by the fetish doctors."

Schweitzer's detailed reply surprised me. He obviously had observed, thought, and studied psychiatric problems among the primitives more extensively than any other native problem I'd heard him discuss. He also was very knowledgeable about modern psychiatric principles.

"I have a terrible ache in my heart for these mental patients," he confessed earnestly. His expression softened. "I know what they are going through. And added to their sickness, they are shunned by families and neighbors as having evil spirits. In some villages, the cure is to throw them in the river—maybe a primitive form of shock therapy. But even here we can't do much more. We treat them with sedatives or Thorazine and just pen up the more destructive ones."

As frequently happened, after about ten minutes our conversation veered off from where it had began. But it was still concerning psychiatry. We eventually got around to the two subjects that I had hoped we could discuss.

One was his *Psychiatric Study of Jesus.* I had read this book of his rather quickly before Phoebe and I came to Lambarene.

The other, of even more importance, was his own bouts with depression. Rumors of this were bruited around the compound; but I had also heard about them from one of his most ardent admirers, Norman Cousins. Schweitzer himself had once alluded to them, in an off-handed although rather personal way, when he let drop, "You can't imagine the utter despair, but more, the impotence, of a person with mental disease trying to get hold of his own mind." It occurred to me that this interest in psychiatry could have been prompted by his own problems.

He continued pensively, "I have carefully watched many of our mental patients with and without drugs. (I remembered how closely he'd observed Mama San Nom.) I've come to feel that maybe mental illness is not caused as much by the stresses of life as Freud believed."

"Do you know Freud's work?" I interrupted.

"Now I do. But I didn't when I wrote my medical school senior dissertation *(The Psychiatric Study of Jesus)*. But in the back of my mind, I have always had a suspicion that there may be a pure biologic reason for mental upsets."

His prescience was extraordinary. Today, with micro-neurologic and genetic research, and the experiments stimulating various areas of the brain to initiate certain emotional responses, a biologic—possibly genetic—basis for mental illness is getting even greater support. The very fact that the use of tranquilizers has allowed the release of almost fifty percent of the patients in mental hospitals makes this theory that much more plausible.

It was surprising that Schweitzer had this thought as far back as 1911 or 1912—long before much was known about psychiatric illness and long before it became a household word.

It was then, for the second time, that he made reference, although a minor one, to his own mental health.

"I guess I researched mental illness more thoroughly than would be expected for a medical school graduation thesis. As busy as I was with concerts to pay for my education, my speaking engagements, preaching, and writing, I was obsessed." He shook his head slowly, "I couldn't get *The Psychiatric Study of Jesus* out of my mind. I worked myself into a terrible mental fatigue and at one point thought of giving the subject up and starting on an easier one." He couldn't, only because of the way it had been initiated.

"Some years earlier I had come across inferences, made by some learned professors, that Jesus was paranoid. It stuck in my mind. So when I was taking the scant psychiatric studies then offered in medical schools, the point I made in the *Historical Jesus*—that Jesus's belief in the supernatural gave credence to those professors and their insanity theory—worried me. This view also cast doubt on my interpretation of Jesus' intellect. Those eminent psychiatrists were misinterpreting the Gospel, exactly as did the Church, and also took things out of context."

So it was partly through the professional pride in his own work and the necessity of defending his thesis that he wrote on that subject. It was another obsessive battle to prove himself right.

He continued, somberly, "Those doctors made the same mistake that the eighteenth- and nineteenth-century Church made: they thought Jesus alone believed that the world was coming to an end, and they ignored the fact that it was actually the common belief among the Jews of that day. Also, they took for granted, just as the Church did, that Jesus thought that He was the son of God—which He didn't—and purportedly announced to the people that He was the Messiah—which He never did. So, with those Church-oriented hypotheses, the psychiatrists were wrong in labeling Him a paranoid with a persecution complex and delusions of grandeur."

Schweitzer seemed to be saying that if the psychiatrists were considered right the *Quest* would be considered wrong. "I was already a heretic among my theologic peers; if the psychiatrists' theories were accepted, my work would be even more denied. But, if I proved them wrong about an insane

Schweitzer with his "dear cousin"

Phoebe's swain, patiently waiting for her to appear

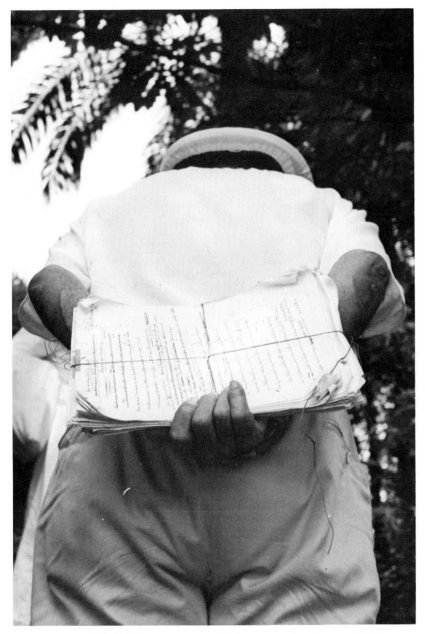

The string-tied manuscript of the second volume of *The Philosophy of Civilization*, snatched from a stealthy nibbling goat

A pensive moment

Jesus, which I think I did, it would add credibility to my work. It was just something I had to do."

I asked Schweitzer how he could disprove the other doctors and determine that Jesus was sane without having a "detailed case history." Didn't he himself tell me that the only reliable accounting of Jesus' entire life was over a period of not less than six months and probably not more than a year? And that was during Christ's last year as a preacher. What's more, it came secondhand from the Gospels which probably were written a hundred or so years later. There was also no valid evidence regarding His family life—His relationships with His mother, His father, or His siblings. And in his own book Schweitzer said Jesus' short ministry came only from certain parts of the Gospels of Mark and Matthew and a little of Luke.

Schweitzer answered obliquely, "It's they who had to prove Him insane; all I am saying is that they couldn't possibly do it on the basis of their knowledge."

What hubris, the faculty leaders must have angrily thought, for a mere student like Schweitzer to try to refute these professors of psychiatry. How could he possibly think he had the knowledge to prove them wrong?

Schweitzer answered the question I had in my mind. "From my research and training, I knew more about the true history of Jesus than they did—which of course is crucial; and they were physicians, not theologians or historians. Furthermore, their critical source material was unhistorical. They may have known more about psychiatry; however, because of my earlier writings, I had as much experience, if not more, in critical writing—which is more important in this instance. As little as my psychiatric experience was, I don't think any psychiatrist in those days had that much more. However, just comparing their bibliography to mine, I'd say theirs was inferior. Besides, even then I had a special feel for the mentally disturbed," he said assuredly.

In this last phrase, again, there was another hint, but certainly no sure indication, of Schweitzer's personal problems.

Schweitzer felt positively about his information concerning Jesus because he was stating facts he had researched himself. He never backed down when he felt he was on sure ground, especially with knowledge from his own findings. Concerning the research of others or hearsay, he acted quite differently and would frequently back off and admit he wasn't sure. But the confident and assured way he expressed his opinion to me was probably the reason that some of his professional critics thought him abrupt, arrogant, and overbearing.

"But," I came back, "suppose someone in Libreville or Berlin or Strasbourg were to start preaching in the streets and implied that he was the Messiah and that he would die for them and would return on a cloud at the right hand of God, surrounded by angels and ready for judgment day, would they think *he* was the true Messiah? Wouldn't most people, especially those who knew Jesus before he became a rabbi, agree with the psychiatrists that He was crazy?"

"Yes, and some did," he admitted. "But Jesus had a huge following who believed in Him. There were also the predictions of the prophets Elijah and Daniel. What's more, most He gave hope to were the poor. They also had great faith in Jesus and His new and revolutionary ethics. Jesus saw the fraudulence of His times and had the nerve to expose it and preach a message in the context of the then-common knowledge. It all boiled down to ethics—especially His concept of love, which was original—which were the keys to the kingdom of a supernatural heaven.

"Not only that, but just the fact of His teachings

lasting so long—history at least has proven Him right. His concepts have also given succor to so many over those years. Even if Jesus thought, as most others did then, that the kingdom was in the supernatural world, He still did much to establish the thought of a "kingdom" here on earth. He was the essence of sanity," Schweitzer said emphatically.

However, I could still see the justification for the psychiatrists' theories. Sure, Jesus was a radical rabbi with a sane and original message. But, as a physician myself, even without a real case history, I felt Jesus could still be a paranoid personality because of His delusions of grandeur and a megalomania—at least as evidenced by some of what He said.

I repeated my ideas in another way. "Dr. Schweitzer, we don't believe in prophets today, and I'm sure you don't believe in fortune tellers and certainly not in palm readers (he smiled at my reference to Phoebe and her palm reading), but there are thousands of people roaming the city streets quoting the prophets and waving signs reading 'Repent, the end is near;' and they're considered fanatics, not Messiahs."

"Yes," he came right back, "but Jesus knew then that there was no possible hope for the masses other than that belief in Elijah and Daniel." Now Schweitzer was preaching more than explaining. "Jesus foresaw the basic problem of mankind and He tried to show the way—although a hard one. He was different from your street-corner prophet because He knew that His preachings would only bring calumny to Himself and show Him to be a pariah to his peers—the Temple priests—then and a danger to His disciples. He was a farseeing farseeing prophet and a possible Messiah in the sense that His teachings could bring inner peace individually and a better world collectively. Also, He preached a spiritual message never preached before—love—and it took root."

There was a long pause; then, looking pained,

Schweitzer said, "Read *The Psychiatric Study* again, carefully, and see if your views don't change. Remember, do it as if you are living in Jesus' time and then let me know how you feel and how you would feel if you were of that hopeless majority."

"Dr. Schweitzer, admitting that Jesus was a true believer and was willing to die to atone and redeem His followers on earth, what about His history from the Gospels? According to the psychiatrists, they quoted His hallucinations, His hearing of voices, and His delusions. Doesn't that clinch the diagnosis of paranoia even more?"

Schweitzer put his hand to his face pensively saying, "Ah, but the psychiatrists took that partly from the book of Luke and John," he remonstrated, "and I have already proven that they were just Greek embellishments, maybe a hundred years after the more believable accounts of Matthew and Mark. I've told you before that the Greek believers wanted to support Jesus' supernatural status—to give it more, not less, credibility."

I thought about the fine line between paranoia and sanity from my own experiences with politicians I've known. Many have a sense of Messiahship and, like Jesus, think in their hearts that they were put on earth to lead and serve, if not to suffer. They also proclaim their views loudly and strongly, and they may not say it but some actually believe they've been anointed by God. Yet they are considered sane.

Schweitzer went right on, "We mustn't forget that in our present-day world our great belief in science is taking the place of the arcane and the mystical of Jesus' time. And in a sense, through His preaching, which has come down with Christianity, life has certainly become somewhat better. Even the rich and powerful atone to a degree, if only under legal compulsion. (How in the world did he know that today much of philanthropy depends on relief from taxes?) However, through this giving they may have learned about the poor and obtained a good feeling from it. Look at what the Christ-given good will of just one day of Christmas has wrought for the poor and what the general good will of just that one day has done for most of mankind. All of this can be seen as sort of an atonement by society, and it seems to get better each year." He said nothing about the commercialism of Christmas. "Then look what Jesus' preachings have started on a worldwide scale among nations, with the Red Cross, UNICEF, the World Bank, and what they have done for the world's ignorant and poor. This was unknown even a hundred years ago. Considering the plight of the poor of thousands of years ago, we may be subtly seeking our own kingdom of heaven."

I looked him right in the eye, with a smile, and said, "Dr. Schweitzer, in appreciation for the peace Jesus has given you, you are repaying it by what you are doing here. You also have a worldwide following. Your philosophy has been worshipped by many more people than Jesus' was in his time. You preach the glories of man, and even the Nobel people think you are a man of peace—couldn't you be the real Messiah?"

He laughed, then grew serious. "But I have no thoughts of having been anointed. I don't think of myself as a Messiah. I preach to only a few; I'm not doing what I do for others; my atonement is personal. What's more, my inner thoughts are as sinful as most."

"Then why don't you think Jesus' thoughts reflected a type of megalomania—a classic symptom of paranoia?" I interposed quietly.

Schweitzer responded forcefully, "You're making the same mistakes that the psychiatrists made. First, there is a point, albeit a fine point, between megalomania and belief in oneself. Many very sane people with faith in themselves have a megalomania. But remember, this is two thousand years later. We are more educated and we ask for scientifically- and historically-researched evidence for what those psychiatrists took for nonacceptable heresy."

Before he could go on, Dr. Mueller came into the pharmacy and asked Schweitzer to see a patient. He rose, excused himself, and asked me to wait. He returned only a short time later looking preoccupied. But when he took the piece of rubber tubing off the nib of his pen, I knew he had no desire to continue our conversation. "We'll finish this some other day," he said as he started writing.

That same evening he came back to the topic of psychiatry, but not about Jesus.

20

A TROUBLED MIND?

As we finished dinner that evening, the weather had become even more humid and muggy than usual; and no one seemed interested in going back to his room, which would have been even more uncomfortable. I thought about changing into fresh clothes; I was already so sticky. Instead, I stayed to chat with Dr. Friedman and Dr. Mueller for a few minutes.

I mentioned to them that Schweitzer and I had discussed *The Psychiatric Study of Jesus* that morning. I felt he seemed to have an inordinate interest in psychiatry. At that, Friedman noted, "Maybe he has more than a professional interest in it." I didn't question him because I knew that the subject was hush-hush around the hospital. It just added another piece of evidence on one side of the enigma regarding Schweitzer's mental problems.

I didn't mean to play the psychiatrist and attach significance to every word Schweitzer uttered. However, even with my minimum background in psychiatry, there were certain statements that he made, hints he inadvertently dropped, and phrases he used that seemed to be obvious and meaningful leads, not only to his character but also to his rumored mental problems.

Just from the extensive bibliography included in Schweitzer's *Psychiatric Study*, I knew that he spent a great deal of time on his research; so maybe he did have more than a mere professional interest. I wondered if even when young he had had an inward inkling or warning, as some people do, of his own future mental problems. After all, how, back in 1911, could a student get so involved in such an embryonic specialty when even in today's advanced state of psychiatry only a smattering of that specialty is taught in medical schools?

In addition, he had apparently kept up to date with psychiatric literature. So already having Schweitzer's questionable mental status in mind, I was alerted to any small puzzle piece in trying to discern whether he had a real problem. If he did, how long did he have it and how severe was it?

After chatting a while with the two doctors, I went to Schweitzer's room. Continuing where we'd left off after breakfast, I said, "This morning you described yourself as a man with sinful thoughts. But even if you have the same sins as everyone else, haven't you atoned for them, after what you've done here the last fifty years?"

Though my rapport with Schweitzer had become very close, only once had he been direct with me concerning his problem. Otherwise, references to it were always by innuendo or in the abstract, as was his answer now.

"The extent of atonement can never be measured; it is an endless day-by-day job." His forehead creased in concentration. Then, softly, almost as if he were talking to himself, "There are the human faults of pride and egocentricity, which I have and which may be unconsciously hurtful to others. Look how prideful I am in defending my own theories in philosophy, religion, and even in music. And remember how short I was with you on your first day when you didn't take my advice in the operating room—that was a matter of face and officiousness which certainly are not virtues. I know how I also want things done my way. I'm abrupt, and occasionally I don't spare others' feelings."

There was an awkward silence as he looked down and stroked his fawn. Looking back up, he went on, "Sometimes I feel it's more a matter of self-righteousness than principle. Even as a child I had arrogant thoughts, especially about some of my teachers and even my parents. This depresses me greatly." It was the first time he had even used the word "depression" in reference to himself. He continued, with a troubled look, "Usually, the Spirit of Christ brings me back from those depths, but sometimes it's a long, drawn-out process; it doesn't happen overnight. In the interim there is great anguish."

When I first heard of Schweitzer's depressions I thought they were just fleeting episodes. But when he implied that his relief "didn't come overnight" and only Christ "revived" him, I felt his depressions may have been much more serious and prolonged. (In a 1975 biography by George Marshal, a friend and Unitarian Minister, it was conjectured that his depressions lasted five years; I am not so sure.)

After spending only one week with Schweitzer I had seen that one source of his mental troubles may have been a dogged, introspective mind—compulsively and unceasingly at work. This could fatigue the strongest mind, much less one with a possible weakness plagued by emotional pressures.

However, one also could not discount his congenital ultrasensitivity to all of the inadequacies and cruelties of life about him. After reading his *Memoirs of Childhood and*

Youth, (truly a self-analysis) I realized how painfully sentient his searching mind was and how only his mystical or deeply religious faith salved it.

Knowing I was getting close to his partly-kept secret— if the rumors were true and his own offhand admission of being depressed was a clue—I trod very lightly. "But you said that the Spirit always revives you."

He was silent, and then slowly answered, "It isn't that easy. I have to tediously fight hard, very hard, to rationalize my every thought according to my spiritual beliefs. At times this takes weeks and sometimes months. We don't always know what triggers our moods (he didn't say depression) or, in most cases, what brings us back from the depths."

Schweitzer spoke in the abstract, but he could only have been talking about himself, though he certainly never showed any signs of chronic or even intermittent depression during my stay at Lambarene.

The phase of his life that must have triggered his emotional problems was the period between 1916 and 1919. This was the time, during World War I, when so many devastating global and personal events occurred. He was a prisoner of war—first in Lambarene and then in France (imagine this genius dressed in prison garb and wearing wooden clogs). In southern France he was not only continuing his long separation from his wife but, even more anguishing, his hospital—his prime means of expiation.

Then, when he was exchanged and allowed to go back to Gunsbach, he learned of his mother's violent death as the result of an accidental trampling by German cavalry horses that came thundering through the village. He had written and also spoken of his guilt about not showing his love for her at their parting some four years before because he had stubbornly refused to take his mother's pleadings against "wasting his great talent by going to Africa."

Also, of course, there existed the stress on his sensitivities of man still butchering man in the First World War. It must have been a shattering blow to Schweitzer's dream of human beings ever evolving to a "Reverence for Life." And there was the added strain of a personal dilemma: whether he should go back to the work and turmoil of Africa to fulfill his spiritual responsibility.

During the time while Schweitzer was back in Europe, there is a hiatus of some years, largely unaccounted for.

Heaped upon this formidable group of circumstances during that difficult period was the existence of his organic illness. There were two operations, the exact nature of which were never revealed, whose physical and emotional ramifications could have helped wreak havoc with the stability of that great mind. Moreover, during some of this time, when he was a prisoner of war, he didn't even have the means for the release and placidity that his music always gave him.

As I thought about his past, Schweitzer continued, "How and why we act and react to certain people and circumstances in our childhood and youth is another secret that we may recognize only after much thought and may be yet unsolved, even using Freudian techniques." Here was another puzzle piece that implied he may have gone through much more analysis in Switzerland than cited and also that it may not have been of too much help.

Most of my analysis was both from my knowledge of his past and our present talks. But the one absolute fact was that, immediately following the war and while he was still in Europe, he first visited his "friend," a psychiatrist and pastor, Dr. Oscar Phister, in Zurich. No one seems to know how many visits he made or how many years these encompassed. One does know that Schweitzer himself insisted on writing the self analysis of his childhood and youth using the doctor's notes, and that must have taken more than one visit.

I spoke abstractly, just as he had. "Do you think a modern-day psychiatrist helps those who are disturbed?"

Schweitzer shook his head, "Not too much." (It has since been said that even Dr. Phister questioned whether analysis ever helped Schweitzer.) Then he said, "Once when I wasn't feeling well (which may have been a possible euphemism for his depressions), I guess I was about forty-four then, I spent a few hours talking about my youth to an old friend, a physician (this was the psychiatrist, Dr. Phister). He wanted to write about it and publish it. I asked him, 'Could you possibly know me better than I know myself after just talking with me for a few hours?' " This was the first direct admission to me that he had or once had had a problem.

Pointing to himself, "I told my friend to send his notes to me and I would write them up." This resulted in the book *Memoirs of Childhood and Youth.*

I think he was right about who could analyze those notes better. Few analysts could have brought out more about Schweitzer than he did himself in that 108-page book. I think there's no question in my mind that Schweitzer had more than one session with him. Dr. Phister never acknowledged this.

The book was written in German. I had it translated before I went to Lambarene. It gives valuable insights into both his weaknesses and strengths. In essence, what he wrote and expanded upon was partly brought out with Dr. Phister in Zurich. Just writing the book must have been good for his psyche.

From two sources—our conversations and the book— I got a glimpse of the inborn source of his acute sensitivity and his outlook on life and society with all the torment and compulsions it implied for his adult life. I could see the ancillary effect that his upbringing had on his inherited tendencies and also how he disciplined himself to keep some of his problems under control. It certainly showed the beginning and the development of his drives, his self-consciousness, his pride, his need for religion and discipline, his incipient creativeness, and his eventual love of work and music.

However, again, some of what he said was contradictory. For instance, he told me once that he had had a happy childhood. Yet, at another time he vacillated, saying that it's a rare child who is happy. Depending on the circumstances, both statements may be true at different times.

Schweitzer was not only torn by his unusual humanitarian feelings toward playmates, family, and his own radical thoughts on all life, but his psyche was torn by history. He was born and grew up in Alsace, just after the military and political turmoil of 1870. The province had just been taken from Catholic France and placed under the rule of Protestant Germany by the treaty of 1870. A new language had to be learned and a new loyalty had to be acquired, which must have caused a terrible confusion in his young mind.

Aside from this influence, he was weak and thin as a child and he perceived that his mother was ashamed of his appearance. He believed she tried to hide his puniness with clothing, though it was probably to shield him from the unkind comments of other boys. Then, he was brought up in a very religious household with perhaps frightening visions of God on the one side and the devil on the other. This may have made him take comfort in goodness and idealism, but it may also have left him with a residual fear of evil and its proponent, the devil.

Psychiatrists frequently blame the problems of the adult on rigid religious training. I don't think Schweitzer's religious training was rigid or forced; he seemed to accept it naturally. Though there was the constant invoking of God, sin, and redemption at his father's knee and especially in church, he seemed to respond to the actual services with enjoyment and to the theology and history with great curiosity. For a boy of five to love church and the long services was in itself unusual. Yet he remembered enjoying it all: the architecture, the trappings, the ritual, the music, the sermons, and even the smells. He even mentioned it having a tranquillizing effect on him.

However, the constant reminder of sin may also have created a need in him for a savior and an expression of atonement. And these were the very reasons he voiced for his eventually giving up almost everything, studying medicine, and going to Africa.

Schweitzer admitted having had the common childhood penchant for seeking attention; however, his persistence in this was extraordinary. Could this have been what drove him to achieve worldwide recognition? He revealed that in his childhood he faked and even lied to be seen and heard. Was going to Africa at the peak of his European career possibly another way to achieve renown?

He told me that, beginning early in life, he had a great sense of personal freedom and the need to be close to nature, especially to animals, and was entranced by the grandeur of trees. "During my first days at school, I thought I had lost my freedom forever and cried each morning as I walked to class. Later, when I transferred from our village to a larger town school, I missed my lone walks through the meadows and woods." This unconscious need may have also influenced his attraction to the unspoiled natural surroundings of Africa.

In addition, at even a preschool age, Schweitzer's ultrasensitivity was shocked by the callousness of people toward each other, and this had a long-term effect. The few Jews in his village were all tormented by most adults and mimicked by children. "Once I even went along with the other children and unthinkingly helped stone an old Jewish man. I never forgot that episode; it preyed on my mind for years. What obsessively stayed with me was the man's imperturbability in light of our cruelty."

Thus, during his youth, Schweitzer realized that he was just trying to be like the other children. "But in my heart I knew I wasn't. I hated their cruelty." From this and other experiences of this sort, Schweitzer learned early in life: he must be himself and he must go his own way. In this respect he never changed.

As he grew out of his puniness and became big and strong physically this presented another problem. Though not rich, he was taunted by his poorer schoolmates for his relative wealth; the criterion then, according to Schweitzer, was "meat in his soup"—on which they blamed his growing strength. Other boys were also jealous of his leather shoes; they wore wooden clogs. "I grew so ashamed of having so much more than my friends that I stopped eating my soup and wore wooden shoes like the rest of the children." Later, he wouldn't even ride his bicycle because none of the other kids had bicycles.

His father once tried to instill some sense into him regarding his reluctance to count his blessings. His mother continually berated him because he thought more of his classmates' accusations than he did of obedience to his parents. But he never recanted. His feelings about and sensitivity to the plight of others were touched, and they never diminished.

Yet despite his sensitivity, he at times felt superior and even arrogant. At the age of about eight, Schweitzer openly said that he knew more than his first music teacher. Though he was not then adept and would practice and memorize only reluctantly, he knew he was better than she at improvisation, a subject in which the teacher was not interested. Throughout his life his pride and compassion warred with each other.

"However in the case of that teacher," Schweitzer remembered, "I learned something I didn't know before: that was betrayal. I told my best friend in secret what I thought of that teacher and the friend told everyone—the first time I had ever been betrayed. I was crushed. But later in life I became used to betrayal by others on larger issues, such as by my clerical colleagues with the *Quest*, and by many musicians in my interpretations of Bach—and that hurt worse."

In music, as with other aspects of his life, he not only became highly controlled but early on condemned the lack of control in everyone else. Possibly because of this, his music teacher thought, long before he went to gymnasium, young Albert showed no heart when practicing a beautiful piece of music. According to Schweitzer, "I personally loathed to be sentimental or show emotion in any way at that time, however strongly I may have felt about a piece of music."

He soon became devoted to one highly disciplined teacher, which made him realize that in order to create one can't just improvise but must be tediously disciplined in every way. His discipline came only with practice and, as we know, it stuck. I think it was one of the major reasons why he could accomplish so much regardless of the environment in which he found himself.

His teacher became convinced of Schweitzer's sensitivity in music only later, when, hardly able to reach the pedals, Schweitzer replaced the village organist at Sunday services. By the time he was fifteen, little doubt existed about the depth of his feelings, especially when he was at the organ.

"At the age of sixteen," he confessed, "I found out for myself and became certain that for myself the only real beauty experienced in the arts was music. Though even then I hated to practice, I forced myself, but I still continued to improvise." It may have been his compulsive improvisation that predicted his future creativity. However, strangely enough, it wasn't in music.

At the age of eleven, in order to get a better education, he was sent to a larger village and stayed with an uncle. He said that he was aware of the other children's inferiority, and he was probably right. In games he was very competitive but had terrible outbreaks of temper. When he didn't win, he would frequently get violent, even with his sister. This worried him and he did something unusual for a child of his age: he gave up the games. However, this was no great sacrifice because even then he was beginning to like books more and like being with other children less. (I had seen signs at Lambarene that his temper hadn't diminished in degree during his later years.)

About this time, Schweitzer experienced a great lust for reading, but only what interested him. He often stayed up and read—not necessarily his school books—well into the early morning hours. During this period, his uncle considered taking him out of school because his reading didn't coincide with his studies, and he was achieving poor grades. This misbehavior was compounded by incessant daydreaming, by pushing himself to be heard, and by questioning everything, especially the Bible. This curiosity in the religious environment in which he lived eventually stimulated his appetite for theology, which led to the researching and writing of one of his greatest works.

Even in his teens, however, his sense of humor was one of the redeeming features counterbalancing his darker moods. In his later years this same humor was one of his most attractive qualities.

Schweitzer confessed that he was a real nuisance between the ages of fourteen and sixteen because he wanted to know the fundamentals of everything anyone mentioned. But he couldn't be satisfied with just anyone's answers; he had to read and research the subject himself. He would not let his curiosity for the truth be satisfied or even colored by the opinions of others, especially when they showed any bowing to dogma, and particularly Church dogma.

As he once said in his later years, "If I ever lost my youthful enthusiasm for truth and ideals, I would die." He never lost it.

Also, Schweitzer could not hide his loathing for small talk or mindlessness. At times he would rebel at inane conversation by just being mute. "I suffer from the foolish everyday conversation of people, and I hate myself when occasionally my disdain bursts through. I'm always sorry for it later, but then it is too late—the damage already has been done."

This feeling of always being "too late for contrition," mentioned both in his self-analysis and to me, seemed particularly strong in regard to his mother. She was always impatient with him for being a mediocre student when she knew he could do better; and she never forgave him for sacrificing his talent to go to Africa. When he left for Lambarene it was not with her loving goodbye. So it was no surprise that he was so deeply disturbed when later she died violently. For then it was too late to see her and make amends.

Along with this revealing insight I remembered another admission of his inner shyness which occurred when as an adolescent, he was finishing gymnasium. He left the home of his aunt and uncle who had fed, clothed, housed, and taught him so much for so long, and he was unable to express his love and appreciation to them at the time. To me, it appeared as if Schweitzer, in youth, had a totally consuming involvement with self and an unthinking attitude toward others.

The shame for not having shown his appreciation to them was always with him. To compensate for this feeling of guilt, he visited his family's graves many years later and whispered then what he believed he should have told them when they were still alive. He often quoted a parable in this vein—about the lepers who didn't think of thanking Jesus for their cure until He was dead.

Schweitzer was not only anguished over the pain and misery around him but was annoyed with himself for taking his luck, his health, and his happiness for granted. This conflict was the one that finally provoked him to make the decision that his ultimate responsibility was to others less fortunate. "Those who receive beauty in life must return it. Those spared of pain must help share that pain with those who have it."

Schweitzer was concerned with the consciousness of life in each minute of one's existence—as was the cousin with whom he'd been close—Jean Paul Sartre: "One should not let these minutes slip by; they should not be taken for granted but should be accounted for," he protested.

This feeling of responsibility to others and expiation for his own great endowments seemed to work on him in dark and frightening ways. How could he ever do enough? Where would it end? "Rarely could I ever get out from under this obsession of responsibility and be master of my life," he said. If Schweitzer had true depressions, this obsession might well be another one of its roots. As he himself reflected, "This compulsiveness of thought darkened my life—growing each year until, like a cloud, it covered the whole sky."

Later that evening, after another prolonged silence, he outlined the rest of his life at the age of twenty: "I made up my mind to write, preach, and dedicate my life to music until I was thirty; then I would serve. My decision to use my life for others after thirty was firm; but how, I did not know."

At that age, already recognized worldwide in theology, philosophy, and music, Schweitzer kept his self-promise and decided to go to Africa. His outward equanimity and confidence in his spiritual urge to go to Africa masked a wrenching inner experience of sacrificing the civilized scholarly things that he was known for. I inferred, from things he said later, there was a deep schism between talent and spirit. But nothing daunted him from his resolve.

I remembered that in his *Childhood Memoirs*, he had contemplated the good and evil in mankind and related this to the experiences of his own youth. He came to believe that good thoughts could not be put into man's mind. They had to be there already, just waiting for someone to kindle a fire under them. Obviously, this philosophy continued for Schweitzer; later he said, "We never know who or how; but we should be grateful to those who light up our lives and bring out our goodness."

Then waxing even more philosophical, he added, "No one, even after years of contact, ever knows the feelings of others completely. We wander together in half darkness and hardly recognize each other. There may be light that illuminates, and we may recognize some faces, but we shouldn't try to penetrate others' minds; it is not noble behavior. We must respect the secrets of each other's minds."

I wondered what he must have thought about my probings of his mind.

He went on, "What counts is giving of oneself." But then he advised, "Do not give all, be cautious; but do not mistrust others. (a fine line to walk) . . . But how much can we hold back and still handle each other tactfully? (something that he practiced so well) . . . Yet no man is a total stranger to others because we are so alike. Reserve must be broken by friendliness and congeniality. The warmth of man has a right to man's warmth."

In his book, Schweitzer went further in explaining his

confidence in the still-uncorrupted mind of youth. "We must go back to the spontaneous truths, ideals, and inspirations of our youth. If only we could keep them and not have them chipped away by maturity and experience. In youth we believe in God and justice; in maturity we don't. We must not resign our youthful ideals even to reason."

Schweitzer cited a parable related by Jesus: "A man was out in a boat during a storm. He lightened the boat by throwing over everything, including his food and water, so that he can keep afloat—only to starve after he survived the storm." Then, once more there was a short silence. Voice growing stronger, he went on, "The practical needs of life and reality should not be completely given away—a pitfall for those whose ideals are too strong."

Again he returned to the subject of his youth. "I was still small and envious. (Here he is talking about Schweitzer the sinner.) I am helpless against dishonesty and lies. My peacefulness is mocked; so maybe it is not strong enough. No one or anything can rule over idealism if one consistently works to be pure."

Yet he knew, as I did, that in the struggle to survive in this world we use every ploy and guile, and consequently we lose our innocence. He protested this was a problem of youth not of maturity, "If the human would be the same at forty as at fourteen, how different the world would be."

Much of what Schweitzer says in *Memoirs of Childhood and Youth* is most illuminating with regard to the basic complexity of the mind and character of this man. I am convinced that much of what he wrote about himself in this book stemmed from the time spent on his "friend's" psychiatric couch.

If at one time he had mental problems, he remained till the end of his life the theologic iconoclast and the ethical Christian he started out.

Yet he also stayed true to his thoughts as they progressed rather than to his background and upbringing. Even at the age of eighty-six he made a radical break with the Church to which he had belonged all his life. It was quite a shock to the Protestant world when he joined the Unitarian movement. For most of his life, he had been loyal to the Lutheran Canons in which he did not really believe. He had thought that it was more rational to try to change the Church's thoughts on Jesus from within. He finally gave up. I'm sure that this was not an easy or happy decision but with an obviously clear mind he left his old Church in gentlemanly style.

On one occasion just before I left Lambarene, he said something which reflected his great self-satisfaction. He mentioned that the Dead Sea Scrolls (then being analyzed) and the new research coming from young theologic thinkers about Jesus' era could possibly have refuted his premises in the *Quest for the Historical Jesus*. He said he could have accepted this. Since most modern scholars concluded that his interpretations were well founded. I don't think anyone with a serious mental affliction could have been so open to new truths, even those possibly reversing the theories he espoused and battled over for half a century, as was Schweitzer. Also, even in his later years, he was still flexible enough to admit to possible mistakes in his Church affiliation and to change.

Schweitzer was the consummate supersensitive revolutionary to the very end. He had his own ideas for just about everything (building a Leper Village against architectural convention, administering a hospital in his own unique way, or shattering the Church's dogmas and teachings about Jesus). He fought those major battles in his own way primarily for the truth in which he passionately believed.

Maybe one of his greatest battles was fought within himself and within his overworked mind. If so, I think he won this battle by the dint of his great spiritual resolve with the aid of the discipline he exercised over himself. It may have involved years of anguish. Most likely much of that anguish stemmed from his temporary inability to control his greatest asset—his mind. From my observations in 1960, there was no vestige of a depressive personality left.

21

PROBLEMS
IN MECCA

I talked almost daily with Schweitzer in the week following the dedication at the old Protestant Mission downriver, sometimes spontaneously, sometimes by invitation, in his room—and these conversations were getting longer, more relaxed, and more candid.

There was very probably a combination of reasons for his being so open with me. First, since he abhorred small talk, I took pains not to indulge in it. Second, Schweitzer was either attracted to someone or he wasn't; and, even if he were attracted, it took a period of time for a rapport to develop. His conversations with distinguished visitors were so short in duration probably because they didn't stay long enough to develop a rapport. Also, Schweitzer liked to dwell on past conversation and come back to the subject a few days later, but this was impossible to do with short-term visitors.

His conversations were strictly business with his regular staff, mostly because their attitude of veneration toward him always kept most relationships distant. Moreover, Schweitzer was overloaded with very real concerns besides running an eight-hundred-patient hospital. Just the correspondence from his worldwide interests in nuclear proliferation and peace, his lecture tours and concerts, and his many famous friends would have kept a dozen men busy. One of his Dutch volunteer physicians, Grett Barthalamew, who, dedicated to his spirit, worked in Lambarene for over five years, said she did not have a speaking relationship with him of more than a few exchanges for the first eight months of her stay.

The Danish philosopher, Dr. Friss, when he had been there for a little over a week had expressed disappointment because he had only talked with Schweitzer for a total of perhaps thirty minutes and only on the subject of whether Schweitzer would act as patron that summer at an African seminar in Denmark.

This lack of rapport with his staff, not wholly purposeful, was the basis of an unhappy group of volunteer doctors and nurses who had come for diverse personal reasons and problems which they thought a closeness to Schweitzer might solve. Without Schweitzer and his fame, Lambarene would not have attracted a tenth of its professional and lay staff. This boded ill for the future of the hospital. This situation was rather fully explored in a conversation between Schweitzer and me near the end of our stay.

Phoebe and I walked over to Schweitzer's room one particularly sweltering evening. He was sitting at his box desk, gazing off almost trancelike, his eyeglasses raised to his forehead, one hand playing with his black-and-yellow-tipped myna bird which was sitting on his shoulder. I think he was trying to teach it some French words. (Friedman had told me that the bird was a gift from someone in the United States, and the little French it spoke was with a Brooklyn accent.)

As we sat down the bird still nestled on Schweitzer's shoulder as he absentmindedly stroked it. Schweitzer almost at once brought up something that was on his mind. He wanted to talk about his old "chicken house" hospital. He asked if I really thought it could actually be renovated as a memento to an old "do-gooder," as I had suggested. (Amazingly, he still remembered that phrase I had used the first day I met him.) Though as I understood, it was unusual for Schweitzer to be interested in the perpetuation of his name by a monument (his work would do that), this idea somehow intrigued him.

"If it were to become a museum," he joked, "what would they do—put my old shoes or my battered old hat in it?"

I told him I thought that, after the fifty years he had spent there, it could just be a memorial to his spirit. Then I added kiddingly, "But to attract tourists they may have to put your old shoes and hat in it and charge twenty-five cents to get in."

Schweitzer laughed heavily at the possibility, but I think the general idea of having a monument to his beginnings in Africa pleased him. He was quite serious as to how he would go about it and had even talked it over with the pastor down at the old refurbished Mission. It would have been no trouble to raise the $1,000 to fix it up.

As we discussed the renovation, he told me how much he loved to build and that if he could have his way he would spend one third of the day building, one third writing, and one third with his music; medicine didn't enter into what he really enjoyed doing. I thought that after almost half a century of the hardships of rendering to those "who bore the mark of pain" he should have had the right, at the age of eighty-five, to divide his day any way he wanted.

I wondered aloud, "With the years left, why not again

play on the best organs in the world, or just write (which he complained he had so little time to do) in an environment you loved, such as in Gunsbach or Paris or wherever?"

Then Schweitzer said something that shocked me. "Do you think I am so narrow that I enjoy living here?" In fact I had thought he did. He continued, "My prime reason for being here hasn't changed in fifty years and it was neither to write nor to play my music.

"I have always been torn. When I was in Europe, I had the desire and sense of duty to get back to try to allay the misery of those people whom I knew and loved. Yet when I'm here I can't say I don't miss the things Europe offers."

Schweitzer seemed especially sad that night. He gazed off more than once with longer-than-usual periods of silence. He seemed preoccupied with some problem or other. Phoebe and I kept the visit short and left early.

The following day the weather was still stifling. Near noon, I entered the noisy, congested pharmacy. Schweitzer's pharmacy desk, like the desk in his family home and now his European retreat in Gunsbach, was off to one side and near a window through which he could look at people and onto the chaotic main street of the hospital grounds. Inside, almost closing in on him, patients were lined up, talking and laughing, waiting for their medication; while cats, dogs, goats, chickens, and ducks ambled about or chased each other underfoot. Once his parrot flew through, squawking out its messages.

Yet he sat in the midst of this absolute madhouse as if he were back in the peaceful village of Gunsbach. Not only that, he was writing a part of the third volume of *Civilization,* which I would have thought needed every erg of concentration. Schweitzer put down his pen and swiveled around toward me.

As I sat down I asked, "Could anyone else in the world write much less run a hospital in this maelstrom?"

"It doesn't bother me," Schweitzer said shaking his head. Then, thinking I was talking more about the general lack of order, he added, "The work gets done, and it'll be up to whomever follows me to run the hospital differently."

This was the first time Schweitzer had ever mentioned the future of the hospital—a worrisome thought among his friends, such as Mark Evans (a television executive and diplomat), Marion Preminger, and Erica Anderson. He said, "The hospital's future is up to the committee in Switzerland which has also helped me raise funds and is the hospital's official link to the outside world. I just hope it's run the way I've set it up. It works this way." About organizations in general, Schweitzer, true to his authoritarian nature, had once said, "Committees are the graveyard of ideas and ideals."

I had talked with two volunteers, Ali Silver and Mathilda Kottman, before about the hospital's future, and my impression was that *they* wanted to maintain the hospital (after he "goes") according to "the way it works"—that living facilities in a rural African hospital should be similar to those from which the patients had come and to which they would be going back. They mentioned a few possible modern improvements. But more than that, they wanted it as a mecca to the worldwide Schweitzer ethic. They wanted his religious and philosophic principles to continue (even if they didn't understand them fully).

But others in the compound, such as Drs. Mueller and Friedman, harbored their own dreams of glory. Their dream was of a clean, efficient, brick-and-mortar modern institution.

Then, too, it was said that the government had plans which differed from those of all the white heirs apparent. It was stated in official circles that the government thought more in terms of a black administration. However, few of the black Gabonese physicians who trained elsewhere came back to the Gabon, and fewer were willing to work in the bush.

As Schweitzer and I sat there together in the pharmacy and talked amid the utter confusion, I finally decided to ask him pointblank about the hospital's future. "Dr. Schweitzer, many people all over the world are interested in this institution. Many have donated to its survival and contributed to what it has achieved under your direction. However, they say that you care little about its future."

"Why should they say that?" he asked, puzzled.

I glanced at him apprehensively. "Because you rarely talk about its future plans, as if it is here more for your own salvation than for the people you serve."

He didn't look startled by this statement. "I don't *wholly* deny that, but I've told you many times that I built the hospital because *I* believed in man's responsibility to man and the affirmation of all life. The hospital is part of it. Friends know what I'd like to see happen here when I leave; but I won't be here to influence it, so why talk about it before it happens?"

Schweitzer went on, "I would like to think that the hospital would serve these people as it always has—simply and plainly—but," he raised an eyebrow, "I hope not as just a museum to me. Anyway for me it's too costly to modernize, and I'm too old to begin now." (He had to raise about $250,000 a year just to maintain it.)

I kidded, "You told me Bach was so stingy; you sound just like him."

"Bach didn't have a family of a thousand," Schweitzer responded, matter-of-factly, "and since when is frugality a vice?"

I knew of his feelings on simplicity, but I also knew

that well-trained young doctors and nurses would never come to work very long under primitive professional conditions. From my experiences with doctors in Latin America who had trained in posh North American hospitals, few ever went back to the bush. First, because they wouldn't have the equipment to practice the standard of medicine they had been trained for; and, second, they wanted the prestige and the Western standard of living.

"Dr. Schweitzer," I said, as gently as possible, "a few months after you leave (my euphemism for his passing, which always brought a fleeting smile to his lips) few of your doctors or nurses will still be here. They'll be gone to less spiritual, more lucrative pastures. Without you, fewer and fewer professionals will be attracted here."

He couldn't deny this, but he still remonstrated that it might not be so. I felt that in his heart he knew differently.

There was another long silence. I'm sure he realized that many of the doctors, maybe secondarily, sought recognition through their association with him. One of them was Dr. Friedman. He had come from Israel not too long after the end of the war (some said without a medical degree but no one knew for sure). He would have liked to succeed Schweitzer, though not to the same extent as would Dr. Mueller. I doubted that Friedman wanted to be Schweitzer's successor for too long but just long enough. (Friedman left the hospital about fifteen months after Schweitzer died.)

Mueller's case was different. He was not only drawn there mainly by Schweitzer's celebrity status but also by his religious motivations. He was competent, though not yet fully trained. He, too, wanted the status of succeeding Schweitzer or at least standing in his shoes for a while, primarily for the prestige it would later give him. I think he would have radically modernized the hospital. Under Mueller it may have been run more efficiently and possibly with better results, but there would be little heart and no philosophy.

Rolf Adler (the doctor who first met us with the *pirogue* on our arrival) was a lovely, gentle man: not aggressive, quite neurotic, and probably not very successful. Although a very ordinary professional man, he was a very good human being. I think he wanted to achieve recognition in some way, if also by association. Mueller and Friedman were constantly at each other's throats; and poor Adler was always in the middle, afraid to go either way. (Adler left soon after I did. He died very young.)

With an eye to the future, both Friedman and Mueller each played up to Silver and Kottman, trying to win their favor, because they knew the women had Schweitzer's ear.

I didn't mention to Schweitzer the not-so-secret ambitions of those doctors. As to the low morale of the hospital, I talked of it at first by citing Siegfried, who, as I told Schweitzer, was totally disillusioned with Lambarene. He was surprised at this and urged me on.

Siegfried was a world wanderer. He had read about Schweitzer and had come to Lambarene to help in his way—as a carpenter, builder, plumber, mechanic—to alleviate the misery of the Africans, to learn about God from Schweitzer, and also to assist Schweitzer in the practical part of his godly work. Though I respected the bright and handsome Siegfried's integrity and honesty, I think he was emotionally upset mainly by his spiritual disappointment in Lambarene and his lack of a close personal rapport with his idol.

One evening Siegfried had gone on at length about how shocked he was by the difference between what Schweitzer wrote and how he acted. "He has been known to strike natives," Siegfried had said. When I pinned him down on this he said it was more like a push—but an angry one. He described some of Schweitzer's rages, one or two of which I had personally witnessed. To my mind, these bouts of anger just made him more human; yet I have never seen anyone as contrite and apologetic as Schweitzer only a few moments after his temper subsided.

Siegfried also told stories about Schweitzer's building expertise, of which Schweitzer was so proud. "Actually, he is a very poor builder," Siegfried had said. One episode somewhat supports Siegfried's allegation. An architect had donated a prefabricated building, which arrived while the architect was away. Schweitzer, not realizing that it was prefabricated, didn't wait for the architect to return. He just went ahead and cut up all of the prefitted parts and put up a building his way, thereby ruining the prefabrication. The building took six weeks to erect instead of six days.

But regardless of Siegfried's opinion and Schweitzer's obvious mistake with the prefab, no one disputed all the clearing and building that Schweitzer oversaw during those first fifteen years alone, using inexperienced labor, inferior tools, and poor supplies. What's more, most of those buildings are still standing.

I also jokingly mentioned Siegfried's allegation that "Schweitzer was totally ruled by women" (meaning Silver and Kottman, whom Siegfried didn't like at all). There was no doubt that those women enjoyed their power which, however, took nothing away from their love and respect for Schweitzer.

Schweitzer smiled at this and said, "It's better to let gossip slide over and around you. Don't take sides; it's usually too trivial and a waste of time. Cliques are for the bored who survive on hate," he nodded sagely.

The truth was that these women did have a large influence over Schweitzer, however, and this did not always contribute to peace on the compound, since they too obviously vied for his favor. Nevertheless, they did take a tremendous amount of work off his shoulders: they worried about the food, laundry, and maintenance; dealt with the workforce; arranged work schedules; and just generally kept the place running. Schweitzer knew they were loyal and would be there as long as he needed them. Their reverence, respect, and being at his beck and call night and day were well worth the power he gave them and some of the decisions he allowed them to make.

Later, when I met Ali in one of the wards, she had heard about my opinions on the women and their power. She claimed it was a total misunderstanding.

Some of the younger women (those in their thirties and forties) at the compound seemed to feel a stronger, almost romantic, attraction to Schweitzer. But I think this had more to do with his power and celebrity status than anything else.

Schweitzer listened closely as I discussed some of his personnel, their motives, and why they wouldn't remain long after he was gone. Then he said, "Is there anything so bad in any of their motives?"

"No," I answered straightforwardly, "but what I am getting at is that *you* are the main reason they are here. When you go, so will they. Regardless of the system or leadership, no one could be the driving force and magnet you have been here. What you have attained may still influence the world, but I think it will disappear here among the staff and natives. The hospital will probably remain as a symbol; but *it* could even disappear unless in some way you or someone else plans now."

"Yes," he agreed, rather morosely. "I won't be around to play the organ and 'sing for my supper' and keep the hospital going."

"But," I injected, somewhat facetiously, "if the Spirit

of Jesus is, as you say, expanding and filling the hearts of men, then there should be a host of people knocking at the door."

At this point I was wondering how frank I should be; I did not want to confront him with all of my gloomy predictions, but I went on.

"Sooner or later, whoever takes over here will have to be subsidized by the government. A few mercenary doctors may still come for a while to pay obeisance to your memory; and probably a lot of new concrete buildings will go up at first. But with no technical expertise to maintain it, later on it will be just another large, dilapidated, government structure. Of course, some of your old buildings will still stand as monuments; and your quarters may be used as a museum to be gawked at by a few tourists, a few philosophers, and by musicians who have read about you. But eventually, even if there is financial planning, all may still recede back into the jungle."

We talked until lunchtime. At that point, Phoebe came in from the *pouponniere*, nudged me, and whispered that Schweitzer might be tired. He raised his pen. "Now stop bothering your husband about me." He then told one of his naive little jokes to chastise her. "A doctor back in Strasbourg used to tell all his female patients to stick out their tongues even though they may have come in with a cut finger. The doctor said he'd rather see their tongues than listen to them."

He then turned back to the future of the hospital, and his face clouded. "I know that much of what you say is true," he said. "And you know much of what I've done may have been a very personal thing; but others must also do it for their own reasons. If the spirit or philosophy I've created does not catch on, then that is too bad because I feel that it is surely one way not only for human survival but for mankind's happiness. I'm too old and tired now to even think about the future."

In an attempt to lighten the mood of our talk, I said, "You are always hiding behind your chronologic age when in your mind you are younger than anyone here—maybe around thirty."

"I'm a long way from thirty," he sighed, looking very sad. He then asked my age and I told him I was forty-three. "That's a good age," he admonished, "but don't waste it, it doesn't stay very long." A momentary smile flickered and was gone.

Then he went off on a related tangent. "Remember when we were talking about the possibility of a new psychiatric wing, you mentioned Dr. Friedman." With a worried look, Schweitzer said, "I like him, but he always seems to be thinking about something other than what he should be thinking about. The other day he again completely forgot to turn on the generator when we needed it badly."

"Dr. Schweitzer." I paused, weighing my words, "Dr. Friedman's absentmindedness may be only a reflection of his underlying unhappiness here."

"Why should he be unhappy?" he asked rather morosely. "He must be doing what he wants to do; he came here voluntarily. I've tried to help him all I could, but I don't have the time to help or listen to all of the thirty or so staff working here—"

I broke in, "I know it's not your fault. It comes back to the self-delusion of most of those who come to work for you. In today's world, it's a rare professional who is charitable, religious, and idealistic enough to continue his job here for any length of time. Ordinarily, when a doctor or nurse comes to work at a hospital they come to practice what they've learned and do what they enjoy. Along with all of that must come comfort, good professional conditions, good pay, and a chance for advancement, which certainly isn't here. (Actually, almost everyone in Lambarene, even the so-called permanent staff, were volunteers, getting paid only for incidentals or their sabbaticals to Europe every few years.)

I went on, "I'd say ninety-nine percent of the doctors and nurses in the U.S. or anywhere else have little feeling of charity, atonement, or the need for penance. It is only the unusual ones who will give up all the good material things and the ease of living to come here and live this hair-shirt, cloistered existence. As you just said, you don't have the time to get close to many of them and that takes away from their desire to stay."

"But," he answered, "if those few come here only for the purposes you say, which evolve around me, they shouldn't."

"Well, some who have deluded themselves know only too late that they had a distorted perception and won't sacrifice for long," I responded.

"You did," he smiled.

"Yes, but I'm only temporary and I told you that first day why I came."

During this part of the conversation, Ali Silver sat there tight-lipped, obviously more intent on listening than interpreting what Schweitzer didn't understand. Her face showed resentment at my bringing up this topic, especially since it involved her.

Disregarding her disapproval, I continued, "To be utterly frank with you, which I think I've tried to be so far, the deep personality problems in this compound which I've talked about are at the core of the staff's disenchantment, and they tend to take it out on you and each other. It's probably none of my business; but since you've been so very kind, generous, and candid with me, I want to be the same with you and let you know that this compound is basically not a happy place."

Schweitzer disregarded the reference to himself and asked searchingly, "How do they take it out on each other?"

For a moment I hesitated, then plunged ahead. "First, many of them rarely speak to each other except regarding hospital matters; and even then they're not too pleasant about it. Right now, it's Friedman and Adler against Mueller. Next week the alliances may change for whatever reason. Most of them need much more training; and, if there was less internal turmoil, they could at least learn something from each other. At the same time, the patients would suffer less because they wouldn't have to take the brunt of the doctor's egos and disappointments, which is usually reflected in abruptness and roughness with patients. All of this is why I think it may be a good idea to look to the future now."

I tried to speak as gently as possible, not as a gossip but to express the problem that faced him. I think he took it that way.

Ali didn't. Whether she was piqued or not, she was the one who brought this conversation to a rather abrupt close. Staring at me rather resentfully, she told Schweitzer that more important things had to be done before he left for lunch. I don't think Schweitzer wholly regretted the conversation's end. I know I didn't.

22

THE LAST FAREWELL

At breakfast the day before we were to leave, Schweitzer announced to everyone that that day was proclaimed a special holiday for Phoebe and me, and we need not follow any bells, rules, or regulations. Jokingly, I asked him if he was proclaiming the holiday because we deserved it—or good riddance.

Raising his eyebrow in mock surprise, he said, "Then stay, and we'll still give you the day off." As we left the dining room he fell into step beside me, putting his head close to mine, whispered, "You don't even have to wear your pith helmet." (He knew I disliked wearing it and had scolded me many times when he caught me without it.)

That evening, Schweitzer surprised us after dinner by asking us directly—not through Silver or Kottman—to come to his room. The invitation was unexpected because that very morning I'd had a long talk with him in front of the dining hall.

Before going over to Schweitzer's, Phoebe and I

stopped at our room. I had a gift for him I had bought (mostly as a gag) in Lambarene. When we arrived at his room, Schweitzer was sitting at his desk, his glasses resting on the end of his nose. He was bent over a reddish, wooden box, writing in indelible ink on the inside of the top. He was going over and over the letters slowly, not in his usual tiny script but in large, bold letters. After greeting us, he gently put the top back on the box, got up, bowed, and took Phoebe's hand. As he handed her the box, he said, "This is my gift to you, dear cousin; first for just being here, and second for working so hard."

Schweitzer explained, "This box is of hard orange-wood and was made by a native priest in the village." It wasn't the most beautiful box, but it was handmade with nicely fitted joinings and was about the size of a cereal carton.

He went on, "I only had two; the other one I gave to Eleanor Roosevelt." Phoebe opened the box and read the inscription: "To Olga Phoebe Rhea Berman." (Though he got her first and second names reversed, he had remembered her maiden name; which she had mentioned to him only once.)

Phoebe kissed him on the cheek; and, kissing her hand again, he said very soberly, "We're all sorry that you are both leaving," and admonished, "Don't wait too long before you return, I'm an old man." Phoebe lovingly kissed him again.

I brought out my gift to him; but, before giving it to him, I made him promise to wear it only on the most festive occasions. He agreed. I opened the box and took out a red silk clip-on bow tie. Schweitzer took it, held it off admiringly, and laughed heartily. "Both of you have implied that I am a Communist; if I wear this, I'll surely be labeled one."

"Wear it on Christmas Day," I kidded him, "and they won't dare accuse you of that."

He tried the tie on. Putting his hand up to hide it, he said, "I'll wear it even if I have to hold my hand here the whole time." Suddenly his mood changed; he seemed terribly sad. Again, he told us not to wait too long to return.

Phoebe, trying to dispell his mood said, "According to 'our' geneaology chart you pinned to my door, you have a long way to go. We Schweitzers live to a much riper age than eighty-five. And even though you wouldn't let me read your palm, I did get a glimpse of it. You have the longest lifeline I've ever seen." (She fibbed.)

Referring to her palm reading, he joked, "You are the only gypsy Schweitzer I've ever met." But the subject of age was still very much on his mind. "I'm getting tired," he sighed, "and one must not be afraid to die."

The direction the conversation was taking was upsetting. I remembered Friedman telling me that Schweitzer did have a fear of dying. I didn't know how Friedman obtained his information because, from my observations, he never spoke that intimately with Schweitzer. However, I tried to steer away from Schweitzer's personal thoughts of death.

"You know, Dr. Schweitzer," I teased, "I have had some experience in transplant surgery. All you have to do is hold on for a few more years, and I guarantee you'll live forever."

He picked up on this with interest and asked about kidney transplants, which he had heard about, and also about my heart transplant experiments. (I don't know how he knew about this work which had been done some three years before.) He paused, then said sadly, "It would be more interesting if you could transplant the spirit."

"That's *your* job; mine is transplanting organs and that's much simpler. Your colleagues have been trying spirit transplantation for some two thousand years with too little success. Anyway, I don't deal with the whole, only with spare parts. However," I added, "if by tomorrow you discover some technique for the spirit, I'll try."

"I've been trying to do it on you since you came here; have I failed?"

"Not totally," I said, "I hope I've come a long way at least in my reverence for life—and isn't that the first step?"

I went on, "We've often talked about how to live, but isn't man just as obsessed with death and dying? Can we have peace of mind and still fear death the way we do?"

He approached the subject quietly. "Everyone eventually dies. How ethically we have lived on earth should determine how peacefully we can take the uncertainty of death. Everyone thinks and feels about death differently. If a person has enjoyed a good, healthy life, he or she may be more reluctant to leave it. If a person has been sick, poor, miserable, and has suffered more, it's different." He went on that the fear of sickness and infirmity of body or mind may be worse than the fear of death. "I have experienced both (here he was no doubt bringing up his two operations and then his depression), and it changes one's attitude about death."

"Are you reluctant to leave this life?" I asked, perhaps too bluntly.

He didn't answer directly. "Well, I know I won't approach it as Bach did. He welcomed death because he believed so literally in the kingdom of God in the hereafter." Schweitzer again looked off, "At one time I welcomed death, but it was for a different reason." (He didn't specify when; but I imagine it was during his most despondent period, between 1919 and 1926.) "I believe more in the living spirit of the kingdom." His voice rose. "I don't fear death; but I have so much to do, so much to finish."

This "so much to finish" was one of the most saddening aspects of his admission to me. It just made no sense that this unique man, so alive with ideas, still seeking answers, and so unafraid of being himself, should ever cease to exist. Whoever devised the system should have made special exceptions.

"If one has adhered to Christ's ethics," he explained, finishing his thought, "I think one dies more peacefully— maybe I shall."

This brought to my mind observations in my own hospital experiences: luckily, as we die physically we also die mentally, and this is a blessing.

"But," I said, "from what I've seen in my practice back in the States, religion does mean something in the way each of us dies. Even a blind faith, which you think so little of, is of great solace. And among all the ordinary people I have seen die, Catholics die most peacefully—mostly with unthinking faith, in a hereafter."

Interrupting me, and with a lift of his shaggy eyebrows, Schweitzer joked, "Yes, but how do they live? I have seen very sick people who have luckily come back after the sacraments; some have said it puts fear in their hearts. No, even with Catholics, without a thinking faith there is a great sense of hopelessness, which makes us even more fearful."

"I'm not so sure," I rejoined. "Even the non-heretical teachings of most of the Christian churches in their wishful rituals, talk of heaven, life after death, and resurrection and make one die better," and then asked, "If last-minute repentance gives someone another chance and some solace, then why not repent? In a sense, isn't death what the dogma, the ritual, and the promise of heaven prepares them for?"

Schweitzer returned to his former argument. "If the Church could teach its faithful how to live better, it wouldn't have to teach them how to die. How can most of us die peacefully if in our hearts we are cognizant of how selfishly we have lived?"

"But, Dr. Schweitzer, most of us don't want to realize

how selfishly we live; we rationalize it on the basis of family, success, or just plain survival."

"And that's what is so wrong," he answered decisively. "The rationalization—going along with the herd, not being an individual."

This was not exactly the warm and sentimental farewell that either Phoebe or I had envisioned. Neither of us thought that the conversation would get this serious. However, we'd gone so far that we couldn't cut it off (in any case, I didn't want to). To me, another piece of the Schweitzerian jigsaw puzzle was dropping into place. He was simply repeating his personal view that there was virtue and peace of soul in living a life according to Jesus' ideals, especially fulfilling man's responsibility to his human brothers. Schweitzer believed this led to grace and a peaceful demise.

Though I knew that spending fifty years in Africa was a rational compulsion for him, I wondered if I couldn't have asked him the same question that he had asked the Catholics: "But how did you live?" This question wasn't meant in the vein that he lived an unselfish life with regard to his brothers. But, after all, did he fulfill most of his God-given talents? As it turned out, his example of living in Africa all those years became so inspirational to so many. Could he have done more had he stayed in Europe?

He continued, "If we live with a reverence for all life, and I know how difficult you say it is in practice, there should be little fear of death. I feel that the people here, in their primitive state, don't fear death as much as the sophisticated man does. Yet after their conversion, it seems the Church inculcates much fear in some of them, especially in the 'fire and brimstone' alternative." Then he put the same question to me. "You've told me you are not a formally religious man. Do you fear death?"

"Well, yes." I reflected, "In some ways it's fear; in

others it's just a reluctance to leave life. One is a reflex; it's automatic—probably a survival instinct that automatically surfaced when I have come close to death, as in an accident. During the war, after we landed on the beach at Okinawa in the midst of battle, fear made me a 'foxhole Christian.' " Schweitzer didn't understand this expression; but, with my poor French and his good knowledge of English, I finally got the idea across. "But," I went on, "typically, the conversion was only temporary, it was forgotten an hour after the battle was over."

What I didn't say is that I have also felt fear at the thought of going into the unknown—in that split second between life and death. When my mother died, only a short time ago, I couldn't get the thought out of my mind after her burial that she was all alone down in the cold grave. It was the nothingness of death, the void, that was frightening—what is nothingness like? My fear was mainly loneliness. I wondered, if we do have a spirit as Schweitzer tried to convince me we do, can that spirit cancel the obsession of the void that I have in my gnostic mind?

On this night of our farewell I was relieved when Schweitzer ended this depressing conversation abruptly. "Let's not be so serious tonight; you weren't asked here for that. Would some of your friends like momentoes of your stay here?" Without waiting for an answer, he went to a shelf full of new books. Disappointed, he muttered that he had no copies of the *Historical Jesus,* about which we had talked so much. Instead, he came back with five books under his arm and sat down and began autographing them. The first was one of his Bibles.

Finishing that, he went over to what looked like a footlocker and took out several pieces of paper. These turned out to be printed layouts of the hospital, first-day issues of envelopes with his picture on the stamps, and some stamps themselves. He spent twenty minutes autographing the lay-outs and envelopes.

Then, with a mischievous look, Schweitzer said, "These envelopes are just to make sure your friends know that you were really here working and not off playing, somewhere in Europe." He asked, "Where are you going when you leave?"

I told him, "We are meeting friends in Paris for a few days, and then we are going home."

He got out a piece of paper and on it wrote, "St. Sulpice" and the name of the organist. "Go to the midnight Mass on Christmas Eve," he said. "There you will hear the greatest organ in the world played by the greatest organist. If that doesn't imbue you with the Spirit, you are lost . . . But I know it will."

It was quite late. Before we left, Phoebe asked him if she would see him in the morning; we were supposed to be leaving around 7:00. He said that she must wait and see.

"It'll be too early and you need your rest," she told him, "so here is a kiss to let you sleep longer and to let you know how much we love you." Then this man, who at times had been described as a cold intellectual, was all warmth and love, his eyes glistened as he held her close.

Early on our last morning, there were the three doctors, also Ali, Marie, Joseph, Pierre, a few other staff members, and even some patients down on the dock. It was a sad leavetaking but primarily because of Schweitzer. Now that I had gotten to know him personally I thought him even greater than I ever imagined he was. He had taught me a great deal. But I had a strange feeling that we would never see him again.

Schweitzer came down to the dock just before we left

and made a little farewell speech. He expressed the hope that
we would return and took Phoebe's hand and kissed it. He
was still waving his pith helmet as we were rowed across the
river to a small airplane by the same leper oarsmen who had
met us the day we arrived. We watched Schweitzer's figure on
the dock, receding as the plane took off.

23

THE METAMORPHOSIS: FROM LAMBARENE TO PARIS

An unpleasant surprise awaited us when we arrived in Libreville. Air France was on strike. The tiny airport was a beehive of stranded travelers. As a last resort, we took a small African airline northward to Chad where we were told we might be able to get transportation to Europe.

I was only vaguely familiar with the nation of Chad or even Fort Lamy, the capital city, where we were scheduled to land. We arrived there about 2:00 p.m. and were taken into a ghost of a city: four or five gray concrete buildings, along unpaved streets, interspersed and surrounded by wooden shacks and tents; all of which was encircled by desert. One of the buildings was a small two-story hotel where we registered.

We were the only occupants; and, though our room was spotlessly clean, the first thing I saw as we unpacked was a hairy tarantula the size of a mouse, sitting on the washstand near our bed. So as not to frighten Phoebe, I gently led it onto a piece of paper, in the Schweitzerian manner, and put it outside. Before coming to Lambarene, I would no doubt have squashed it with the hotel Bible.

After freshening up, we went to the one airline office. We placed our names on a list for the first flight out, which was supposed to be by an Italian airline and "probably" destined for Nice. There was a telegraph but no telephone; and everything was "probable." They weren't even sure that the plane would arrive on a specific day.

At dusk, Phoebe and I turned back toward the hotel. As we walked, to our surprise and enchantment, we were met by a sight right out of the Arabian nights. Down the main street, in a cloud of dust, came a charge of about twelve beautiful Arabian horses. They were ridden by fierce-looking mustachioed and turbanned men dressed in colorful tunics and pantaloons, seated on embossed, silver-studded saddles. Old-fashioned curved scimitars hung from the sides of the saddles, and we could see the butts of ancient long rifles on the other side. They didn't stop but flashed right through the center of town.

The incident illustrated, rather romantically, the stage of civilization of the country of Chad. At the hotel, we learned that there was a huge bazaar and a tent city oasis located not far from where we were staying. If the French fort still existed we never saw it.

We had a sparse dinner that night and went to bed. As hot as it had been during the day, the night winds from the desert had us sleeping under blankets. The next day, with nothing to do but wait, we went out to the bazaar. It was a scene with a feeling of the Old Testament. There were only a few "permanent" buildings of mud and stucco; tented living quarters clustered around a few palm trees and some shallow wells.

Tethered near a corral were small desert horses, short-legged and pony-sized, and a number of camels on their knees, placidly chewing their cuds. In front of each tent opening was a circle of stones enclosing an open fire over which hung a huge kettle. Goats, sheep, scrawny pigs, and chickens wandered aimlessly; others, which were for sale, were penned in small enclosures made of brambly wood that was tied crudely with handmade cord. From other tents, spotted around the periphery of the bazaar, we could see smoke and smell pungent cooking aromas as we approached.

The people seemed to live the biblical life as I imagined it to be in those times. Surrounding the shallow well were women drawing buckets of water and pouring the water into huge earthenware jars, which must have weighed fifteen or twenty pounds when empty. The women, mostly veiled, carried the jars away on their heads.

In the business center of the bazaar, rugged-looking men and women of all hues, from white to black, sat cross-legged before their wares. They shouted at anyone who passed by. Some held up what looked like tuberous roots of various sorts, and displayed black beans and pealike vegetables. Others sold tinware, sandals, faggots of wood, rope hammocks, and roughly-woven but colorful blouses and pants.

Many of the people were unlike any I had ever seen before. They were very tall with Caucasian features, but with pitch-black skin, and deep blue eyes.

At one location we came upon a group of what seemed to be ladies in waiting surrounding a very beautiful woman of about thirty. This woman must have been at least six feet tall and she sat on a stool, her back straight as a rod. Beautifully dressed in a multicolored gown, holding a mirror in each hand, she was probably desert royalty. Some of her ladies were grooming her hair into long, thin braids. Others rubbed her legs with oil, while two painted her toenails. We stopped to watch. Noticing us, she smiled a sort of Mona Lisa smile while looking straight ahead. Then she whispered to the others. They all turned to look at us and began giggling. We smiled, then they all broke into laughter.

As we went on we saw the Arabian horses that we had seen the night before. They were different from the other, pony-sized, horses. These were all tethered, brushed, and shiny; their ornate saddles and bridles neatly stacked on nearby wooden stands. There were no motorized vehicles to be seen anywhere. As we walked around, people with goats, chickens, and produce kept coming and going; some were on small donkeys heavily laden with full saddlebags or stacked high with faggots of firewood.

On our walk back to the hotel, we stopped at the airline office. There was still no word on an available flight. We were told that planes did not come in and out on a regular schedule and rarely were there more than two flights a week. Phoebe and I were beginning to get nervous, because we thought we might be stranded in this primitive stop for some time. We had a late lunch, and because it was so beastly hot we took a nap.

About 5:00 p.m. there was a rap on our door. A message was delivered that our plane had landed and would take off about 7:00 a.m. the following day. We were so relieved that we celebrated by sharing a bottle of wine at dinner with the dark, rather dapper, Algerian hotel keeper; he seemed happy to have company.

The next morning we arrived at the airport at 6:30. It was only about five minutes from the hotel. The plane didn't take off for Nice until about 8:30. It was the morning of

Christmas Eve. In Nice snow flurries began while we waited to change planes.

We were able to make a connection early that afternoon for Paris. As we had planned months before, friends were staying at the luxurious Plaza Athenée and had reserved rooms for us. We called them from Nice and told them the hour of our expected arrival.

We arrived in Paris on schedule, picked up our bags, took a cab to the hotel, and registered in the sumptuous lobby. Before going to our room, we went to our friends' suite. They welcomed us with a pound of gray Iranian Beluga caviar and chilled champagne. After Lambarene and Chad the contrast was almost unbelievable. We ate, drank, and talked for about an hour then told our friends we'd meet them about 10:30 and we'd all go to the midnight Mass. Then we went to our rooms for the *piece de resistance:* a hot shower with scented French soap, super-large fluffy towels, terry-cloth bathrobes, and lovely beds with down comforters. Phoebe and I each stayed in the shower for at least half an hour and went to bed in happy exhaustion.

When the operator rang with our wake-up call I couldn't believe where I was; the change was such a shock. I took out the one dress suit and shirt which I had brought along, and Phoebe unpacked an elegant dress, neither of which had seen daylight for months. Because neither the suit nor the dress had been touched since Lambarene, they were wrinkled messes. We sent them down for pressing, which was done almost immediately. Then we dressed and went down to meet our friends, who were waiting in the bar.

Again we toasted our return to civilization, with shining crystal glassware and perfect service. As I relaxed with our friends and a cocktail, I thought of the delightful amenities of European life that Schweitzer had given up in order to live his spartan jungle existence. I realized then that no amount of spiritual longing could force me to change places with him. I knew that in these opulent surroundings it was impossible for me to even contemplate it. I was close to the spirit in Lambarene, but now I knew how fleeting it was—all now lost to the flesh in Paris.

As we entered a cab to go to St. Sulpice, a light snowfall began. We reached the church as people streamed into the beautiful baroque structure with its ancient stone floors, its huge naves, the many paintings around its periphery, the votary candles flickering before them. The smell of incense mixed with the musty odor of ages. The darkened old interior was lighted by lanterns, which emphasized the jewel-like colors of the stained-glass windows. There was a hushed whispering until the priest and his acolytes entered and the rhythmic chanting of the Latin text began. Interspersed were the beautiful voices of a full choir. When the organ music began, the resonance could only be described as heavenly. All sounds melodiously melded together with the responses of the faithful to the prayers of the priest.

The thought I had had while sitting in the Athenée's bar—that no religious experience could lead me back to a Schweitzerian ambience with all of its spiritual upliftment—was wrong. As Schweitzer told me once, "Hearing Bach played on an old European church organ could convert the most meager surroundings into a place of worship." He should also have added that it could transmute the most recalcitrant soul into a believer. The majestic soaring of Bach's music in this solemn Mass almost reverted this heathen's fleshpot mentality to the incipient spirituality that Schweitzer had tried to inculcate. Not unlike that evening of Schweitzer's unintended duet with the native drummer, time stood suspended. Even though the Mass lasted over an hour, it seemed it was over almost as soon as it had begun. We departed St. Sulpice in a transcendental state only to be brought back to reality by the wetness of the quiet, soft snow.

We were hungry and it was late. Taking a chance, we went to a tiny restaurant which had been recommended to us before we left home—La Mere Michele, on the Right Bank just near the Etoile. It was locked, but we could see that a few guests were still eating. After our knocking on the door for some minutes, a lovely rosy-cheeked, aproned, motherly type woman with her hair up in a bun opened the door to tell us, in broken English, that she was closing for the night. I asked how she could turn away four wanderers from a distant shore while the Eastern star was still shining brightly in the snowy night. She laughed and said if the wanderers would like to eat with the help her door was open.

She threw the door open wider, took our coats, seated us, and we immediately ordered a bottle of wine. We invited her to eat with us. Accepting, she said that she would order the meal and hoped it pleased us. After we drank the delicious Pouilly Fuisse, the whole kitchen staff entered with the meal we were to eat. It featured a flaky broiled stuffed turbot surrounded by a variety of crisp sauteed vegetables. We ordered more wine for the whole staff and ate a meal never to be forgotten, even in Paris. We toasted Christmas Day and each other between courses.

Lifting my glass, I looked through the sparkling goblet of wine remembering our last toast with Schweitzer the night before we left. In Lambarene we had raised our heavy, peanut-butter-jar glasses with advertisements shining through the almost-sour Bordeaux.

Here, at Mere Michele's, the impeccable china, crystal, silverware, and napery were far removed from the wooden table, the tin trays, the steel cutlery of mongrel design, and the paper napkins in Lambarene. Even the comraderie (with the chef and waiters) of La Mere and the general festive spirit was in sharp contrast to the somber "last supper" ambience at Schweitzer's table. Our hostess had made the dessert herself, as if to show she still had her hand in the restaurant's cuisine. It was a luscious lemon souffle, which we ate with a liquored capuccino.

We left the restaurant around 5:30 in the morning; everyone kissed and hugged each other. The huge flakes of snow were still coming down. Enveloped by a joyous glow, we walked back to the Plaza Athenée through the soft, white morning after a Christmas Eve that will never be forgotten.

Phoebe and I slept that next morning away between smooth, soft, white cotton sheets with fluffy pillows that didn't crackle when we turned and on a mattress that felt like a cloud. There was no awakening from our sleep that night, neither by sudden downpours nor by the bomblike blast of the heavy breadfruit dropping on the iron roof. There were no bells to tell us it was time to climb the hill again.

We woke naturally and comfortably (not sweating in a moist heat) around noon. We did not have to step gingerly from our beds onto old newspapers to prevent a Bilharzia invasion. Instead, we slipped our feet into terrycloth slippers and walked on the silken, antique Persian rug.

Our shoes were shined and waiting outside the door: not even a spider lurked in any one of them. There was no embarrassing lineup outside our bathroom. A steamy hot shower was ready at the turn of a handle. At the beck of just one buzz for the floor maid, coffee and the International Herald Tribune were at our door.

Somehow, comfort and services temporarily negated my conscience and my responsibility for "those who bore the mark of pain." After my return to the United States, with the press of catching up on my professional life, the spirituality I had absorbed retreated even further from my mind. It only returned on rare occasions when I thought back to Schweitzer and the man's dedication, which was so far removed from my own and that of most others. On these occasions, to me his greatness was even more magnified. I realized anew, and still do, how rare a human being he really was.

An Afterword

In 1983, twenty-three years after Phoebe and I took leave of Albert Schweitzer as he waved his pith helmet from the hospital landing on the bank of the Ogowe River, we went back to Lambarene. Entering the village of Lambarene, we saw that the now perfectly dry Ogowe River was spanned by a huge steel-girdered bridge for the occasional trucks that came through.

We went directly to the old Relais Hotel, where we used to indulge ourselves with a Saturday afternoon hot shower and a civilized meal. The once-popular barroom still had its large crystal chandeliers hanging in the center. Everything else was tattered and worn. The lumbermen, miners, and merchants were all relegated to the past. There were three customers, including a peace corps volunteer, sipping their afternoon beer in the sweltering heat. We stayed only long enough to refresh ourselves with a cold drink and were happy to leave, going directly to the hospital.

As we entered the hospital grounds, we were directed to the administration building. Schweitzer's rough-hewn hospital had been replaced by a modern concrete, glass, and steel building, all centrally air-conditioned. Inside the building was a marble-floored foyer, and the only reminder that we were back at the Albert Schweitzer Hospital was his bust on a pedestal opposite the reception desk.

After we'd been ushered through a sumptuous office, with a perfunctory introduction to Dr. Schoenlaub, the middle-aged *Chef de Medicine,* our bags were transferred to a jeep and we were driven to the exact quarters we had stayed in before. Its comfort had improved measurably. There were now "beauty rest" mattresses, hot and cold running water, and electricity lighting everything, including the porch.

We unpacked and rested until a knock sounded on the door. There stood our old friend, nurse Marie Langendyk. She was the only one left from the entire former staff. With tears in her eyes she welcomed us back. As she said, everyone had gone within eighteen months after Schweitzer died and only one or two people had returned in the past fifteen years. Marie had aged perceptibly but was still soft spoken and gentle. She volunteered to show Phoebe and me around the next day.

That evening on the way up to the old dining hall, I suddenly realized that there were absolutely no animals anywhere. Not a chimp, a monkey, a goat—not even a dog—was visible. As we later found out, that was part of the new policy—hardly an example of "Reverence for Life." On my walk up the hill I couldn't help but recall the night of the "concert." But now the flickering kerosene lanterns were no longer necessary—the paths between the buildings were all electrically lit. And there was no organ—much less a master to play it.

That evening, dinner was a bigger shock. Most of the staff, many of them new, had voted down reading aloud parts of Schweitzer's works at dinner. After that, the Bible readings and hymns were dispensed with (a pastor came on Sunday mornings for services). Finally the long "last supper" table was taken out and his empty chair not kept there as a remembrance. Small four-seated bridge tables were substituted.

Only a few doctors were having dinner that evening. Most of the new professional staff, now with wives and children, had modern kitchens in their own apartments. They preferred dinner on their own. The staff got together only at lunch, usually for assignments and announcements. However, one tradition was still maintained—the absence of any black staff eating there.

The next morning, Marie met us after our breakfast with a nurse and three other rather sullen doctors. When they left, Phoebe and I sat for a long time and talked with Marie. She told us of Schweitzer's last days.

In the early winter of 1965 Schweitzer began going downhill. He had lapses of memory, frequently not knowing where he was. In June he became worse but at times was able to work on his correspondence and see some important visitors.

By late July he was more or less confined to his room and bed. Not long afterwards, he had to be fed by hand. His appetite declined but he refused all medication and any intravenous nutriment. He talked frenetically about nuclear peace, knowing that time was running out.

Weak as he was, he insisted on once more inspecting the entire hospital one day late in August. He made his last rounds driven in a jeep to every building including the leprosarium, where the saddened lepers came out to pay him tribute. When taken back to his room, he collapsed and was semiconscious for almost a whole week.

As Marie related it, the word got around that he was dying. The natives, always in awe of him, marveled at his fight to keep living. The few days before his death, hundreds of them and other friends came by foot, road, and *pirogue* to file past his bed.

At 11:30 p.m. on Saturday, September 4, he quietly died. At 5:00 a.m., the prearranged signal went out to the Mission and the neighboring villages via one of the bells which Marie herself rang for half an hour.

That Sunday afternoon, with staff, Gabonese dignitaries, and hundreds of natives from miles around, a simple ceremony was held from the same porch on which we had seen him shave and where his pelican roosted and his pet pig slept. There he lay, unembalmed, replete with his white shirt, clip-on bow tie and his "European" hat, in the coffin that he himself had the woodworking shop build almost a year before. His casket was carried down the hill and he was interred beside his wife Helene and his first volunteer nurse Emma Hausnecht. A simple homemade concrete cross, similar to the others, with his name and dates on it was placed over him. Letters, wires, and messages of sorrow flooded in from leaders of nations, former patients, and ordinary people from all over the world.

Marie and I left the dining room and, as we walked, she told of the nasty infighting of the staff to get control, even before he died, as he lay unconscious. Rhena, his daughter, had come back, and everyone—Mueller, Friedman, and nurses Kottman and Silver—had played up to her. They had heard that his will, written a month or so before, had left the hospital in charge of Rhena along with the weak *Medicine de Chef* Dr. Munch. Everyone knew Rhena wouldn't stay long and guessed Munch would not last. Mueller soon gave up and left. Friedman vowed that he wouldn't leave before Munch, whom he considered unfit to run the hospital. He outlasted Munch by a few months. Ali and most of the nurses left soon afterward.

By then the Swiss committee took over. And as the old guard left, a new, well-paid staff—all white Europeans—was being recruited. The spirit of Schweitzer left with his old staff. I couldn't help remembering my conversations with Schweitzer about this and the confidence he had that the hospital would go on with the same staff.

Marie showed me through the new spotless, terrazzo-floored, air-conditioned, fully equipped modern operating room. There were also now a separate maternity ward, a well equipped laboratory, up-to-date x-ray equipment, and even a research center. In one large building there was a generating plant that could have easily electrified all of the town of Lambarene.

We walked down past Schweitzer's grave. Two others, besides Helene Schweitzer and Emma Hausnecht, were now buried there: nurse Kottman and Schweitzer's photographer friend Erica Anderson. Four of the five concrete crosses were yellow with age. The old hospital square, once so busy as a social center with families cooking for their sick, children playing, and chimpanzees, goats, and dogs scurrying about, was empty. There was a separate place for the natives to cook, a commissary for the purchase of packaged and canned goods, and a place for them to stay. There was a social center on the drawing board. Patients were now charged three dollars a day and had to feed themselves.

The old hospital was still there, rotting away as the new center of concrete and steel, private rooms, private staff living quarters even an accounting office, and specialty buildings looked down on it from its crescent of buildings higher on the hill.

Most of the old wards and the operating room literally hand built by Schweitzer were in ruins and padlocked. The old TB ward was inhabited by the elderly. However, the five reinforced cells for psychiatric patients, of which Schweitzer was so ashamed, were still used. One patient lodged there.

The new hospital seemed sterile in spirit and as dead as the man who created it.

A few of the old buildings were opened for me to browse around in. There in the O.R. was the old pressure cooker for the sterilization of instruments and the ancient, chipped, enamel operating table. The *pouponniere*, with its shelves for holding infants, was now a woodworking shop, and Schweitzer's office, in the once-busy pharmacy looking out on the square, was shrouded in cobwebs. A snake slithered away as we came in.

The room where Schweitzer had worked and slept was now the *Musée de Schweitzer*, something which we once had kidded about and which he would never have tolerated. The pelican, the pig, the owl and the fawn were, of course, long gone. But, true to his ironic predictions, there was a price for tourists to see his old iron bedstead, his shaving strop hanging on the wall with the straight razor beneath it. And—something else he once joked about—his old beaten-up work shoes stood in a corner on the floor. The now-quiet piano from the dining room had been moved down to replace his old zinc-lined organ which Ali Silver had shipped back to Gunsbach.

As we left his former quarters, the death of both the spirit and example of Lambarene was readily apparent. There, near the old plaza, once the center of hospital activity, was a caged "zoo" of six or seven antelopes. It was an abomination against both his philosophy of "reverence" and the hospital's tradition. Perhaps, with everything else, I shouldn't have been surprised. But I was.

His family medical system was also gone: poor patients and poor families had to bring or buy their own food, and had no chance of working in lieu of paying for the treatment of their sick. Even his musical legacy seemed flouted by bringing down that old piano from the dining room as a tourist substitute for Schweitzer's piano-organ given him by the French Bach Society. It was all too saddening.

Marie and I walked to the nearby village where Nyama, the elderly *infirmier* once in charge of the O.R., was still living with his wife. He was still huge but hobbled with arthritis, and walked with a cane. His hut, like the others, was the same, but the thatched roof had been replaced by asbestos shingles. There was still no running water or bathroom facilities and the cooking was done on an open fire. He told us how Joseph, Schweitzer's most loyal and talented *infirmier*, became an alcoholic after Schweitzer died, and Pierre, that extraordinary handler of instruments and the best surgical aide anywhere, had died and that black aides no longer worked as O.R. assistants. He also told us that Mama San Nom had perished in the name of civilization: she was made to wear a tutu which caught fire in one of her dances and burned her to death.

The following day I went back alone to the first and only Mission the Church would give Schweitzer in 1913 because of his then-heretical book on the historical Jesus. The pastor's house, which we all helped dedicate with Schweitzer in 1960, had been taken back over by the jungle. Schweitzer's old chicken coop hospital, the one he had so proudly pointed out to me, was hidden by weeds and was now lived in by squatters. The simple old church down the hill was empty and sagging. The path leading to it was grown over with shoulder-high flora. The large handmade wooden cross outside was askew but the all-but-faded mauve asbestos shingles on the caved-in steeple were still intact. Inside, long-stemmed African grass pushed up through the floor boards.

I came back to the hospital from my visit to the old Mission and roamed around by myself for an hour or so. Then I had a long conversation with Dr. Schoenlaub in his office. He talked of the strictures the hospital now worked under. All flagrant drunkeness, laziness or derelection of any duty by the native help had to be immediately reported to the government. Public health had not made many inroads, as they were treating the same diseases. Bilharzia, infant diarrhea, malaria, elephantiasis, tuberculosis, and leprosy were still rampant. Mental disease was now being treated mainly with tranquilizers. Even Schweitzer's preventive health legacy was short-lived.

During my stay I heard not one word of his "Reverence for Life" theory, his *Quest for the Historical Jesus,* nor his music. There was no mention by anyone of his nuclear peace initiatives nor his convictions about man's relationship to man.

Moreover, with all of the polished glass and shining chrome instruments and equipment, the surgical mortality rate was not much better than before. And the heart, lung, and brain cases still could not be handled by Libreville but sent by the government to France and Switzerland.

The new-found wealth of Libreville from their natural resources was wasted on showy bridges, office buildings, elegant hotels, and a pervasive corruption. There were still no rural electrification, wells for clean water, nor agricultural extension services, despite the starvation which was now much worse than in 1960. In every bush village, the huts still had dirt floors and no cooking stoves. The birth rate among teenagers was as high as any place in the world. There was no reverence for animal life—the keystone of Schweitzer's religious philosophy: white hunters and local poachers were still gradually depleting the jungle of any and all wild life.

Dr. Schoenlaub was terribly pessimistic about the future of the hospital. European doctors and nurses were getting impossible to find; only the good salary recruited the few applicants. Fund raising was getting impossible as Schweitzer's name receded in history.

I hated to hear this confirmation that my predictions to Schweitzer twenty-three years before were more accurate than his hopes.

On the trip back to the United States, I couldn't help thinking of the legacy of Schweitzer's single-handed fifty-year alleviation of misery, in his spirit of "man's responsibility to man." Maybe we are not far enough evolved as humans to appreciate what was offered for our own well being and longevity as a society. It seemed that such a short span of the influence of his life's work is a sad commentary on society's ever living together in peace.

However, as Schweitzer once said, what he did was for his own redemption. He did what he had to do for "those who bore the mark of pain." For him that sufficed. Only mankind will be the loser if it is indifferent to the thoughts and reverence for life of one of the rare minds of our times.